Welcome to

Official GRE® Quantitative Reasoning Practice Questions, Volume 1

The book you are holding offers 150 real GRE practice questions directly from the maker of the *GRE*® revised General Test. This book is specially created to give you in-depth practice and accurate test preparation for the Quantitative Reasoning measure.

Here's what you will find inside:

- **Authentic GRE Quantitative Reasoning test questions** arranged by content and question type—to help you build your test-taking skills. Plus, mixed practice sets.

- **Answers and explanations** for every question!

- **ETS's own test-taking strategies.** Learn valuable hints and tips that can help you get your best score.

- **GRE Math Review** covering math topics you need to know for the test.

- **Official information on the GRE Quantitative Reasoning measure.** Get the facts about the test content, structure, scoring, and more—straight from ETS.

About ETS

At ETS, we advance quality and equity in education for people worldwide by creating assessments based on rigorous research. ETS serves individuals, educational institutions, and government agencies by providing customized solutions for teacher certification, English language learning, and elementary, secondary, and post-secondary education, as well as conducting educational research, analysis, and policy studies. Founded as a nonprofit in 1947, ETS develops, administers, and scores more than 50 million tests annually—including the *TOEFL*® and *TOEIC*® tests, the *GRE*® tests, and *The Praxis Series*™ assessments—in more than 180 countries at over 9,000 locations worldwide. For more information, visit **www.ets.org**.

IMPORTANT

ETS makes available free test preparation materials for individuals planning to take a GRE test. *POWERPREP® II* software is available for individuals planning to take the computer-delivered GRE revised General Test, and the *Practice Book for the Paper-based GRE revised General Test*, Second edition, is available for individuals planning to take the paper-delivered test. The information about how to prepare for the Quantitative Reasoning measure of the GRE revised General Test, including test-taking strategies, question strategies, etc., that is included in the free test preparation is also included in this publication. This publication also provides you with 150 brand new practice questions with answers and explanations.

**For more information about the GRE revised General Test, free and low-cost
GRE test preparation materials, and other GRE products and services,
please visit the GRE website at:**

www.ets.org/gre

**Inquiries concerning the practice test questions in this book
should be sent to the GRE testing program at:**

GRETestQuestionInquiries@ets.org

Volume 1

Official
GRE®
QUANTITATIVE
REASONING
Practice Questions

New York | Chicago | San Francisco | Athens | London | Madrid
Mexico City | Milan | New Delhi | Singapore | Sydney | Toronto

7 8 9 10   QVS/QVS   1 0 9 8 7 6 5

ISBN 978-0-07-183432-2
MHID 0-07-183432-X

e-ISBN 978-0-07-183431-5
e-MHID 0-07-183431-1

Library of Congress Control Number 2014932104

McGraw-Hill Education products are available at special quantity discounts to use as premiums and sales promotions or for use in corporate training programs. To contact a representative, please visit the Contact Us pages at www.mhprofessional.com.

Sponsoring Editor: Charles Wall
Interior Designer: Jane Tenenbaum
Typesetters: MPS Limited

Contents

1 Overview of the *GRE*® Quantitative Reasoning Measure   1

2 Test Content   7

3 Arithmetic   43

7 Mixed Practice Sets 139

Appendix A: *GRE*® Math Review 229

Appendix B: Mathematical Conventions for the Quantitative Reasoning Measure of the *GRE*® revised General Test 329

How to Use This Book

This book provides important information about the Quantitative Reasoning measure of the GRE revised General Test, including the knowledge and skills that are assessed and the types of questions that appear. The book will help you:

- Familiarize yourself with the test format and test question types
- Learn valuable test-taking strategies for each question type
- Review the math topics you need to know for the test
- Check your progress with Quantitative Reasoning practice questions

The following four-step program has been designed to help you make the best use of this book.

STEP 1 Learn About the GRE Quantitative Reasoning Measure

Chapter 1 of this book provides an overview of the GRE Quantitative Reasoning measure. Read this chapter to learn about the number of questions, time limits, and the test design features. You will also find valuable test-taking strategies from ETS and important information about how the measure is scored.

STEP 2 Study the Different GRE Quantitative Reasoning Question Types

Chapter 2 of this book describes the types of questions you will encounter in the Quantitative Reasoning measure. You will learn what the questions are designed to measure, and you will get tips for answering each question type. You will also see samples of each question type, with helpful explanations.

STEP 3 Practice Answering GRE Quantitative Reasoning Questions

Chapters 3, 4, 5, and 6 contain sets of authentic Quantitative Reasoning practice questions in the content areas of Arithmetic, Algebra, Geometry, and Data Analysis, respectively. Answer the questions in each set, and then read through the explanations to see which questions you found most challenging. Look for patterns. Did specific content areas give you trouble? You can refresh your math skills in these areas with the GRE Math Review in Appendix A. The GRE Math Review is a review of the math topics that are likely to appear on the Quantitative Reasoning measure. Each section of the GRE Math Review ends with exercises that will help you see how well you have mastered the material. Note that Appendix B provides information about the mathematical conventions that are used on the Quantitative Reasoning measure. Prior to answering the practice questions, it might be helpful to review these conventions.

STEP 4 Test Yourself With the Mixed Practice Sets

Once you have completed the practice sets for each content area in Chapters 3–6, it is time to practice with authentic GRE questions in the Mixed Practice Sets in Chapter 7. Each Mixed Practice Set includes the question types and content areas contained in an actual Quantitative Reasoning section of the GRE revised General Test.

1 Overview of the *GRE*® Quantitative Reasoning Measure

Your goal for this chapter	⇨ Review basic information on the structure of the *GRE*® Quantitative Reasoning measure, test-taking strategies, and scoring

Introduction to the *GRE*® revised General Test

The *GRE*® revised General Test—the most widely accepted graduate admissions test worldwide—measures verbal reasoning, quantitative reasoning, critical thinking, and analytical writing skills that are necessary for success in graduate and business school.

Prospective graduate and business school applicants from all around the world take the GRE revised General Test. Although applicants come from varying educational and cultural backgrounds, the GRE revised General Test provides a common measure for comparing candidates' qualifications. GRE scores are used by admissions committees and fellowship panels to supplement undergraduate records, recommendation letters, and other qualifications for graduate-level study.

The GRE revised General Test is available at test centers in more than 160 countries. In most regions of the world, the computer-delivered test is available on a continuous basis throughout the year. In areas of the world where computer-delivered testing is not available, the test is administered in a paper-delivered format up to three times a year.

Before taking the GRE revised General Test, it is important to become familiar with the content and structure of the test, and with each of the three measures—Verbal Reasoning, Quantitative Reasoning, and Analytical Writing. This book provides a close look at the GRE Quantitative Reasoning measure. Chapter 1 provides an overview of the structure and scoring of the Quantitative Reasoning measure. In Chapters 2 through 7, you will find information specific to the content of the Quantitative Reasoning measure. You can use the information in this publication to help you understand the type of material on which you will be tested. For the most up-to-date information about the GRE revised General Test, visit the GRE website at **www.ets.org/gre**.

The Quantitative Reasoning Measure of the Computer-delivered GRE revised General Test

Structure of the Quantitative Reasoning Measure

Measure	Number of Questions	Allotted Time
Quantitative Reasoning (Two sections)	20 questions per section	35 minutes per section

The Quantitative Reasoning sections may appear anytime in the test after section 1. The directions at the beginning of each Quantitative Reasoning section specify the total number of questions in the section and the time allowed for the section.

Test Design Features

The Quantitative Reasoning measure of the computer-delivered GRE revised General Test is section-level adaptive. This means the computer selects the second section of a measure based on your performance on the first section.

The advanced adaptive design also means you can freely move forward and backward throughout an entire section. Specific features include:

- Preview and review capabilities within a section
- "Mark" and "Review" features to tag questions, so you can skip them and return later if you have time remaining in the section
- The ability to change/edit answers within a section
- An on-screen calculator (More information about the calculator is given in Chapter 2.)

Test-taking Strategies

The questions in the Quantitative Reasoning measure are presented in a variety of formats. Some require you to select a single answer choice, others require you to select one or more answer choices, and yet others require you to enter a numeric answer. Make sure when answering a question that you understand what response is required. An on-screen calculator will be provided at the test center for use during the Quantitative Reasoning sections.

When taking the Quantitative Reasoning measure of the computer-delivered GRE revised General Test, you are free to skip questions that you might have difficulty answering within a section. The testing software has a "Mark" feature that enables you to mark questions you would like to revisit during the time provided to work on that section. The testing software also has a "Review" feature that lets you view a complete list of all the questions in the section on which you are working, that indicates whether you have answered each question, and that identifies the questions you have marked for review. Additionally, you can review questions you have already answered and change your answers, provided you still have time remaining to work on that section.

A sample review screen appears below. The review screen is intended to help you keep track of your progress on the test. Do not spend too much time on the review screen, as this will take away from the time allotted to read and answer the questions on the test.

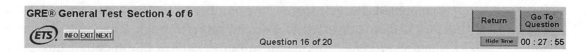

GRE® General Test Section 4 of 6

INFO EXIT NEXT   Question 16 of 20   Return | Go To Question | Hide Time 00 : 27 : 55

Below is the list of questions in the current section. The question you were on is highlighted. Questions you have seen are labeled **Answered**, **Incomplete**, or **Not Answered**. A question is labeled **Incomplete** if the question requires you to select a certain number of answer choices and you have selected more or fewer than that number. Questions you have marked are indicated with a ✔.

To return to the question you were on, click **Return**.

To go to a different question, click on that question to highlight it, then click **Go To Question**.

Question Number	Status	Marked	Question Number	Status	Marked
1	Answered		11	Answered	
2	Answered		12	Incomplete	
3	Answered		13	Incomplete	
4	Answered		14	Incomplete	✔
5	Answered		15	Incomplete	✔
6	Incomplete		16	Answered	
7	Answered	✔	17	Answered	
8	Answered		18	Answered	✔
9	Answered		19	Not seen	
10	Answered		20	Not seen	

Your Quantitative Reasoning score will be determined by the number of questions you answer correctly. Nothing is subtracted from a score if you answer a question incorrectly. Therefore, to maximize your scores on the Quantitative Reasoning measure, it is best to answer every question.

Work as rapidly as you can without being careless. Since no question carries greater weight than any other, do not waste time pondering individual questions you find extremely difficult or unfamiliar.

You may want to go through each of the Quantitative Reasoning sections rapidly first, stopping only to answer questions you can answer with certainty. Then go back and answer the questions that require greater thought, concluding with the difficult questions if you have time.

During the actual administration of the revised General Test, you may work only on one section at a time and only for the time allowed. Once you have completed a section, you may not go back to it.

Scratch Paper

You will receive a supply of scratch paper before you begin the test. You can replenish your supply of scratch paper as necessary throughout the test by asking the test administrator.

How the Quantitative Reasoning Measure Is Scored

The Quantitative Reasoning measure is section-level adaptive. This means the computer selects the second section of a measure based on your performance on the first section. Within each section, all questions contribute equally to the final score. First a raw score is computed. The raw score is the number of questions you answered correctly. The raw score is then converted to a scaled score through a process known as equating. The equating process accounts for minor variations in difficulty from test to test as well as the differences introduced by the section-level adaptation. Thus a given scaled score reflects the same level of performance regardless of which second section was selected and when the test was taken.

The Quantitative Reasoning Measure of the Paper-delivered GRE revised General Test

Structure of the Quantitative Reasoning Measure

Measure	Number of Questions	Allotted Time
Quantitative Reasoning (Two sections)	25 questions per section	40 minutes per section

The Quantitative Reasoning sections may appear in any order after section 2. The directions at the beginning of each section specify the total number of questions in the section and the time allowed for the section.

Test Design Features

- You are free, within any section, to skip questions and come back to them later or change the answer to a question.
- Answers are entered in the test book, rather than a separate answer sheet.
- You will be provided with an ETS calculator to use during the Quantitative Reasoning section; you may not use your own calculator.

Test-taking Strategies

The questions in the Quantitative Reasoning measure have a variety of formats. Some require you to select a single answer choice, others require you to select one or more answer choices, and yet others require you to enter a numeric answer. Make sure when answering a question that you understand what response is required. A calculator will be provided at the test center for use during the Quantitative Reasoning sections.

When taking a Quantitative Reasoning section, you are free, within that section, to skip questions that you might have difficulty answering and come back to them later during the time provided to work on that section. Also during that time you may change the answer to any question in that section by erasing it completely and filling in an alternative answer. Be careful not to leave any stray marks in the answer area, as they may be interpreted as incorrect responses. You can, however, safely make notes or perform calculations on other parts of the page. No additional scratch paper will be provided.

Your Quantitative Reasoning score will be determined by the number of questions you answer correctly. Nothing is subtracted from a score if you answer a question incorrectly. Therefore, to maximize your score on the Quantitative Reasoning measure, it is best to answer every question.

Work as rapidly as you can without being careless. Since no question carries greater weight than any other, do not waste time pondering individual questions you find extremely difficult or unfamiliar.

You may want to go through each of the Quantitative Reasoning sections rapidly first, stopping only to answer questions you can answer with certainty. Then go back and answer the questions that require greater thought, concluding with the difficult questions if you have time.

During the actual administration of the revised General Test, you may work only on the section the test center supervisor designates and only for the time allowed. You may *not* go back to an earlier section of the test after the supervisor announces, "Please stop work" for that section. The supervisor is authorized to dismiss you from the center for doing so.

All answers must be recorded in the test book.

How the Quantitative Reasoning Measure Is Scored

Scoring of the Quantitative Reasoning measure is essentially a two-step process. First a raw score is computed. The raw score is the number of questions answered correctly in the two sections for the measure. The raw score is then converted to a scaled score through a process known as equating. The equating process accounts for minor variations in difficulty among the different test editions. Thus a given scaled score reflects the same level of performance regardless of which edition of the test was taken.

Score Reporting

A Quantitative Reasoning score is reported on a 130–170 score scale, in 1-point increments. If you do not answer any questions at all for the measure, you will receive a No Score (NS) for that measure.

The *ScoreSelect*® Option

The *ScoreSelect*® option is available for both the GRE revised General Test and GRE Subject Tests and can be used by anyone with reportable scores from the last five years. This option lets you send institutions your best scores. For your four free score reports, you can send scores from your *Most Recent* test administration or scores from *All* test administrations in your reportable history. After test day, you can send scores from your *Most Recent, All,* or *Any* specific test administration(s) for a fee when ordering

Additional Score Reports. Just remember, scores for a test administration must be reported in their entirety. For more information, visit **www.ets.org/gre/scoreselect**.

Score Reporting Time Frames

Scores from computer-delivered GRE revised General Test administrations are reported approximately 10 to 15 days after the test date. Scores from paper-delivered administrations are reported within six weeks after the test date. If you are applying to a graduate or business school program, be sure to review the appropriate admissions deadlines and plan to take the test in time for your scores to reach the institution.

For more information on score reporting, visit the GRE website at **www.ets.org/gre/scores/get**.

2 Test Content

Your goals for this chapter

⇨ Learn general problem-solving steps and strategies
⇨ Learn the four types of *GRE*® Quantitative Reasoning questions and get tips for answering each question type
⇨ Study sample Quantitative Reasoning questions with solutions
⇨ Learn how to use the on-screen calculator

Overview of the Quantitative Reasoning Measure

The Quantitative Reasoning measure of the GRE revised General Test assesses your:

- basic mathematical skills
- understanding of elementary mathematical concepts
- ability to reason quantitatively and to model and solve problems with quantitative methods

Some of the Quantitative Reasoning questions are posed in real-life settings, while others are posed in purely mathematical settings. Many of the questions are "word problems," which must be translated and modeled mathematically. The skills, concepts, and abilities are assessed in the four content areas below.

Arithmetic topics include properties and types of integers, such as divisibility, factorization, prime numbers, remainders, and odd and even integers; arithmetic operations, exponents, and roots; and concepts such as estimation, percent, ratio, rate, absolute value, the number line, decimal representation, and sequences of numbers.

Algebra topics include operations with exponents; factoring and simplifying algebraic expressions; relations, functions, equations, and inequalities; solving linear and quadratic equations and inequalities; solving simultaneous equations and inequalities; setting up equations to solve word problems; and coordinate geometry, including graphs of functions, equations, and inequalities, intercepts, and slopes of lines.

Geometry topics include parallel and perpendicular lines, circles, triangles—including isosceles, equilateral, and 30°-60°-90° triangles—quadrilaterals, other polygons, congruent and similar figures, three-dimensional figures, area, perimeter, volume, the Pythagorean theorem, and angle measurement in degrees. The ability to construct proofs is not tested.

Data analysis topics include basic descriptive statistics, such as mean, median, mode, range, standard deviation, interquartile range, quartiles, and percentiles; interpretation of data in tables and graphs, such as line graphs, bar graphs, circle graphs, boxplots, scatterplots, and frequency distributions; elementary probability, such as probabilities of compound events and independent events; random variables and probability distributions, including normal distributions; and counting methods, such as combinations, permutations, and Venn diagrams. These topics are typically taught in high school algebra courses or introductory statistics courses. Inferential statistics is not tested.

The content in these areas includes high school mathematics and statistics at a level that is generally no higher than a second course in algebra; it does not include trigonometry, calculus, or other higher-level mathematics. The publication *Math Review for the GRE revised General Test,* which is available in Appendix A, provides detailed information about the content of the Quantitative Reasoning measure.

The mathematical symbols, terminology, and conventions used in the Quantitative Reasoning measure are those that are standard at the high school level. For example, the positive direction of a number line is to the right, distances are nonnegative, and prime numbers are greater than 1. Whenever nonstandard notation is used in a question, it is explicitly introduced in the question.

In addition to conventions, there are some important assumptions about numbers and figures that are listed in the Quantitative Reasoning section directions:

- All numbers used are real numbers.
- All figures are assumed to lie in a plane unless otherwise indicated.
- Geometric figures, such as lines, circles, triangles, and quadrilaterals, **are not necessarily** drawn to scale. That is, you should **not** assume that quantities such as lengths and angle measures are as they appear in a figure. You should assume, however, that lines shown as straight are actually straight, points on a line are in the order shown, and more generally, all geometric objects are in the relative positions shown. For questions with geometric figures, you should base your answers on geometric reasoning, not on estimating or comparing quantities by sight or by measurement.
- Coordinate systems, such as *xy*-planes and number lines, **are** drawn to scale; therefore, you can read, estimate, or compare quantities in such figures by sight or by measurement.
- Graphical data presentations, such as bar graphs, circle graphs, and line graphs, **are** drawn to scale; therefore, you can read, estimate, or compare data values by sight or by measurement.

More about conventions and assumptions appears in the publication *Mathematical Conventions for the GRE revised General Test,* which is available in Appendix B.

General Problem-solving Steps

Questions in the Quantitative Reasoning measure ask you to model and solve problems using quantitative, or mathematical, methods. Generally, there are three basic steps in solving a mathematics problem:

Step 1: Understand the problem
Step 2: Carry out a strategy for solving the problem
Step 3: Check your answer

Here is a description of the three steps, followed by a list of useful strategies for solving mathematics problems.

Step 1: Understand the Problem

The first step is to read the statement of the problem carefully to make sure you understand the information given and the problem you are being asked to solve.

Some information may describe certain quantities. Quantitative information may be given in words or mathematical expressions, or a combination of both. Also, in some problems you may need to read and understand quantitative information in data presentations, geometric figures, or coordinate systems. Other information may take the form of formulas, definitions, or conditions that must be satisfied by the quantities. For example, the conditions may be equations or inequalities, or may be words that can be translated into equations or inequalities.

In addition to understanding the information you are given, it is important to understand what you need to accomplish in order to solve the problem. For example, what unknown quantities must be found? In what form must they be expressed?

Step 2: Carry Out a Strategy for Solving the Problem

Solving a mathematics problem requires more than understanding a description of the problem, that is, more than understanding the quantities, the data, the conditions, the unknowns, and all other mathematical facts related to the problem. It requires determining *what* mathematical facts to use and *when* and *how* to use those facts to develop a solution to the problem. It requires a strategy.

Mathematics problems are solved by using a wide variety of strategies. Also, there may be different ways to solve a given problem. Therefore, you should develop a repertoire of problem-solving strategies, as well as a sense of which strategies are likely to work best in solving particular problems. Attempting to solve a problem without a strategy may lead to a lot of work without producing a correct solution.

After you determine a strategy, you must carry it out. If you get stuck, check your work to see if you made an error in your solution. It is important to have a flexible, open mind-set. If you check your solution and cannot find an error or if your solution strategy is simply not working, look for a different strategy.

Step 3: Check Your Answer

When you arrive at an answer, you should check that it is reasonable and computationally correct.

- Have you answered the question that was asked?
- Is your answer reasonable in the context of the question? Checking that an answer is reasonable can be as simple as recalling a basic mathematical fact and checking whether your answer is consistent with that fact. For example, the probability of an event must be between 0 and 1, inclusive, and the area of a geometric figure must be positive. In other cases, you can use estimation to check that your answer is reasonable. For example, if your solution involves adding three numbers, each of which is between 100 and 200, estimating the sum tells you that the sum must be between 300 and 600.
- Did you make a computational mistake in arriving at your answer? A key-entry error using the calculator? You can check for errors in each step in your solution. Or you may be able to check directly that your solution is correct. For example, if you solved the equation $7(3x - 2) + 4 = 95$ for x and got the answer $x = 5$, you can check your answer by substituting $x = 5$ into the equation to see that $7(3(5) - 2) + 4 = 95$.

Strategies

There are no set rules—applicable to all mathematics problems—to determine the best strategy. The ability to determine a strategy that will work grows as you solve more and more problems. What follows are brief descriptions of useful strategies, along with references to questions in this chapter that you can answer with the help of particular strategies. These strategies do not form a complete list, and, aside from grouping the first four strategies together, they are not presented in any particular order.

The first four strategies are translation strategies, where one representation of a mathematics problem is translated into another.

Strategy 1: Translate from Words to an Arithmetic or Algebraic Representation

Word problems are often solved by translating textual information into an arithmetic or algebraic representation. For example, an "odd integer" can be represented by the expression $2n + 1$, where n is an integer; and the statement "the cost of a taxi trip is $3.00, plus $1.25 for each mile" can be represented by the expression $c = 3 + 1.25m$. More generally, translation occurs when you understand a word problem in mathematical terms in order to model the problem mathematically.

- See question 4 on page 27 and question 5 on page 35.

Strategy 2: Translate from Words to a Figure or Diagram

To solve a problem in which a figure is described but not shown, draw your own figure. Draw the figure as accurately as possible, labeling as many parts as possible, including any unknowns.

Drawing figures can help in geometry problems as well as in other types of problems. For example, in probability and counting problems, drawing a diagram can sometimes make it easier to analyze the relevant data and to notice relationships and dependencies.

- See question 2 on page 25.

Strategy 3: Translate from an Algebraic to a Graphical Representation

Many algebra problems can be represented graphically in a coordinate system, whether the system is a number line if the problem involves one variable, or a coordinate plane if the problem involves two variables. Such graphs can clarify relationships that may be less obvious in algebraic presentations.

- See question 3 on page 26.

Strategy 4: Translate from a Figure to an Arithmetic or Algebraic Representation

When a figure is given in a problem, it may be effective to express relationships among the various parts of the figure using arithmetic or algebra.

- See question 4 on page 18 and question 3 on page 34.

Strategy 5: Simplify an Arithmetic or Algebraic Representation

Arithmetic and algebraic representations include both expressions and equations. Your facility in simplifying a representation can often lead to a quick solution. Examples include converting from a percent to a decimal, converting from one measurement unit to another, combining like terms in an algebraic expression, and simplifying an equation until its solutions are evident.

- See question 6 on page 20 and question 4 on page 35.

Strategy 6: Add to a Geometric Figure

Sometimes you can add useful lines, points, or circles to a geometric figure to facilitate solving a problem. You can also add any given information—as well as any new information as you derive it—to the figure to help you see relationships within the figure more easily, for example, the length of a line segment or the measure of an angle.

- See question 3 on page 26.

Strategy 7: Find a Pattern

Patterns are found throughout mathematics. Identifying a pattern is often the first step in understanding a complex mathematical situation. Pattern recognition yields insight that may point in the direction of a complete solution to the problem or simply help you generate a hypothesis, which requires further exploration using another strategy. In a problem where you suspect there is a pattern but don't recognize it yet, working with particular instances can help you identify the pattern. Once a pattern is identified, it can be used to answer questions.

- See question 4 on page 31.

Strategy 8: Search for a Mathematical Relationship

More general than patterns, mathematical relationships exist throughout mathematics. Problems may involve quantities that are related algebraically, sets that are related logically, or figures that are related geometrically. Also, there may be relationships between information given textually, algebraically, graphically, etc. To express relationships between quantities, it is often helpful to introduce one or more variables to represent the quantities. Once a relationship is understood and expressed, it is often the key to solving a problem.

- See question 8 on page 22 and question 3 on page 30.

Strategy 9: Estimate

Sometimes it is not necessary to perform extensive calculations to solve a problem—it is sufficient to estimate the answer. The degree of accuracy needed depends on the particular question being asked. Care should be taken to determine how far off your estimate could possibly be from the actual answer to the question. Estimation can also be used to check whether the answer to a question is reasonable.

- See question 3 on page 17 and question 4 on page 27.

Strategy 10: Trial and Error

Version 1: Make a Reasonable Guess and then Refine It

For some problems, the fastest way to a solution is to make a reasonable guess at the answer, check it, and then improve on your guess. This is especially useful if the number of possible answers is limited. In other problems, this approach may help you at least to understand better what is going on in the problem.

- See question 1 on page 29.

Version 2: Try More Than One Value of a Variable

To explore problems containing variables, it is useful to substitute values for the variables. It often helps to substitute more than one value for each variable. How many values to choose and what values are good choices depends on the problem. Also dependent on the problem is whether this approach, by itself, will yield a solution or whether the approach will simply help you generate a hypothesis that requires further exploration using another strategy.

- See question 2 on page 17 and question 5 on page 19.

Strategy 11: Divide into Cases

Some problems are quite complex. To solve such problems you may need to divide them into smaller, less complex problems, which are restricted cases of the original problem. When you divide a problem into cases, you should consider whether or not to include all possibilities. For example, if you want to prove that a certain statement is true for all integers, it may be best to show that it is true for all positive integers, then show it is true for all negative integers, and then show it is true for zero. In doing that, you will have shown that the statement is true for all integers, because each integer is either positive, negative, or zero.

- See question 1 on page 16 and question 2 on page 30.

Strategy 12: Adapt Solutions to Related Problems

When solving a new problem that seems similar to a problem that you know how to solve, you can try to solve the new problem by adapting the solution—both the strategies and the results—of the problem you know how to solve.

If the differences between the new problem and the problem you know how to solve are only surface features—for example, different numbers, different labels, or different categories—that is, features that are not fundamental to the structure of the problem, then solve the new problem using the same strategy as you used before.

If the differences between the new problem and the problem you know how to solve are more than just surface features, try to modify the solution to the problem you know how to solve to fit the conditions given in the new problem.

- See question 3 on page 30 and question 4 on page 31.

Strategy 13: Determine Whether a Conclusion Follows from the Information Given

In some problems, you are given information and a statement describing a possible conclusion, which may or may not follow from the information. You need to determine whether or not the conclusion is a logical consequence of the information given.

If you think that the conclusion follows from the information, try to show it. Using the information and any relevant mathematical relationships, try to reason step-by-step from the information to the conclusion. Another way to show that the conclusion follows from the information, is to show that in *all* cases in which the information is true, the conclusion is also true.

If you think that the conclusion does *not* follow from the information, try to show that instead. One way to show that a conclusion does not follow from the information is to produce a counterexample. A counterexample is a case where the given information is true but the conclusion is false. If you are unsuccessful in producing a counterexample, it does not necessarily mean that the conclusion does not follow from the information—it may mean that although a counterexample exists, you were not successful in finding it.

- See question 9 on page 23 and question 3 on page 38.

Strategy 14: Determine What Additional Information Is Sufficient to Solve a Problem

Some problems cannot be solved directly from the information given, and you need to determine what other information will help you answer the question. In that case, it is useful to list all the information given in the problem, along with the information that would be contained in a complete solution, and then evaluate what is missing. Sometimes the missing information can be derived from the information given, and sometimes it cannot.

- See question 3 on page 38.

Quantitative Reasoning Question Types

The Quantitative Reasoning measure has four types of questions:

Calc only →
- Quantitative Comparison questions
- Multiple-choice questions—Select One Answer Choice
- Multiple-choice questions—Select One or More Answer Choices
- Numeric Entry questions

Each question appears either independently as a discrete question or as part of a set of questions called a Data Interpretation set. All of the questions in a Data Interpretation set are based on the same data presented in tables, graphs, or other displays of data.

In the computer-delivered test, you are allowed to use a basic calculator—provided on-screen—on the Quantitative Reasoning measure. Information about using the calculator appears later in this chapter.

For the paper-delivered test, handheld calculators are provided at the test center for use during the test. Information about using the handheld calculator to help you answer questions appears in the free *Practice Book for the Paper-based GRE revised General Test*, which is available at **www.ets.org/gre/prepare**.

Quantitative Comparison Questions

Description

Questions of this type ask you to compare two quantities—Quantity A and Quantity B— and then determine which of the following statements describes the comparison.

- Quantity A is greater.
- Quantity B is greater.
- The two quantities are equal.
- The relationship cannot be determined from the information given.

Tips for Answering

- **Become familiar with the answer choices.** Quantitative Comparison questions always have the same answer choices, so get to know them, especially the last choice, "The relationship cannot be determined from the information given." Never select this last choice if it is clear that the values of the two quantities can be determined by computation. Also, if you determine that one quantity is greater than the other, make sure you carefully select the corresponding choice so as not to reverse the first two choices.

- **Avoid unnecessary computations.** Don't waste time performing needless computations in order to compare the two quantities. Simplify, transform, or estimate one or both of the given quantities only as much as is necessary to compare them.

- **Remember that geometric figures are not necessarily drawn to scale.** If any aspect of a given geometric figure is not fully determined, try to redraw the figure, keeping those aspects that are completely determined by the given information fixed but changing the aspects of the figure that are not determined. Examine the results. What variations are possible in the relative lengths of line segments or measures of angles?

- **Plug in numbers.** If one or both of the quantities are algebraic expressions, you can substitute easy numbers for the variables and compare the resulting quantities in your analysis. Consider all kinds of appropriate numbers before you give an answer: e.g., zero, positive and negative numbers, small and large numbers, fractions and decimals. If you see that Quantity A is greater than Quantity B in one case and Quantity B is greater than Quantity A in another case, choose "The relationship cannot be determined from the information given."

- **Simplify the comparison.** If both quantities are algebraic or arithmetic expressions and you cannot easily see a relationship between them, you can try to simplify the comparison. Try a step-by-step simplification that is similar to the steps involved when you solve the equation $5 = 4x + 3$ for x, or similar to the steps involved when you determine that the inequality $\dfrac{3y + 2}{5} < y$ is equivalent to the simpler inequality $1 < y$. Begin by setting up a comparison involving the two quantities, as follows:

Quantity A ▢ Quantity B

where ▢ is a "placeholder" that could represent the relationship *greater than* (>), *less than* (<), or *equal to* (=) or could represent the fact that the relationship cannot be determined from the information given. Then try to simplify the comparison, step by step, until you can determine a relationship between simplified quantities. For example, you may conclude after the last step that ▢ represents equal to (=). Based on this conclusion, you may be able to compare Quantities A and B. To understand this strategy more fully, see sample questions 6 to 9.

Sample Questions

Compare Quantity A and Quantity B, using additional information centered above the two quantities if such information is given, and select one of the following four answer choices:

Ⓐ Quantity A is greater.

Ⓑ Quantity B is greater.

Ⓒ The two quantities are equal.

Ⓓ The relationship cannot be determined from the information given.

A symbol that appears more than once in a question has the same meaning throughout the question.

Quantity A	Quantity B

1. The least prime number greater than 24 — The greatest prime number less than 28

Ⓐ Quantity A is greater.

Ⓑ Quantity B is greater.

Ⓒ The two quantities are equal.

Ⓓ The relationship cannot be determined from the information given.

Explanation

For the integers greater than 24, note that 25, 26, 27, and 28 are not prime numbers, but 29 is a prime number, as are 31 and many other greater integers. Thus, 29 is the least prime number greater than 24, and Quantity A is 29. For the integers less than 28, note that 27, 26, 25, and 24 are not prime numbers, but 23 is a prime number, as are 19 and several other lesser integers. Thus 23 is the greatest prime number less than 28, and Quantity B is 23.

The correct answer is Choice A, Quantity A is greater.

This explanation uses the following strategy.
Strategy 11: Divide into Cases

Lionel is younger than Maria.

	Quantity A	Quantity B
2.	Twice Lionel's age	Maria's age

- (A) Quantity A is greater.
- (B) Quantity B is greater.
- (C) The two quantities are equal.
- (D) The relationship cannot be determined from the information given.

Explanation

If Lionel's age is 6 years and Maria's age is 10 years, then Quantity A is greater, but if Lionel's age is 4 years and Maria's age is 10 years, then Quantity B is greater. Thus the relationship cannot be determined.

The correct answer is Choice D, the relationship cannot be determined from the information given.

This explanation uses the following strategies.
Strategy 10: Trial and Error
Strategy 13: Determine Whether a Conclusion Follows from the Information Given

---

	Quantity A	Quantity B
3.	54% of 360	150

- (A) Quantity A is greater.
- (B) Quantity B is greater.
- (C) The two quantities are equal.
- (D) The relationship cannot be determined from the information given.

Explanation

Without doing the exact computation, you can see that 54 percent of 360 is greater than $\frac{1}{2}$ of 360, which is 180, and 180 is greater than Quantity B, 150.

Thus the correct answer is Choice A, Quantity A is greater.

This explanation uses the following strategy.
Strategy 9: Estimate

Figure 1

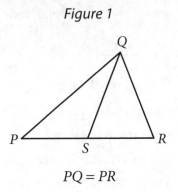

$$PQ = PR$$

Quantity A	Quantity B

4.   *PS*   *SR*

    Ⓐ Quantity A is greater.

    Ⓑ Quantity B is greater.

    Ⓒ The two quantities are equal.

    Ⓓ The relationship cannot be determined from the information given.

Explanation

From Figure 1, you know that *PQR* is a triangle and that point *S* is between points *P* and *R*, so $PS < PR$ and $SR < PR$. You are also given that $PQ = PR$. However, this information is not sufficient to compare *PS* and *SR*. Furthermore, because the figure is not necessarily drawn to scale, you cannot determine the relative sizes of *PS* and *SR* visually from the figure, though they may appear to be equal. The position of *S* can vary along side *PR* anywhere between *P* and *R*. Following are two possible variations of Figure 1, each of which is drawn to be consistent with the information $PQ = PR$.

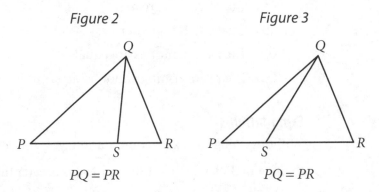

Figure 2   *Figure 3*

$$PQ = PR \qquad\qquad PQ = PR$$

Note that Quantity A is greater in Figure 2 and Quantity B is greater in Figure 3.

    Thus the correct answer is Choice D, the relationship cannot be determined from the information given.

This explanation uses the following strategies.

Strategy 4: Translate from a Figure to an Arithmetic or Algebraic Representation

Strategy 13: Determine Whether a Conclusion Follows from the Information Given

$$y = 2x^2 + 7x - 3$$

Quantity A	Quantity B

5. x y

    (A) Quantity A is greater.

    (B) Quantity B is greater.

    (C) The two quantities are equal.

    (D) The relationship cannot be determined from the information given.

Explanation

If $x = 0$, then $y = 2(0^2) + 7(0) - 3 = -3$, so in this case, $x > y$; but if $x = 1$, then $y = 2(1^2) + 7(1) - 3 = 6$, so in that case, $y > x$.

    Thus the correct answer is Choice D, the relationship cannot be determined from the information given.

This explanation uses the following strategies.
Strategy 10: Trial and Error
Strategy 13: Determine Whether a Conclusion Follows from the Information Given

Note that plugging numbers into expressions *may* not be conclusive. It *is* conclusive, however, if you get different results after plugging in different numbers: the conclusion is that the relationship cannot be determined from the information given. It is also conclusive if there are only a small number of possible numbers to plug in and all of them yield the same result, say, that Quantity B is greater.

    Now suppose that there are an infinite number of possible numbers to plug in. If you plug many of them in and each time the result is, for example, that Quantity A is greater, you still cannot conclude that Quantity A is greater for every possible number that could be plugged in. Further analysis would be necessary and should focus on whether Quantity A is greater for all possible numbers or whether there are numbers for which Quantity A is not greater.

The following sample questions focus on simplifying the comparison.

$$y > 4$$

Quantity A	Quantity B
6. $\dfrac{3y + 2}{5}$	y

(A) Quantity A is greater.

(B) Quantity B is greater.

(C) The two quantities are equal.

(D) The relationship cannot be determined from the information given.

Explanation

Set up the initial comparison:

$$\frac{3y + 2}{5} \; ? \; y$$

Then simplify:

Step 1: Multiply both sides by 5 to get

$$3y + 2 \; ? \; 5y$$

Step 2: Subtract $3y$ from both sides to get

$$2 \; ? \; 2y$$

Step 3: Divide both sides by 2 to get

$$1 \; ? \; y$$

The comparison is now simplified as much as possible. In order to compare 1 and y, note that you are given the information $y > 4$ (above Quantities A and B). It follows from $y > 4$ that $y > 1$, or $1 < y$, so that in the comparison $1 \; ? \; y$, the placeholder ? represents *less than* (<): $1 < y$.

However, the problem asks for a comparison between Quantity A and Quantity B, not a comparison between 1 and y. To go from the comparison between 1 and y to a comparison between Quantities A and B, start with the last comparison, $1 < y$, and carefully consider each simplification step in reverse order to determine what each comparison implies about the preceding comparison, all the way back to the comparison between Quantities A and B if possible. Since step 3 was "*divide* both sides by 2," *multiplying* both sides of the comparison $1 < y$ by 2 implies the preceding comparison $2 < 2y$, thus reversing step 3. Each simplification step can be reversed as follows:

- Reverse step 3: *multiply* both sides by 2.
- Reverse step 2: *add* $3y$ to both sides.
- Reverse step 1: *divide* both sides by 5.

When each step is reversed, the relationship remains *less than* (<), so Quantity A is less than Quantity B.

Thus the correct answer is Choice B, Quantity B is greater.

This explanation uses the following strategy.
Strategy 5: Simplify an Arithmetic or Algebraic Representation

While some simplification steps like subtracting 3 from both sides or dividing both sides by 10 are always reversible, it is important to note that some steps, like squaring both sides, may not be reversible.

Also, note that when you simplify an *inequality*, the steps of multiplying or dividing both sides by a negative number change the direction of the inequality; for example, if $x < y$, then $-x > -y$. So the relationship in the final, simplified inequality may be the *opposite* of the relationship between Quantities A and B. This is another reason to consider the impact of each step carefully.

	Quantity A	Quantity B
7.	$\dfrac{2^{30} - 2^{29}}{2}$	2^{28}

    Ⓐ Quantity A is greater.

    Ⓑ Quantity B is greater.

    Ⓒ The two quantities are equal.

    Ⓓ The relationship cannot be determined from the information given.

Explanation

Set up the initial comparison:

$$\frac{2^{30} - 2^{29}}{2} \;?\; 2^{28}$$

Then simplify:

Step 1: Multiply both sides by 2 to get

$$2^{30} - 2^{29} \;?\; 2^{29}$$

Step 2: Add 2^{29} to both sides to get

$$2^{30} \;?\; 2^{29} + 2^{29}$$

Step 3: Simplify the right-hand side using the fact that $(2)(2^{29}) = 2^{30}$ to get

$$2^{30} \;?\; 2^{30}$$

The resulting relationship is *equal to* (=). In reverse order, each simplification step implies *equal to* in the preceding comparison. So Quantities A and B are also equal. **Thus the correct answer is Choice C, the two quantities are equal.**

This explanation uses the following strategy.
Strategy 5: Simplify an Arithmetic or Algebraic Representation

---

	Quantity A	Quantity B
8.	$x^2 + 1$	$2x - 1$

   Ⓐ Quantity A is greater.

   Ⓑ Quantity B is greater.

   Ⓒ The two quantities are equal.

   Ⓓ The relationship cannot be determined from the information given.

Explanation

Set up the initial comparison:

$$x^2 + 1 \; ? \; 2x - 1$$

Then simplify by noting that the quadratic polynomial $x^2 - 2x + 1$ can be factored:

Step 1: Subtract $2x$ from both sides to get

$$x^2 - 2x + 1 \; ? \; -1$$

Step 2: Factor the left-hand side to get

$$(x - 1)^2 \; ? \; -1$$

The left-hand side of the comparison is the square of a number. Since the square of a number is always greater than or equal to 0, and 0 is greater than −1, the simplified comparison is the inequality $(x - 1)^2 > -1$ and the resulting relationship is *greater than* (>). In reverse order, each simplification step implies the inequality *greater than* (>) in the preceding comparison. Therefore Quantity A is greater than Quantity B.

The correct answer is Choice A, Quantity A is greater.

This explanation uses the following strategies.
Strategy 5: Simplify an Arithmetic or Algebraic Representation
Strategy 8: Search for a Mathematical Relationship

$$w > 1$$

Quantity A	Quantity B

9. $\qquad$ $7w - 4$ $\qquad\qquad\qquad\qquad$ $2w + 5$

    Ⓐ Quantity A is greater.

    Ⓑ Quantity B is greater.

    Ⓒ The two quantities are equal.

    Ⓓ The relationship cannot be determined from the information given.

Explanation

Set up the initial comparison:

$$7w - 4 \;\boxed{?}\; 2w + 5$$

Then simplify:

Step 1: Subtract $2w$ from both sides and add 4 to both sides to get

$$5w \;\boxed{?}\; 9$$

Step 2: Divide both sides by 5 to get

$$w \;\boxed{?}\; \frac{9}{5}$$

The comparison cannot be simplified any further. Although you are given that $w > 1$, you still don't know how w compares to $\frac{9}{5}$, or 1.8. For example, if $w = 1.5$, then $w < 1.8$, but if $w = 2$, then $w > 1.8$. In other words, the relationship between w and $\frac{9}{5}$ cannot be determined.

    Note that each of these simplification steps is reversible, so in reverse order, each simplification step implies that the *relationship cannot be determined* in the preceding comparison. Thus the relationship between Quantities A and B cannot be determined.

    The correct answer is Choice D, the relationship cannot be determined from the information given.

This explanation uses the following strategies.
Strategy 5: Simplify an Arithmetic or Algebraic Representation
Strategy 13: Determine Whether a Conclusion Follows from the Information Given

The strategy of simplifying the comparison works most efficiently when you note that a simplification step is reversible while actually taking the step. Here are some common steps that are always reversible:

- Adding any number or expression to both sides of a comparison
- Subtracting any number or expression from both sides
- Multiplying both sides by any nonzero number or expression
- Dividing both sides by any nonzero number or expression

Remember that if the relationship is an inequality, multiplying or dividing both sides by any *negative* number or expression will yield the opposite inequality. Be aware that some common operations like squaring both sides are generally not reversible and may require further analysis using other information given in the question in order to justify reversing such steps.

Multiple-choice Questions—Select One Answer Choice

Description

These questions are multiple-choice questions that ask you to select only one answer choice from a list of five choices.

> #### Tips for Answering
>
> - **Use the fact that the answer is there.** If your answer is not one of the five answer choices given, you should assume that your answer is incorrect and do the following:
>   - Reread the question carefully—you may have missed an important detail or misinterpreted some information.
>   - Check your computations—you may have made a mistake, such as mis-keying a number on the calculator.
>   - Reevaluate your solution method—you may have a flaw in your reasoning.
> - **Examine the answer choices.** In some questions you are asked explicitly which of the choices has a certain property. You may have to consider each choice separately, or you may be able to see a relationship between the choices that will help you find the answer more quickly. In other questions, it may be helpful to work backward from the choices, say, by substituting the choices in an equation or inequality to see which one works. However, be careful, as that method may take more time than using reasoning.
> - **For questions that require approximations, scan the answer choices to see how close an approximation is needed.** In other questions, too, it may be helpful to scan the choices briefly before solving the problem to get a better sense of what the question is asking. If computations are involved in the solution, it may be necessary to carry out all computations exactly and round only your final answer in order to get the required degree of accuracy. In other questions, you may find that estimation is sufficient and will help you avoid spending time on long computations.

Sample Questions

Select a single answer choice.

1. If $5x + 32 = 4 - 2x$, what is the value of x?

  (A) −4
  (B) −3
  (C) 4
  (D) 7
  (E) 12

Explanation

Solving the equation for x, you get $7x = -28$, and so $x = -4$.
  The correct answer is Choice A, −4.

This explanation uses the following strategy.
Strategy 5: Simplify an Arithmetic or Algebraic Representation

---

2. Which of the following numbers is farthest from the number 1 on the number line?

  (A) −10
  (B) −5
  (C) 0
  (D) 5
  (E) 10

Explanation

Circling each of the answer choices in a sketch of the number line (Figure 4) shows that of the given numbers, −10 is the greatest distance from 1.

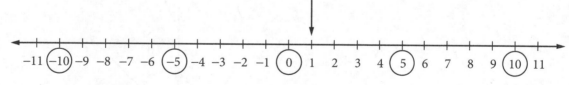

Figure 4

Another way to answer the question is to remember that the distance between two numbers on the number line is equal to the absolute value of the difference of the two numbers. For example, the distance between −10 and 1 is $|-10 - 1| = 11$, and the distance between 10 and 1 is $|10 - 1| = |9| = 9$.
  The correct answer is Choice A, −10.

This explanation uses the following strategy.
Strategy 2: Translate from Words to a Figure or Diagram

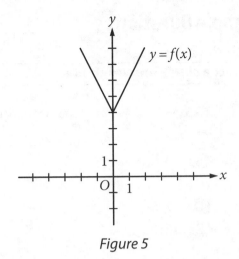

Figure 5

3.   The figure above shows the graph of the function *f* defined by $f(x) = |2x| + 4$ for all numbers *x*. For which of the following functions *g*, defined for all numbers *x*, does the graph of *g* intersect the graph of *f*?

(A) $g(x) = x - 2$

(B) $g(x) = x + 3$

(C) $g(x) = 2x - 2$

(D) $g(x) = 2x + 3$

(E) $g(x) = 3x - 2$

Explanation

You can see that all five choices are linear functions whose graphs are lines with various slopes and *y*-intercepts. The graph of Choice A is a line with slope 1 and *y*-intercept −2, shown in Figure 6.

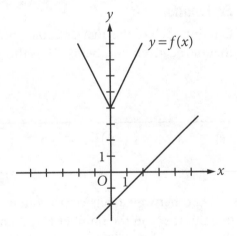

Figure 6

It is clear that this line will not intersect the graph of f to the left of the y-axis. To the right of the y-axis, the graph of f is a line with slope 2, which is greater than slope 1. Consequently, as the value of x increases, the value of y increases faster for f than for g, and therefore the graphs do not intersect to the right of the y-axis. Choice B is similarly ruled out. Note that if the y-intercept of either of the lines in Choices A and B were greater than or equal to 4 instead of less than 4, they would intersect the graph of f.

Choices C and D are lines with slope 2 and y-intercepts less than 4. Hence, they are parallel to the graph of f (to the right of the y-axis) and therefore will not intersect it. Any line with a slope greater than 2 and a y-intercept less than 4, like the line in Choice E, will intersect the graph of f (to the right of the y-axis).

The correct answer is Choice E, $g(x) = 3x - 2$.

This explanation uses the following strategies.
Strategy 3: Translate from an Algebraic to a Graphical Representation
Strategy 6: Add to a Geometric Figure
Strategy 8: Search for a Mathematical Relationship

---

4. A car got 33 miles per gallon using gasoline that cost $2.95 per gallon. Approximately what was the cost, in dollars, of the gasoline used in driving the car 350 miles?

    Ⓐ $10
    Ⓑ $20
    Ⓒ $30
    Ⓓ $40
    Ⓔ $50

Explanation

Scanning the answer choices indicates that you can do at least some estimation and still answer confidently. The car used $\frac{350}{33}$ gallons of gasoline, so the cost was $\left(\frac{350}{33}\right)(2.95)$ dollars You can estimate the product $\left(\frac{350}{33}\right)(2.95)$ by estimating $\frac{350}{33}$ a little low, 10, and estimating 2.95 a little high, 3, to get approximately $(10)(3) = 30$ dollars. You can also use the calculator to compute a more exact answer and then round the answer to the nearest 10 dollars, as suggested by the answer choices. The calculator yields the decimal 31.287..., which rounds to 30 dollars.

Thus the correct answer is Choice C, $30.

This explanation uses the following strategies.
Strategy 1: Translate from Words to an Arithmetic or Algebraic Representation
Strategy 9: Estimate

5. A certain jar contains 60 jelly beans—22 white, 18 green, 11 yellow, 5 red, and 4 purple. If a jelly bean is to be chosen at random, what is the probability that the jelly bean will be neither red nor purple?

Ⓐ 0.09

Ⓑ 0.15

Ⓒ 0.54

Ⓓ 0.85

Ⓔ 0.91

Explanation

Since there are 5 red and 4 purple jelly beans in the jar, there are 51 that are neither red nor purple, and the probability of selecting one of these is $\frac{51}{60}$. Since all of the answer choices are decimals, you must convert the fraction to its decimal equivalent, 0.85.

Thus the correct answer is Choice D, 0.85.

This explanation uses the following strategies.
Strategy 1: Translate from Words to an Arithmetic or Algebraic Representation
Strategy 5: Simplify an Arithmetic or Algebraic Representation

Multiple-choice Questions—Select One or More Answer Choices

Description

These questions are multiple-choice questions that ask you to select one or more answer choices from a list of choices. A question may or may not specify the number of choices to select. These questions are marked with square boxes beside the answer choices, not circles or ovals.

Tips for Answering

- **Note whether you are asked to indicate a specific number of answer choices or all choices that apply.** In the latter case, be sure to consider all of the choices, determine which ones are correct, and select all of those and only those choices. Note that there may be only one correct choice.
- **In some questions that involve conditions that limit the possible values of numerical answer choices, it may be efficient to determine the least and/or the greatest possible value.** Knowing the least and/or greatest possible value may enable you to quickly determine all of the choices that are correct.
- **Avoid lengthy calculations by recognizing and continuing numerical patterns.**

Sample Questions

> Select one or more answer choices according to the specific question directions.
>
> If the question does not specify how many answer choices to select, select all that apply.
>
> - The correct answer may be just one of the choices or as many as all of the choices, depending on the question.
> - No credit is given unless you select all of the correct choices and no others.
>
> If the question specifies how many answer choices to select, select exactly that number of choices.

1. Which two of the following numbers have a product that is between -1 and 0 ?

    Indicate both of the numbers.

    A -20
    B -10
    C 2^{-4}
    D 3^{-2}

Explanation

For this question, you must select a pair of answer choices. The product of the pair must be negative, so the possible products are $(-20)(2^{-4})$, $(-20)(3^{-2})$, $(-10)(2^{-4})$, and $(-10)(3^{-2})$. The product must also be greater than -1. The first product is

$\dfrac{-20}{2^4} = -\dfrac{20}{16} < -1$, the second product is $\dfrac{-20}{3^2} = -\dfrac{20}{9} < -1$, and the third product is

$\dfrac{-10}{2^4} = -\dfrac{10}{16} > -1$, so you can stop there.

The correct answer consists of Choices B (-10) and C (2^{-4}).

This explanation uses the following strategies.
Strategy 1: Translate from Words to an Arithmetic or Algebraic Representation
Strategy 10: Trial and Error

2.   Which of the following integers are multiples of both 2 and 3 ?

Indicate all such integers.

A   8
B   9
C   12
D   18
E   21
F   36

Explanation

You can first identify the multiples of 2, which are 8, 12, 18, and 36, and then among the multiples of 2 identify the multiples of 3, which are 12, 18, and 36. Alternatively, if you realize that every number that is a multiple of 2 and 3 is also a multiple of 6, you can identify the choices that are multiples of 6.
   The correct answer consists of Choices C (12), D (18), and F (36).

This explanation uses the following strategies.
Strategy 1: Translate from Words to an Arithmetic or Algebraic Representation
Strategy 11: Divide into Cases

---

3.   Each employee of a certain company is in either Department X or Department Y, and there are more than twice as many employees in Department X as in Department Y. The average (arithmetic mean) salary is $25,000 for the employees in Department X and $35,000 for the employees in Department Y. Which of the following amounts could be the average salary for all of the employees of the company?

Indicate all such amounts.

A $26,000
B $28,000
C $29,000
D $30,000
E $31,000
F $32,000
G $34,000

Explanation

One strategy for answering this kind of question is to find the least and/or greatest possible value. Clearly the average salary is between $25,000 and $35,000, and all of the answer choices are in this interval. Since you are told that there are more employees with the lower average salary, the average salary of all employees must be less than the average of $25,000 and $35,000, which is $30,000. If there were exactly twice as many employees in Department X as in Department Y, then the average salary for all employees would be, to the nearest dollar, the following weighted mean,

$$\frac{(2)(25,000) + (1)(35,000)}{2 + 1} \approx 28,333 \text{ dollars}$$

where the weight for $25,000 is 2 and the weight for $35,000 is 1. Since there are *more* than twice as many employees in Department X as in Department Y, the actual average salary must be even closer to $25,000 because the weight for $25,000 is greater than 2. This means that $28,333 is the greatest possible average. Among the choices given, the possible values of the average are therefore $26,000 and $28,000.

Thus the correct answer consists of Choices A ($26,000) and B ($28,000).

Intuitively, you might expect that any amount between $25,000 and $28,333 is a possible value of the average salary. To see that $26,000 is possible, in the weighted mean above, use the respective weights 9 and 1 instead of 2 and 1. To see that $28,000 is possible, use the respective weights 7 and 3.

This explanation uses the following strategies.
Strategy 1: Translate from Words to an Arithmetic or Algebraic Representation
Strategy 8: Search for a Mathematical Relationship
Strategy 12: Adapt Solutions to Related Problems

---

4. Which of the following could be the units digit of 57^n, where n is a positive integer?

    Indicate <u>all</u> such digits.

    A 0
    B 1
    C 2
    D 3
    E 4
    F 5
    G 6
    H 7
    I 8
    J 9

Explanation

The units digit of 57^n is the same as the units digit of 7^n for all positive integers n. To see why this is true for $n = 2$, compute 57^2 by hand and observe how its units digit results from the units digit of 7^2. Because this is true for every positive integer n, you need to consider only powers of 7. Beginning with $n = 1$ and proceeding consecutively, the units digits of 7, 7^2, 7^3, 7^4, and 7^5 are 7, 9, 3, 1, and 7, respectively. In this sequence, the first digit, 7, appears again, and the pattern of four digits, 7, 9, 3, 1, repeats without end. Hence, these four digits are the only possible units digits of 7^n and therefore of 57^n.

The correct answer consists of Choices B (1), D (3), H (7), and J (9).

This explanation uses the following strategies.
Strategy 7: Find a Pattern
Strategy 12: Adapt Solutions to Related Problems

Numeric Entry Questions

Description

Questions of this type ask you either to enter your answer as an integer or a decimal in a single answer box or to enter it as a fraction in two separate boxes—one for the numerator and one for the denominator. In the computer-delivered test, use the computer mouse and keyboard to enter your answer.

> ### *Tips for Answering*
>
> - **Make sure you answer the question that is asked.** Since there are no answer choices to guide you, read the question carefully and make sure you provide the type of answer required. Sometimes there will be labels before or after the answer box to indicate the appropriate type of answer. Pay special attention to units such as feet or miles, to orders of magnitude such as millions or billions, and to percents as compared with decimals.
> - **If you are asked to round your answer, make sure you round to the required degree of accuracy.** For example, if an answer of 46.7 is to be rounded to the nearest integer, you need to enter the number 47. If your solution strategy involves intermediate computations, you should carry out all computations exactly and round only your final answer in order to get the required degree of accuracy. If no rounding instructions are given, enter the exact answer.
> - **Examine your answer to see if it is reasonable with respect to the information given.** You may want to use estimation or another solution path to double-check your answer.

Sample Questions

Enter your answer as an integer or a decimal if there is a single answer box OR as a fraction if there are two separate boxes—one for the numerator and one for the denominator.

To enter an integer or a decimal, either type the number in the answer box using the keyboard or use the Transfer Display button on the calculator.

- First, click on the answer box—a cursor will appear in the box—and then type the number.
- To erase a number, use the Backspace key.
- For a negative sign, type a hyphen. For a decimal point, type a period.
- To remove a negative sign, type the hyphen again and it will disappear; the number will remain.
- The Transfer Display button on the calculator will transfer the calculator display to the answer box.
- Equivalent forms of the correct answer, such as 2.5 and 2.50, are all correct.
- Enter the exact answer unless the question asks you to round your answer.

To enter a fraction, type the numerator and the denominator in the respective boxes using the keyboard.

- For a negative sign, type a hyphen; to remove it, type the hyphen again. A decimal point cannot be used in a fraction.
- The Transfer Display button on the calculator cannot be used for a fraction.
- Fractions do not need to be reduced to lowest terms, though you may need to reduce your fraction to fit in the boxes.

1. One pen costs $0.25 and one marker costs $0.35. At those prices, what is the total cost of 18 pens and 100 markers?

$ ☐

Explanation

Multiplying $0.25 by 18 yields $4.50, which is the cost of the 18 pens; and multiplying $0.35 by 100 yields $35.00, which is the cost of the 100 markers. The total cost is therefore $4.50 + $35.00 = $39.50. Equivalent decimals, such as $39.5 or $39.500, are considered correct.

Thus the correct answer is $39.50 (or equivalent).

Note that the dollar symbol is in front of the answer box, so the symbol $ does not need to be entered in the box. In fact, only numbers, a decimal point, and a negative sign can be entered in the answer box.

This explanation uses the following strategy.
Strategy 1: Translate from Words to an Arithmetic or Algebraic Representation

2. Rectangle R has length 30 and width 10, and square S has length 5. The perimeter of S is what fraction of the perimeter of R ?

Explanation

The perimeter of R is $30 + 10 + 30 + 10 = 80$, and the perimeter of S is $(4)(5) = 20$. Therefore, the perimeter of S is $\frac{20}{80}$ of the perimeter of R. To enter the answer $\frac{20}{80}$, you should enter the numerator 20 in the top box and the denominator 80 in the bottom box. Because the fraction does not need to be reduced to lowest terms, any fraction that is equivalent to $\frac{20}{80}$ is also considered correct, as long as it fits in the boxes. For example, both of the fractions $\frac{2}{8}$ and $\frac{1}{4}$ are considered correct.

Thus the correct answer is $\frac{20}{80}$ (or any equivalent fraction).

This explanation uses the following strategy.
Strategy 1: Translate from Words to an Arithmetic or Algebraic Representation

---

RESULTS OF A USED-CAR AUCTION

	Small Cars	Large Cars
Number of cars offered	32	23
Number of cars sold	16	20
Projected sales total for cars offered (in thousands)	$70	$150
Actual sales total (in thousands)	$41	$120

Figure 7

3. For the large cars sold at an auction that is summarized in the table above, what was the average sale price per car?

$

Explanation

From Figure 7, you see that the number of large cars sold was 20 and the sales total for large cars was $120,000 (not $120). Thus the average sale price per car was

$$\frac{\$120,000}{20} = \$6,000.$$

The correct answer is $6,000 (or equivalent).

(Note that the comma in 6,000 will appear automatically in the answer box in the computer-delivered test.)

This explanation uses the following strategy.
Strategy 4: Translate from a Figure to an Arithmetic or Algebraic Representation

4. A merchant made a profit of \$5 on the sale of a sweater that cost the merchant \$15. What is the profit expressed as a percent of the merchant's cost?

Give your answer to the <u>nearest whole percent</u>.

 %

Explanation

The percent profit is $\left(\dfrac{5}{15}\right)(100) = 33.333\ldots = 33.\overline{3}$ percent, which is 33%, to the nearest whole percent.

Thus the correct answer is 33% (or equivalent).

If you use the calculator and the Transfer Display button, the number that will be transferred to the answer box is 33.333333, which is incorrect since it is not given to the nearest whole percent. You will need to adjust the number in the answer box by deleting all of the digits to the right of the decimal point (using the Backspace key).

Also, since you are asked to give the answer as a percent, the decimal equivalent of 33 percent, which is 0.33, is incorrect. The percent symbol next to the answer box indicates that the form of the answer must be a percent. Entering 0.33 in the box would give the erroneous answer 0.33%.

This explanation uses the following strategies.
Strategy 1: Translate from Words to an Arithmetic or Algebraic Representation
Strategy 5: Simplify an Arithmetic or Algebraic Representation

---

5. Working alone at its constant rate, machine A produces k liters of a chemical in 10 minutes. Working alone at its constant rate, machine B produces k liters of the chemical in 15 minutes. How many minutes does it take machines A and B, working simultaneously at their respective constant rates, to produce k liters of the chemical?

 minutes

Explanation

Machine A produces $\dfrac{k}{10}$ liters per minute, and machine B produces $\dfrac{k}{15}$ liters per minute. So when the machines work simultaneously, the rate at which the chemical is produced is the sum of these two rates, which is $\dfrac{k}{10} + \dfrac{k}{15} = k\left(\dfrac{1}{10} + \dfrac{1}{15}\right) = k\left(\dfrac{25}{150}\right) = \dfrac{k}{6}$ liters per minute. To compute the time required to produce k liters at this rate, divide the amount k by the rate $\dfrac{k}{6}$ to get $\dfrac{k}{\frac{k}{6}} = 6$.

Therefore, the correct answer is 6 minutes (or equivalent).

One way to check that the answer of 6 minutes is reasonable is to observe that if the slower rate of machine *B* were the same as machine *A*'s faster rate of *k* liters in 10 minutes, then the two machines, working simultaneously, would take half the time, or 5 minutes, to produce the *k* liters. So the answer has to be *greater than 5 minutes*. Similarly, if the faster rate of machine *A* were the same as machine *B*'s slower rate of *k* liters in 15 minutes, then the two machines would take half the time, or 7.5 minutes, to produce the *k* liters. So the answer has to be *less than 7.5 minutes*. Thus the answer of 6 minutes is reasonable compared to the lower estimate of 5 minutes and the upper estimate of 7.5 minutes.

This explanation uses the following strategies.
Strategy 1: Translate from Words to an Arithmetic or Algebraic Representation
Strategy 5: Simplify an Arithmetic or Algebraic Representation
Strategy 8: Search for a Mathematical Relationship

Data Interpretation Sets

Description

Data Interpretation questions are grouped together and refer to the same table, graph, or other data presentation. These questions ask you to interpret or analyze the given data. The types of questions may be Multiple-choice (both types) or Numeric Entry.

> ### *Tips for Answering*
>
> - **Scan the data presentation briefly to see what it is about, but do not spend time studying all of the information in detail.** Focus on those aspects of the data that are necessary to answer the questions. Pay attention to the axes and scales of graphs; to the units of measurement or orders of magnitude (such as *billions*) that are given in the titles, labels, and legends; and to any notes that clarify the data.
> - **Bar graphs and circle graphs, as well as other graphical displays of data, are drawn to scale, so you can read or estimate data visually from such graphs.** For example, you can use the relative sizes of bars or sectors to compare the quantities that they represent, but be aware of broken scales and of bars that do not start at 0.
> - **The questions are to be answered only on the basis of the data presented, everyday facts (such as the number of days in a year), and your knowledge of mathematics.** Do not make use of specialized information you may recall from other sources about the particular context on which the questions are based unless the information can be derived from the data presented.

Sample Questions

Questions 1 to 3 are based on the following data.

ANNUAL PERCENT CHANGE IN DOLLAR AMOUNT OF SALES
AT FIVE RETAIL STORES FROM 2006 TO 2008

Store	Percent Change from 2006 to 2007	Percent Change from 2007 to 2008
P	10	−10
Q	−20	9
R	5	12
S	−7	−15
T	17	−8

Figure 8

1. If the dollar amount of sales at Store *P* was $800,000 for 2006, what was the dollar amount of sales at that store for 2008 ?

   Ⓐ $727,200

   Ⓑ $792,000

   Ⓒ $800,000

   Ⓓ $880,000

   Ⓔ $968,000

Explanation

According to Figure 8, if the dollar amount of sales at Store *P* was $800,000 for 2006, then it was 10 percent greater for 2007, which is 110 percent of that amount, or $880,000. For 2008 the amount was 90 percent of $880,000, which is $792,000.

The correct answer is Choice B, $792,000.

Note that an increase of 10 percent for one year and a decrease of 10 percent for the following year does not result in the same dollar amount as the original dollar amount because the base that is used in computing the percents is $800,000 for the first change but $880,000 for the second change.

This explanation uses the following strategies.
Strategy 4: Translate from a Figure to an Arithmetic or Algebraic Representation
Strategy 5: Simplify an Arithmetic or Algebraic Representation

2. At Store *T*, the dollar amount of sales for 2007 was what percent of the dollar amount of sales for 2008 ?

   Give your answer to the <u>nearest 0.1 percent</u>.

   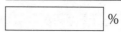 %

Explanation

If *A* is the dollar amount of sales at Store *T* for 2007, then 8 percent of *A*, or $0.08A$, is the amount of decrease from 2007 to 2008. Thus $A - 0.08A = 0.92A$ is the dollar amount for 2008. Therefore, the desired percent can be obtained by dividing *A* by $0.92A$, which equals $\dfrac{A}{0.92A} = \dfrac{1}{0.92} = 1.0869565\ldots$ Expressed as a percent and rounded to the nearest 0.1 percent, this number is 108.7%.

Thus the correct answer is 108.7% (or equivalent).

This explanation uses the following strategies.
Strategy 4: Translate from a Figure to an Arithmetic or Algebraic Representation
Strategy 5: Simplify an Arithmetic or Algebraic Representation

---

3. Based on the information given, which of the following statements must be true?

   Indicate <u>all</u> such statements.

   [A] For 2008 the dollar amount of sales at Store *R* was greater than that at each of the other four stores.

   [B] The dollar amount of sales at Store *S* for 2008 was 22 percent less than that for 2006.

   [C] The dollar amount of sales at Store *R* for 2008 was more than 17 percent greater than that for 2006.

Explanation

For Choice A, since the only data given in Figure 8 are percent changes from year to year, there is no way to compare the actual dollar amount of sales at the stores for 2008 or for any other year. Even though Store *R* had the greatest percent increase from 2006 to 2008, its actual dollar amount of sales for 2008 may have been much smaller than that for any of the other four stores, and therefore Choice A is not necessarily true.

For Choice B, even though the sum of the two percent decreases would suggest a 22 percent decrease, the bases of the percents are different. If *B* is the dollar amount of sales at Store *S* for 2006, then the dollar amount for 2007 is 93 percent of *B*, or $0.93B$, and the dollar amount for 2008 is given by $(0.85)(0.93)B$, which is $0.7905B$. Note that this represents a percent decrease of $100 - 79.05 = 20.95$ percent, which is not equal to 22 percent, and so Choice B is not true.

For Choice C, if *C* is the dollar amount of sales at Store *R* for 2006, then the dollar amount for 2007 is given by $1.05C$ and the dollar amount for 2008 is given by $(1.12)(1.05)C$, which is $1.176C$. Note that this represents a 17.6 percent increase, which is greater than 17 percent, so Choice C must be true.

Therefore the correct answer consists of only Choice C (The dollar amount of sales at Store *R* for 2008 was more than 17 percent greater than that for 2006).

This explanation uses the following strategies.
Strategy 1: Translate from Words to an Arithmetic or Algebraic Representation
Strategy 4: Translate from a Figure to an Arithmetic or Algebraic Representation
Strategy 5: Simplify an Arithmetic or Algebraic Representation
Strategy 13: Determine Whether a Conclusion Follows from the Information Given
Strategy 14: Determine What Additional Information Is Sufficient to Solve a Problem

Using the Calculator

Sometimes the computations you need to do in order to answer a question in the Quantitative Reasoning measure are somewhat time-consuming, like long division, or involve square roots. For such computations, you can use the on-screen calculator provided in the computer-delivered test. The on-screen calculator is shown in Figure 9.

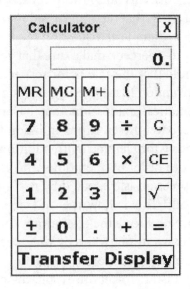

Figure 9

Although the calculator can shorten the time it takes to perform computations, keep in mind that the calculator provides results that supplement, but do not replace, your knowledge of mathematics. You must use your mathematical knowledge to determine whether the calculator's results are reasonable and how the results can be used to answer a question.

Here are some general guidelines for calculator use in the Quantitative Reasoning measure:

- Most of the questions don't require difficult computations, so don't use the calculator just because it's available.
- Use it for calculations that you know are tedious, such as long division, square roots, and addition, subtraction, or multiplication of numbers that have several digits.

- Avoid using it for simple computations that are quicker to do mentally, such as $10 - 490$, $(4)(70)$, $\dfrac{4{,}300}{10}$, $\sqrt{25}$, and 30^2.

- Avoid using it to introduce decimals if you are asked to give an answer as a fraction.

- Some questions can be answered more quickly by reasoning and estimating than by using the calculator.

- If you use the calculator, estimate the answer beforehand so that you can determine whether the calculator's answer is "in the ballpark." This may help you avoid key-entry errors.

The following guidelines are specific to the on-screen calculator in the computer-delivered test:

- When you use the computer mouse or the keyboard to operate the calculator, take care not to mis-key a number or operation.

- Note all of the calculator's buttons, including Transfer Display.

- The Transfer Display button can be used on Numeric Entry questions with a single answer box. This button will transfer the calculator display to the answer box. You should check that the transferred number has the correct form to answer the question. For example, if a question requires you to round your answer or convert your answer to a percent, make sure that you adjust the transferred number accordingly.

- Take note that the calculator respects *order of operations*, which is a mathematical convention that establishes which operations are performed before others in a mathematical expression that has more than one operation. The order is as follows: parentheses, exponentiation (including square roots), multiplications and divisions (from left to right), additions and subtractions (from left to right). With respect to order of operations, the value of the expression $1 + 2 \times 4$ is 9 because the expression is evaluated by first multiplying 2 and 4 and then by adding 1 to the result. This is how the on-screen calculator in the Quantitative Reasoning measure performs the operations. (Note that many basic calculators follow a different convention, whereby they perform multiple operations in the order that they are entered into the calculator. For such calculators, the result of entering $1 + 2 \times 4$ is 12. To get this result, the calculator adds 1 and 2, displays a result of 3, then multiplies 3 and 4, and displays a result of 12.)

- In addition to parentheses, the on-screen calculator has one memory location and three memory buttons that govern it: memory recall $\boxed{\text{MR}}$, memory clear $\boxed{\text{MC}}$, and memory sum $\boxed{\text{M+}}$. These buttons function as they normally do on most basic calculators.

- Some computations are not defined for real numbers: for example, division by zero or taking the square root of a negative number. If you enter $6 \boxed{\div} 0 \boxed{=}$, the word **Error** will be displayed. Similarly, if you enter $1 \boxed{\pm} \boxed{\sqrt{\ }}$, then **Error** will be displayed. To clear the display, you must press the clear button $\boxed{\text{C}}$.

- The calculator displays up to eight digits. If a computation results in a number greater than 99,999,999, then **Error** will be displayed. For example, the calculation $10{,}000{,}000 \boxed{\times} 10 \boxed{=}$ results in **Error**. The clear button $\boxed{\text{C}}$ must be used to clear the display. If a computation results in a positive number less than 0.00000001, or 10^{-8}, then 0 will be displayed.

Below are some examples of computations using the calculator.

1. Compute $4 + \dfrac{6.73}{2}$.

Explanation

Enter 4 [+] 6.73 [÷] 2 [=] to get 7.365. Alternatively, enter 6.73 [÷] 2 [=] to get 3.365, and then enter [+] 4 [=] to get **7.365**.

---

2. Compute $-\dfrac{8.4 + 9.3}{70}$.

Explanation

Since division takes precedence over addition in the order of operations, you need to override that precedence in order to compute this fraction. Here are two ways to do that. You can use the parentheses for the addition in the numerator, entering [(] 8.4 [+] 9.3 [)] [÷] 70 [=] [±] to get −0.2528571. Or you can use the equals sign after 9.3, entering 8.4 [+] 9.3 [=] [÷] 70 [=] [±] to get the same result. In the second way, note that pressing the first [=] is essential, because without it, 8.4 [+] 9.3 [÷] 70 [=] [±]

would erroneously compute $-\left(8.4 + \dfrac{9.3}{70}\right)$ instead.

Incidentally, the exact value of the expression $-\dfrac{8.4 + 9.3}{70}$ is the repeating decimal $-0.25\overline{285714}$, where the digits 285714 repeat without end, but the calculator rounds the decimal to **−0.2528571.**

---

3. Find the length, to the nearest 0.01, of the hypotenuse of a right triangle with legs of length 21 and 54; that is, use the Pythagorean theorem and calculate $\sqrt{21^2 + 54^2}$.

Explanation

Enter 21 [×] 21 [+] 54 [×] 54 [=] [√] to get 57.939624. Again, pressing the [=] before the [√] is essential because 21 [×] 21 [+] 54 [×] 54 [√] [=] would erroneously compute $21^2 + 54\sqrt{54}$. This is because the square root would take precedence over the multiplication in the order of operations. Note that parentheses could be used, as in [(] 21 [×] 21 [)] [+] [(] 54 [×] 54 [)] [=] [√], but they are not necessary because the multiplications already take precedence over the addition.

Incidentally, the exact answer is a nonterminating, nonrepeating decimal, or an irrational number, but the calculator rounds the decimal to 57.939624. Finally, note that the problem asks for the answer to the nearest 0.01, so the correct answer is **57.94.**

4. Compute $(-15)^3$.

Explanation

Enter 15 $\boxed{\pm}$ $\boxed{\times}$ 15 $\boxed{\pm}$ $\boxed{\times}$ 15 $\boxed{\pm}$ $\boxed{=}$ to get **−3,375.**

---

5. Convert 6 miles per hour to feet per second.

Explanation

The solution to this problem uses the conversion factors 1 mile = 5,280 feet and 1 hour = 3,600 seconds as follows:

$$\left(\frac{6 \text{ miles}}{1 \text{ hour}}\right)\left(\frac{5,280 \text{ feet}}{1 \text{ mile}}\right)\left(\frac{1 \text{ hour}}{3,600 \text{ seconds}}\right) = ? \frac{\text{feet}}{\text{second}}$$

Enter 6 $\boxed{\times}$ 5280 $\boxed{\div}$ 3600 $\boxed{=}$ to get 8.8. Alternatively, enter 6 $\boxed{\times}$ 5280 $\boxed{=}$ to get the result 31,680, and then enter $\boxed{\div}$ 3600 $\boxed{=}$ to get **8.8 feet per second.**

---

6. At a fund-raising event, 43 participants donated $60 each, 21 participants donated $80 each, and 16 participants donated $100 each. What was the average (arithmetic mean) donation per participant, in dollars?

Explanation

The solution to this problem is to compute the weighted mean

$\dfrac{(43)(60) + (21)(80) + (16)(100)}{43 + 21 + 16}$. You can use the memory buttons and parentheses for this computation as follows:

Enter 43 $\boxed{\times}$ 60 $\boxed{=}$ $\boxed{M+}$ 21 $\boxed{\times}$ 80 $\boxed{=}$ $\boxed{M+}$ 16 $\boxed{\times}$ 100 $\boxed{=}$ $\boxed{M+}$ $\boxed{MR}$ $\boxed{\div}$ $\boxed{(}$ 43 $\boxed{+}$ 21 $\boxed{+}$ 16 $\boxed{)}$ $\boxed{=}$ to get 73.25, or **$73.25 per participant.**

When the $\boxed{M+}$ button is first used, the number in the calculator display is stored in memory and an **M** appears to the left of the display to show that the memory function is in use. Each subsequent use of the $\boxed{M+}$ button adds the number in the current display to the number stored in memory and replaces the number stored in memory by the sum. When the $\boxed{MR}$ button is pressed in the computation above, the current value in memory, 5,860, is displayed. To clear the memory, use the $\boxed{MC}$ button, and the **M** next to the display disappears.

3 Arithmetic

<table>
<tr>
<td>Your goals for this chapter</td>
<td>⇨ Practice answering GRE® questions in arithmetic
⇨ Review answers and explanations, particularly for questions you answered incorrectly</td>
</tr>
</table>

This chapter contains GRE Quantitative Reasoning practice questions that involve arithmetic.

Arithmetic topics include properties and types of integers, such as divisibility, factorization, prime numbers, remainders, and odd and even integers; arithmetic operations, exponents, and roots; and concepts such as estimation, percent, ratio, rate, absolute value, the number line, decimal representation, and sequences of numbers.

The questions are arranged by question type: Quantitative Comparison questions, followed by both types of Multiple-choice questions, and then Numeric Entry questions.

Following the questions is an answer key for quick reference. Then, at the end of the chapter, you will find complete explanations for every question. Each explanation is presented with the corresponding question for easy reference.

Review the answers and explanations carefully, paying particular attention to explanations for questions that you answered incorrectly.

Before answering the practice questions, read the Quantitative Reasoning section directions that begin on the following page. Also, review the directions that precede each question type to make sure you understand how to answer the questions.

Quantitative Reasoning Section Directions

For each question, indicate the best answer, using the directions given.

Notes: All numbers used are real numbers.

All figures are assumed to lie in a plane unless otherwise indicated.

Geometric figures, such as lines, circles, triangles, and quadrilaterals, **are not necessarily** drawn to scale. That is, you should **not** assume that quantities such as lengths and angle measures are as they appear in a figure. You should assume, however, that lines shown as straight are actually straight, points on a line are in the order shown, and more generally, all geometric objects are in the relative positions shown. For questions with geometric figures, you should base your answers on geometric reasoning, not on estimating or comparing quantities by sight or by measurement.

Coordinate systems, such as *xy*-planes and number lines, **are** drawn to scale; therefore, you can read, estimate, or compare quantities in such figures by sight or by measurement.

Graphical data presentations, such as bar graphs, circle graphs, and line graphs, **are** drawn to scale; therefore, you can read, estimate, or compare data values by sight or by measurement.

Quantitative Comparison Questions

For Questions 1 to 7, compare Quantity A and Quantity B, using additional information centered above the two quantities if such information is given. Select one of the following four answer choices and fill in the corresponding oval to the right of the question.

(A) Quantity A is greater.

(B) Quantity B is greater.

(C) The two quantities are equal.

(D) The relationship cannot be determined from the information given.

A symbol that appears more than once in a question has the same meaning throughout the question.

	Quantity A	Quantity B	Correct Answer
Example 1:	(2)(6)	2 + 6	Ⓐ Ⓑ Ⓒ Ⓓ

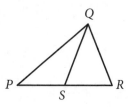

	Quantity A	Quantity B	Correct Answer
Example 2:	PS	SR	Ⓐ Ⓑ Ⓒ Ⓓ

(since equal lengths cannot be assumed, even though PS and SR appear equal)

D is the decimal form of the fraction $\dfrac{4}{11}$.

	Quantity A	Quantity B	
1.	The 25th digit to the right of the decimal point in D	4	Ⓒ Ⓓ

	Quantity A	Quantity B	
2.	$\sqrt[3]{270} - \sqrt[3]{10}$	$\sqrt[3]{80}$	Ⓑ Ⓒ

n is a positive integer, $x = 7n + 2$, and $y = 6n + 3$.

	Quantity A	Quantity B	
3.	The ones digit of $x + y$	5	Ⓐ Ⓑ Ⓒ Ⓓ

$$r = 2$$
$$s = -7$$

	Quantity A	Quantity B	
4.	$(r - s)^4$	$r^4 - s^4$	Ⓐ Ⓑ Ⓒ Ⓓ

---

n is an even negative integer.

	Quantity A	Quantity B	
5.	$\left(\dfrac{1}{3}\right)^n$	$(-3)^n$	Ⓐ Ⓑ Ⓒ Ⓓ

Today the price of a table was reduced by 20 percent from what it was yesterday, and the price of a lamp was reduced by 30 percent from what it was yesterday.

	Quantity A	Quantity B	
6.	The dollar amount of the reduction in the price of the table	The dollar amount of the reduction in the price of the lamp	Ⓐ Ⓑ Ⓒ Ⓓ

For 5 hours, a photocopier copied at a constant rate of 2 pages every 3 seconds.

	Quantity A	Quantity B	
7.	The number of pages the photocopier copied in the 5 hours	12,000	Ⓐ Ⓑ Ⓒ Ⓓ

Multiple-choice Questions—Select One Answer Choice

For Questions 8 to 13, select a single answer choice.

8. For each integer $n > 1$, let $A(n)$ denote the sum of the integers from 1 to n. For example, $A(100) = 1 + 2 + 3 + \cdots + 100 = 5{,}050$. What is the value of $A(200)$?

   (A) 10,100

   (B) 15,050

   (C) 15,150

   (D) 20,100

   (E) 21,500

9. Which of the following integers CANNOT be expressed as the sum of two prime numbers?

   (A) 8

   (B) 9

   (C) 10

   (D) 11

   (E) 12

10. When the positive integer n is divided by 45, the remainder is 18. Which of the following must be a divisor of n?

    (A) 11

    (B) 9

    (C) 7

    (D) 6

    (E) 4

11. Points A, B, C, and D are on the number line above, and $AB = CD = \frac{1}{3}(BC)$. What is the coordinate of C?

(A) $\dfrac{13}{30}$

(B) $\dfrac{9}{20}$

(C) $\dfrac{11}{24}$

(D) $\dfrac{7}{15}$

(E) $\dfrac{29}{60}$

12. Which of the following represents the total dollar amount that a customer would have to pay for an item that costs s dollars plus a sales tax of 8 percent, in terms of s?

(A) $\dfrac{s}{0.08}$

(B) $\dfrac{s}{1.08}$

(C) $\dfrac{s}{8}$

(D) $0.08s$

(E) $1.08s$

13. Marie earned $0.75 for every mile she walked in a charity walkathon. If she earned a total of $18.00 at that rate, how many miles did she walk?

(A) 13.5

(B) 17.5

(C) 21

(D) 22.5

(E) 24

Multiple-choice Questions—Select One or More Answer Choices

For Questions 14 to 16, select all the answer choices that apply.

14. Which of the following operations carried out on both the numerator and the denominator of a fraction will always produce an equivalent fraction?

    Indicate <u>all</u> such operations.

    [A] Adding 2
    [B] Multiplying by 5
    [C] Dividing by 100

15. If $|z| \leq 1,$ which of the following statements must be true?

    Indicate <u>all</u> such statements.

    [A] $z^2 \leq 1$
    [B] $z^2 \leq z$
    [C] $z^3 \leq z$

16. In a certain medical group, Dr. Schwartz schedules appointments to begin 30 minutes apart, Dr. Ramirez schedules appointments to begin 25 minutes apart, and Dr. Wu schedules appointments to begin 50 minutes apart. All three doctors schedule their first appointments to begin at 8:00 in the morning, which are followed by their successive appointments throughout the day without breaks. Other than at 8:00 in the morning, at what times before 1:30 in the afternoon do all three doctors schedule their appointments to begin at the same time?

    Indicate <u>all</u> such times.

    [A] 9:30 in the morning
    [B] 10:00 in the morning
    [C] 10:30 in the morning
    [D] 11:00 in the morning
    [E] 11:30 in the morning
    [F] 12:00 noon
    [G] 12:30 in the afternoon
    [H] 1:00 in the afternoon

Numeric Entry Questions

For Questions 17 to 19, enter your answer in the answer box(es) below the question.

- Your answer may be an integer, a decimal, or a fraction, and it may be negative.
- If a question asks for a fraction, there will be two boxes—one for the numerator and one for the denominator. A decimal point cannot be used in a fraction.
- Equivalent forms of the correct answer, such as 2.5 and 2.50, are all correct. Fractions do not need to be reduced to lowest terms, though you may need to reduce your fraction to fit in the boxes.
- Enter the exact answer unless the question asks you to round your answer.

17. The integers x and y are greater than 1. If $(4x)(7y) = 756$, what is the value of $x + y$?

$$x + y = \boxed{}$$

$$1, -3, 4, 1, -3, 4, 1, -3, 4, \ldots$$

18. In the sequence above, the first 3 terms repeat without end. What is the sum of the terms of the sequence from the 150th term to the 154th term?

$$\boxed{}$$

---

19. A manufacturing company has plants in three locations: Indonesia, Mexico, and Pakistan. The company has 6,000 employees, and each of the employees works at only one of the plants. If $\dfrac{3}{8}$ of the employees work at the plant in Indonesia and if twice as many employees work at the plant in Mexico as work at the plant in Pakistan, how many employees work at the plant in Mexico?

$$\boxed{} \text{ employees}$$

ANSWER KEY

1. **Choice B**: Quantity B is greater.
2. **Choice C**: The two quantities are equal.
3. **Choice D**: The relationship cannot be determined from the information given.
4. **Choice A**: Quantity A is greater.
5. **Choice A**: Quantity A is greater.
6. **Choice D**: The relationship cannot be determined from the information given.
7. **Choice C**: The two quantities are equal.
8. **Choice D**: 20,100
9. **Choice D**: 11
10. **Choice B**: 9
11. **Choice D**: $\dfrac{7}{15}$
12. **Choice E**: $1.08s$
13. **Choice E**: 24
14. **Choice B**: Multiplying by 5
    AND
    Choice C: Dividing by 100
15. **Choice A**: $z^2 \leq 1$
16. **Choice C**: 10:30 in the morning
    AND
    Choice H: 1:00 in the afternoon
17. **12**
18. **7**
19. **2,500**

Answers and Explanations

D is the decimal form of the fraction $\dfrac{4}{11}$.

	Quantity A	Quantity B	
1.	The 25th digit to the right of the decimal point in D	4	Ⓐ Ⓑ Ⓒ Ⓓ

Explanation

By dividing 4 by 11, you get the decimal form $D = 0.363636\ldots$, where the sequence of two digits "36" repeats without end. Continuing the repeating pattern, you see that the 1st digit, the 3rd digit, the 5th digit, and every subsequent odd-numbered digit to the right of the decimal point is 3. Therefore, Quantity A, the 25th digit to the right of the decimal point, is 3. Since Quantity A is 3 and Quantity B is 4, the correct answer is **Choice B**.

This explanation uses the following strategy.
Strategy 7: Find a Pattern

	Quantity A	Quantity B	
2.	$\sqrt[3]{270} - \sqrt[3]{10}$	$\sqrt[3]{80}$	Ⓐ Ⓑ Ⓒ Ⓓ

Explanation

You can simplify both quantities. Quantity A can be simplified as follows:

$$\sqrt[3]{270} - \sqrt[3]{10} = \left(\sqrt[3]{27}\right)\left(\sqrt[3]{10}\right) - \sqrt[3]{10} = 3\sqrt[3]{10} - \sqrt[3]{10} = 2\sqrt[3]{10}$$

Quantity B can be simplified as follows:

$$\sqrt[3]{80} = \left(\sqrt[3]{8}\right)\left(\sqrt[3]{10}\right) = 2\sqrt[3]{10}$$

Thus the correct answer is **Choice C**.

This explanation uses the following strategy.
Strategy 5: Simplify an Arithmetic or Algebraic Representation

n is a positive integer, $x = 7n + 2$, and $y = 6n + 3$.

Quantity A	Quantity B	
3. The ones digit of $x + y$	5	

Explanation

In the question, you are given that $x = 7n + 2$ and $y = 6n + 3$. Substituting the given expressions for x and y in Quantity A, you get $x + y = 13n + 5$.

Using trial and error, you can compare Quantity A, the ones digit of $13n + 5$, and Quantity B, 5, by plugging in a few values for the positive integer n.

If $n = 1$, then $x + y = 18$ and the ones digit is 8, which is greater than 5. So in this case Quantity A is greater than Quantity B.

If $n = 2$, then $x + y = 31$ and the ones digit is 1, which is less than 5. So in this case Quantity B is greater than Quantity A.

Since in one case Quantity A is greater than Quantity B, and in the other case Quantity B is greater than Quantity A, you can conclude that the correct answer is **Choice D**.

This explanation uses the following strategies.
Strategy 10: Trial and Error
Strategy 13: Determine Whether a Conclusion Follows from the Information Given

---

$$r = 2$$
$$s = -7$$

Quantity A	Quantity B	
4. $(r - s)^4$	$r^4 - s^4$	

Explanation

If you substitute the given numbers into the expressions in Quantities A and B, you can compare them.

Substituting in Quantity A gives $(r - s)^4 = (2 - (-7))^4 = 9^4$.

Substituting in Quantity B gives $r^4 - s^4 = 2^4 - (-7)^4 = 2^4 - 7^4$.

Without further calculation, you see that Quantity A is positive and Quantity B is negative. Thus the correct answer is **Choice A**.

This explanation uses the following strategy.
Strategy 5: Simplify an Arithmetic or Algebraic Representation

n is an even negative integer.

Quantity A	Quantity B

5. $\left(\dfrac{1}{3}\right)^{n}$ $(-3)^{n}$ Ⓐ Ⓑ Ⓒ Ⓓ

Explanation

Try plugging the first few even negative integers into the expressions in Quantity A and Quantity B to see if a pattern emerges.

If $n = -2$, Quantity A is $\left(\dfrac{1}{3}\right)^{-2} = 3^{2}$ and Quantity B is $(-3)^{-2} = \dfrac{1}{(-3)^{2}} = \dfrac{1}{3^{2}}$.

If $n = -4$, Quantity A is $\left(\dfrac{1}{3}\right)^{-4} = 3^{4}$ and Quantity B is $(-3)^{-4} = \dfrac{1}{(-3)^{4}} = \dfrac{1}{3^{4}}$.

If $n = -6$, Quantity A is $\left(\dfrac{1}{3}\right)^{-6} = 3^{6}$ and Quantity B is $(-3)^{-6} = \dfrac{1}{(-3)^{6}} = \dfrac{1}{3^{6}}$.

From these three examples, it looks like Quantity A and Quantity B may always be reciprocals of each other, with Quantity A greater than 1 and Quantity B less than 1. You can see this as follows.

If n is an even negative integer, then n can be expressed as $-2k$ where k is a positive integer. Substituting $-2k$ for n in Quantity A and Quantity B, you get that Quantity A is $\left(\dfrac{1}{3}\right)^{n} = \left(\dfrac{1}{3}\right)^{-2k} = 3^{2k}$ and Quantity B is $(-3)^{n} = (-3)^{-2k} = \left(\dfrac{1}{3}\right)^{2k}$. Since for all positive integers k the value of 3^{2k} is greater than 1 and the value of $\left(\dfrac{1}{3}\right)^{2k}$ is less than 1, it follows that the correct answer is **Choice A**.

This explanation uses the following strategies.
Strategy 7: Find a Pattern
Strategy 8: Search for a Mathematical Relationship

Today the price of a table was reduced by 20 percent from what it was yesterday, and the price of a lamp was reduced by 30 percent from what it was yesterday.

	Quantity A	Quantity B	
6.	The dollar amount of the reduction in the price of the table	The dollar amount of the reduction in the price of the lamp	Ⓐ Ⓑ Ⓒ Ⓓ

Explanation

Quantity A is 20 percent of yesterday's price of the table. Since yesterday's price is not given, you cannot calculate this quantity. Similarly, you cannot calculate Quantity B. In the absence of further information with which to compare the two quantities, the correct answer is **Choice D**.

This explanation uses the following strategy.
Strategy 13: Determine Whether a Conclusion Follows from the Information Given

---

For 5 hours, a photocopier copied at a constant rate of 2 pages every 3 seconds.

	Quantity A	Quantity B	
7.	The number of pages the photocopier copied in the 5 hours	12,000	Ⓐ Ⓑ Ⓒ Ⓓ

Explanation

Translating the given information, you can calculate Quantity A, the number of pages the photocopier copied in the 5 hours. Copying at the rate of 2 pages every 3 seconds is the same as copying at a rate of 40 pages every 60 seconds, or 40 pages per minute. This rate is the same as copying 2,400 pages every hour, or 12,000 pages in 5 hours. Since Quantity A is equal to 12,000 and Quantity B is 12,000, the correct answer is **Choice C**.

This explanation uses the following strategy.
Strategy 1: Translate from Words to an Arithmetic or Algebraic Representation

8. For each integer $n > 1$, let $A(n)$ denote the sum of the integers from 1 to n. For example, $A(100) = 1 + 2 + 3 + \cdots + 100 = 5{,}050$. What is the value of $A(200)$?

(A) 10,100

(B) 15,050

(C) 15,150

(D) 20,100

(E) 21,500

Explanation

In the question, you are given that $A(n)$ is equal to the sum of the integers from 1 to n, so $A(200) = 1 + 2 + 3 + \cdots + 100 + 101 + 102 + 103 + \cdots + 200$. In order to be able to use the given value of $A(100) = 5{,}050$, you can rewrite the sum as

$$
\begin{aligned}
A(200) &= A(100) + 101 + 102 + 103 + \cdots + 200 \\
&= A(100) + (100+1) + (100+2) + (100+3) + \cdots + (100+100) \\
&= A(100) + (1+2+3+\cdots+100) + (100)(100) \\
&= A(100) + A(100) + (100)(100) \\
&= 5{,}050 + 5{,}050 + 10{,}000 \\
&= 20{,}100
\end{aligned}
$$

Thus the correct answer is **Choice D**.

This explanation uses the following strategy.
Strategy 12: Adapt Solutions to Related Problems

---

9. Which of the following integers CANNOT be expressed as the sum of two prime numbers?

(A) 8

(B) 9

(C) 10

(D) 11

(E) 12

Explanation

Trying to write each answer choice as a sum of two prime numbers by trial and error, you get:

Choice A: $8 = 3 + 5$
Choice B: $9 = 2 + 7$
Choice C: $10 = 3 + 7$
Choice D: $11 = 1 + 10 = 2 + 9 = 3 + 8 = 4 + 7 = 5 + 6$
Choice E: $12 = 5 + 7$

Of the answer choices given, only 11 cannot be expressed as the sum of two prime numbers. The correct answer is **Choice D**.

This explanation uses the following strategy.
Strategy 10: Trial and Error

10. When the positive integer n is divided by 45, the remainder is 18. Which of the following must be a divisor of n ?

 Ⓐ 11

 Ⓑ 9

 Ⓒ 7

 Ⓓ 6

 Ⓔ 4

Explanation

The given information tells you that n can be expressed in the form $n = 45k + 18$, where k can be any nonnegative integer. Consider how the divisors of 45 and 18 may be related to the divisors of n. Every common divisor of 45 and 18 is also a divisor of any sum of multiples of 45 and 18, like $45k + 18$. So any common divisor of 45 and 18 is also a divisor of n. Of the answer choices given, only 9 is a common divisor of 45 and 18. Thus the correct answer is **Choice B**.

This explanation uses the following strategies.
Strategy 1: Translate from Words to an Arithmetic or Algebraic Representation
Strategy 8: Search for a Mathematical Relationship

11. Points A, B, C, and D are on the number line above, and $AB = CD = \frac{1}{3}(BC)$. What is the coordinate of C ?

 Ⓐ $\dfrac{13}{30}$

 Ⓑ $\dfrac{9}{20}$

 Ⓒ $\dfrac{11}{24}$

 Ⓓ $\dfrac{7}{15}$

 Ⓔ $\dfrac{29}{60}$

Explanation

From the figure you can see that since the coordinate of A is $\frac{1}{3}$, it follows that the coordinate of C is $\frac{1}{3} + AB + BC$. Since you are given that $AB = \frac{1}{3}(BC)$, the coordinate of C can be rewritten in terms of AB as follows:

$$\frac{1}{3} + AB + BC = \frac{1}{3} + AB + 3(AB) = \frac{1}{3} + 4(AB)$$

To find the coordinate of C, you need to know AB. From the figure, you know that $AD = AB + BC + CD = AB + 3(AB) + AB = 5(AB)$. On the other hand, since the coordinate of A is $\dfrac{1}{3}$ and the coordinate of D is $\dfrac{1}{2}$, it follows that $AD = \dfrac{1}{2} - \dfrac{1}{3} = \dfrac{1}{6}$.

Therefore you can conclude that $\dfrac{1}{6} = 5(AB)$ and $AB = \dfrac{1}{30}$. Thus the coordinate of C is $\dfrac{1}{3} + 4(AB) = \dfrac{1}{3} + 4\left(\dfrac{1}{30}\right)$, or $\dfrac{7}{15}$. The correct answer is **Choice D**.

This explanation uses the following strategies.
Strategy 4: Translate from a Figure to an Arithmetic or Algebraic Representation
Strategy 8: Search for a Mathematical Relationship

---

12. Which of the following represents the total dollar amount that a customer would have to pay for an item that costs s dollars plus a sales tax of 8 percent, in terms of s?

(A) $\dfrac{s}{0.08}$

(B) $\dfrac{s}{1.08}$

(C) $\dfrac{s}{8}$

(D) $0.08s$

(E) $1.08s$

Explanation

The total dollar amount that the customer would have to pay is equal to the cost plus 8 percent of the cost. Translating to an algebraic expression, you get that the total amount is $s + 0.08s$, or $1.08s$. Thus the correct answer is **Choice E**.

This explanation uses the following strategy.
Strategy 1: Translate from Words to an Arithmetic or Algebraic Representation

13. Marie earned $0.75 for every mile she walked in a charity walkathon. If she earned a total of $18.00 at that rate, how many miles did she walk?

   (A) 13.5

   (B) 17.5

   (C) 21

   (D) 22.5

   (E) 24

Explanation

You can translate the given information into an algebraic equation. If Marie walks m miles, she earns $0.75m$ dollars. Since you know that she earned a total of $18, you get $0.75m = 18$. Solving for m, you have $m = \dfrac{18}{0.75} = 24$. Thus the correct answer is **Choice E**.

This explanation uses the following strategy.
Strategy 1: Translate from Words to an Arithmetic or Algebraic Representation

---

14. Which of the following operations carried out on both the numerator and the denominator of a fraction will always produce an equivalent fraction?

   Indicate <u>all</u> such operations.

   A   Adding 2

   B   Multiplying by 5

   C   Dividing by 100

Explanation

Multiplying both the numerator and the denominator of a fraction by the same nonzero number is equivalent to multiplying the fraction by 1, thus producing an equivalent fraction. The same is true for division. However, adding the same number to both the numerator and denominator does not usually produce an equivalent fraction. Here is an example:

$$\frac{1}{2} \neq \frac{1+2}{2+2} = \frac{3}{4}$$

Thus the correct answer consists of **Choices B and C**.

This explanation uses the following strategy.
Strategy 13: Determine Whether a Conclusion Follows from the Information Given

15. If $|z| \leq 1$, which of the following statements must be true?

   Indicate <u>all</u> such statements.

   $\boxed{A}$ $z^2 \leq 1$

   $\boxed{B}$ $z^2 \leq z$

   $\boxed{C}$ $z^3 \leq z$

Explanation

The condition stated in the question, $|z| \leq 1$, includes both positive and negative values of z. For example, both $\dfrac{1}{2}$ and $-\dfrac{1}{2}$ are possible values of z. Keep this in mind as you evaluate each of the inequalities in the answer choices to see whether the inequality must be true.

   Choice A: $z^2 \leq 1$. First look at what happens for a positive and a negative value of z for which $|z| \leq 1$, say, $z = \dfrac{1}{2}$ and $z = -\dfrac{1}{2}$. If $z = \dfrac{1}{2}$, then $z^2 = \dfrac{1}{4}$. If $z = -\dfrac{1}{2}$, then $z^2 = \dfrac{1}{4}$. So in both these cases it is true that $z^2 \leq 1$.

   Since the inequality $z^2 \leq 1$ is true for a positive and a negative value of z, try to prove that it is true for all values of z such that $|z| \leq 1$. Recall that if $0 \leq c \leq 1$, then $c^2 \leq 1$. Since $0 \leq |z| \leq 1$, letting $c = |z|$ yields $|z|^2 \leq 1$. Also, it is always true that $|z|^2 = z^2$, and so $z^2 \leq 1$.

   Choice B: $z^2 \leq z$. As before, look at what happens when $z = \dfrac{1}{2}$ and when $z = -\dfrac{1}{2}$. If $z = \dfrac{1}{2}$, then $z^2 = \dfrac{1}{4}$. If $z = -\dfrac{1}{2}$, then $z^2 = \dfrac{1}{4}$. So when $z = \dfrac{1}{2}$, the inequality $z^2 \leq z$ is true, and when $z = -\dfrac{1}{2}$, the inequality $z^2 \leq z$ is false. Therefore you can conclude that if $|z| \leq 1$, it is not necessarily true that $z^2 \leq z$.

   Choice C: $z^3 \leq z$. As before, look at what happens when $z = \dfrac{1}{2}$ and when $z = -\dfrac{1}{2}$. If $z = \dfrac{1}{2}$, then $z^3 = \dfrac{1}{8}$. If $z = -\dfrac{1}{2}$, then $z^3 = -\dfrac{1}{8}$. So when $z = \dfrac{1}{2}$, the inequality $z^3 \leq z$ is true, and when $z = -\dfrac{1}{2}$, the inequality $z^3 \leq z$ is false. Therefore, you can conclude that if $|z| \leq 1$, it is not necessarily true that $z^3 \leq z$.

   Thus when $|z| \leq 1$, Choice A, $z^2 \leq 1$, must be true, but the other two choices are not necessarily true. The correct answer consists of **Choice A**.

This explanation uses the following strategies.

Strategy 8: Search for a Mathematical Relationship
Strategy 10: Trial and Error
Strategy 13: Determine Whether a Conclusion Follows from the Information Given

16. In a certain medical group, Dr. Schwartz schedules appointments to begin 30 minutes apart, Dr. Ramirez schedules appointments to begin 25 minutes apart, and Dr. Wu schedules appointments to begin 50 minutes apart. All three doctors schedule their first appointments to begin at 8:00 in the morning, which are followed by their successive appointments throughout the day without breaks. Other than at 8:00 in the morning, at what times before 1:30 in the afternoon do all three doctors schedule their appointments to begin at the same time?

Indicate <u>all</u> such times.

A   9:30 in the morning
B   10:00 in the morning
C   10:30 in the morning
D   11:00 in the morning
E   11:30 in the morning
F   12:00 noon
G   12:30 in the afternoon
H   1:00 in the afternoon

Explanation

By examining the pattern of beginning times for the three types of appointments, you can see that the times will coincide when the number of minutes after 8:00 in the morning is a common multiple of 30, 25, and 50. The least common multiple of 30, 25, and 50 is 150, which represents 150 minutes, or 2.5 hours. So the times coincide every 2.5 hours after 8:00 in the morning, that is, at 10:30 in the morning, at 1:00 in the afternoon, and so on. The correct answer consists of **Choices C and H**.

This explanation uses the following strategy.
Strategy 7: Find a Pattern

17. The integers x and y are greater than 1. If $(4x)(7y) = 756$, what is the value of $x + y$?

$$x + y = \boxed{}$$

Explanation

You can solve the given equation, $(4x)(7y) = 756$, for the product xy:

$$(4x)(7y) = 756$$
$$28xy = 756$$
$$xy = 27$$

By trial and error, you find that 3 and 9 are the only two integers greater than 1 whose product is 27. So $x + y = 12$, and the correct answer is **12**.

This explanation uses the following strategy.
Strategy 10: Trial and Error

$$1, -3, 4, 1, -3, 4, 1, -3, 4, \ldots$$

18. In the sequence above, the first 3 terms repeat without end. What is the sum of the terms of the sequence from the 150th term to the 154th term?

$$\boxed{}$$

Explanation

Examining the repeating pattern, you see that the 3rd term is 4, and every 3rd term after that, in other words, the 6th, 9th, 12th, 15th, and so on, is 4. Since 150 is a multiple of 3, the 150th term is 4. Therefore the 150th to the 154th terms are 4, 1, −3, 4, 1. The sum of these 5 terms is 7, so the correct answer is **7**.

This explanation uses the following strategy.
Strategy 7: Find a Pattern

19. A manufacturing company has plants in three locations: Indonesia, Mexico, and Pakistan. The company has 6,000 employees, and each of the employees works at only one of the plants. If $\frac{3}{8}$ of the employees work at the plant in Indonesia and if twice as many employees work at the plant in Mexico as work at the plant in Pakistan, how many employees work at the plant in Mexico?

> [   ] employees

Explanation

Three-eighths of the company's 6,000 employees work in Indonesia, so the number of employees that do not work in Indonesia is $\frac{5}{8}(6,000)$, or 3,750. Of those employees, twice as many work in Mexico as work in Pakistan, so the number working in Mexico is $\frac{2}{3}(3,750)$, or 2,500. Thus the correct answer is **2,500** employees.

This explanation uses the following strategy.
Strategy 1: Translate from Words to an Arithmetic or Algebraic Representation

4 Algebra

This chapter contains GRE Quantitative Reasoning practice questions that involve algebra.

Algebra topics include operations with exponents; factoring and simplifying algebraic expressions; relations, functions, equations, and inequalities; solving linear and quadratic equations and inequalities; solving simultaneous equations and inequalities; setting up equations to solve word problems; and coordinate geometry, including graphs of functions, equations, and inequalities, intercepts, and slopes of lines.

The questions are arranged by question type: Quantitative Comparison questions, followed by both types of Multiple-choice questions, and then Numeric Entry questions.

Following the questions is an answer key for quick reference. Then, at the end of the chapter, you will find complete explanations for every question. Each explanation is presented with the corresponding question for easy reference.

Review the answers and explanations carefully, paying particular attention to explanations for questions that you answered incorrectly.

Before answering the practice questions, read the Quantitative Reasoning section directions that begin on the following page. Also, review the directions that precede each question type to make sure you understand how to answer the questions.

Quantitative Reasoning Section Directions

For each question, indicate the best answer, using the directions given.

Notes: All numbers used are real numbers.

All figures are assumed to lie in a plane unless otherwise indicated.

Geometric figures, such as lines, circles, triangles, and quadrilaterals, **are not necessarily** drawn to scale. That is, you should **not** assume that quantities such as lengths and angle measures are as they appear in a figure. You should assume, however, that lines shown as straight are actually straight, points on a line are in the order shown, and more generally, all geometric objects are in the relative positions shown. For questions with geometric figures, you should base your answers on geometric reasoning, not on estimating or comparing quantities by sight or by measurement.

Coordinate systems, such as *xy*-planes and number lines, **are** drawn to scale; therefore, you can read, estimate, or compare quantities in such figures by sight or by measurement.

Graphical data presentations, such as bar graphs, circle graphs, and line graphs, **are** drawn to scale; therefore, you can read, estimate, or compare data values by sight or by measurement.

Quantitative Comparison Questions

For Questions 1 to 7, compare Quantity A and Quantity B, using additional information centered above the two quantities if such information is given. Select one of the following four answer choices and fill in the corresponding oval to the right of the question.

Ⓐ Quantity A is greater.

Ⓑ Quantity B is greater.

Ⓒ The two quantities are equal.

Ⓓ The relationship cannot be determined from the information given.

A symbol that appears more than once in a question has the same meaning throughout the question.

	Quantity A	Quantity B	Correct Answer
Example 1:	$(2)(6)$	$2+6$	

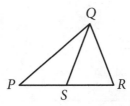

	Quantity A	Quantity B	Correct Answer
Example 2:	PS	SR	

(since equal lengths cannot be assumed, even though PS and SR appear equal)

$$\frac{x(x-2)}{(x+3)(x-4)^2}=0$$

	Quantity A	Quantity B	
1.	x	-2	Ⓐ Ⓑ Ⓒ Ⓓ

$$x > 0$$

	Quantity A	Quantity B	
2.	$\dfrac{1}{x}$	$\dfrac{x+1}{x^2}$	Ⓐ Ⓑ Ⓒ Ⓓ

	Quantity A	Quantity B	
3.	$\left|m+25\right|$	$25-m$	Ⓐ Ⓑ Ⓒ Ⓓ

During an experiment, the pressure of a fixed mass of gas increased from 40 pounds per square inch (psi) to 50 psi. Throughout the experiment, the pressure, P psi, and the volume, V cubic inches, of the gas varied in such a way that the value of the product PV was constant.

	Quantity A	Quantity B	
4.	The volume of the gas when the pressure was 40 psi	1.2 times the volume of the gas when the pressure was 50 psi	Ⓐ Ⓑ Ⓒ Ⓓ

$$x > 0$$

	Quantity A	Quantity B	
5.	x percent of $100x$	x^2	Ⓐ Ⓑ Ⓒ Ⓓ

$$(4x-2y)(6x+3y)=18$$

	Quantity A	Quantity B	
6.	$4x^2 - y^2$	6	Ⓐ Ⓑ Ⓒ Ⓓ

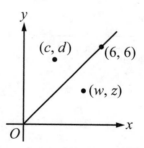

	Quantity A	Quantity B	
7.	$w+d$	$c+z$	Ⓐ Ⓑ Ⓒ Ⓓ

Multiple-choice Questions—Select One Answer Choice

For Questions 8 to 13, select a single answer choice.

8. If $xy^2 = 12$ and $xy = 4,$ then $x =$

   (A) 1

   (B) 2

   (C) $\sqrt{3}$

   (D) $\dfrac{2}{3}$

   (E) $\dfrac{4}{3}$

9. The total cost of 8 bagels at a bakery is x dollars. At this cost per bagel, which of the following represents the total cost, in dollars, of y bagels?

   (A) $\dfrac{8}{xy}$

   (B) $\dfrac{8x}{y}$

   (C) $\dfrac{8y}{x}$

   (D) $\dfrac{xy}{8}$

   (E) $\dfrac{x}{8y}$

10. Which of the following is equal to $\dfrac{2^{x-y}}{2^{x+y}}$ for all integers x and y ?

   (A) 4^{-x}

   (B) 4^{-y}

   (C) 2^{xy}

   (D) 4^{x}

   (E) 4^{y}

11. How many integers are in the solution set of the inequality $x^2 - 10 < 0$?

    (A) Two

    (B) Five

    (C) Six

    (D) Seven

    (E) Ten

12. A group of 5,000 investors responded to a survey asking whether they owned stocks and whether they owned bonds. Of the group, 20 percent responded that they owned only one of the two types of investments. If r is the number of investors in the group who owned stocks but not bonds, which of the following represents the number of investors in the group who owned bonds but not stocks, in terms of r ?

    (A) $5,000 - r$

    (B) $1,000 - r$

    (C) $r - 1,000$

    (D) $1,000r$

    (E) $(0.2)(5,000 - r)$

13. If $\dfrac{m+n}{4+5} = \dfrac{m}{4} + \dfrac{n}{5}$, which of the following statements must be true?

    (A) $m = n$

    (B) $5m = 4n$

    (C) $5m = -4n$

    (D) $25m = 16n$

    (E) $25m = -16n$

Multiple-choice Questions—Select One or More Answer Choices

For Questions 14 to 15, select all the answer choices that apply.

14. In the xy-plane, triangular region R is bounded by the lines $x = 0$, $y = 0$, and $4x + 3y = 60$. Which of the following points lie inside region R ?

    Indicate all such points.

    A (2, 18)
    B (5, 12)
    C (10, 7)
    D (12, 3)
    E (15, 2)

15. At the beginning of a trip, the tank of Diana's car was filled with gasoline to half of its capacity. During the trip, Diana used 30 percent of the gasoline in the tank. At the end of the trip, Diana added 8 gallons of gasoline to the tank. The capacity of the tank of Diana's car was x gallons. Which of the following expressions represent the number of gallons of gasoline in the tank after Diana added gasoline to the tank at the end of the trip?

    Indicate all such expressions.

    A $\dfrac{x}{2} - \dfrac{3x}{20} + 8$

    B $\dfrac{7x}{20} + 8$

    C $\dfrac{3x}{20} + 8$

    D $\dfrac{x}{2} + \dfrac{3x}{20} - 8$

    E $\dfrac{7x}{20} - 8$

Numeric Entry Questions

For Questions 16 to 17, enter your answer in the answer box(es) below the question.

- **Your answer may be an integer, a decimal, or a fraction, and it may be negative.**
- **If a question asks for a fraction, there will be two boxes—one for the numerator and one for the denominator. A decimal point cannot be used in a fraction.**
- **Equivalent forms of the correct answer, such as 2.5 and 2.50, are all correct. Fractions do not need to be reduced to lowest terms, though you may need to reduce your fraction to fit in the boxes.**
- **Enter the exact answer unless the question asks you to round your answer.**

16. Machine A, working alone at its constant rate, produces x pounds of peanut butter in 12 minutes. Machine B, working alone at its constant rate, produces x pounds of peanut butter in 18 minutes. How many minutes will it take machines A and B, working simultaneously at their respective constant rates, to produce x pounds of peanut butter?

minutes

17. The function f has the property that $f(x) = f(x + 1)$ for all numbers x. If $f(4) = 17$, what is the value of $f(8)$?

ANSWER KEY

1. **Choice A**: Quantity A is greater.
2. **Choice B**: Quantity B is greater.
3. **Choice D**: The relationship cannot be determined from the information given.
4. **Choice A**: Quantity A is greater.
5. **Choice C**: The two quantities are equal.
6. **Choice B**: Quantity B is greater.
7. **Choice A**: Quantity A is greater.
8. **Choice E**: $\dfrac{4}{3}$
9. **Choice D**: $\dfrac{xy}{8}$
10. **Choice B**: 4^{-y}
11. **Choice D**: Seven
12. **Choice B**: $1,000 - r$
13. **Choice E**: $25m = -16n$
14. **Choice B**: $(5, 12)$
    AND
    Choice D: $(12, 3)$
15. **Choice A**: $\dfrac{x}{2} - \dfrac{3x}{20} + 8$

    AND

    Choice B: $\dfrac{7x}{20} + 8$
16. **7.2**
17. **17**

Answers and Explanations

$$\frac{x(x-2)}{(x+3)(x-4)^2}=0$$

	Quantity A	Quantity B	
1.	x	-2	Ⓐ Ⓑ Ⓒ Ⓓ

Explanation

To compare x with -2, you should first solve the equation $\dfrac{x(x-2)}{(x+3)(x-4)^2}=0$ for x.

To solve the equation, recall that a fraction $\dfrac{a}{b}$ is equal to 0 only if $a=0$ and $b\neq 0$.

So the fraction $\dfrac{x(x-2)}{(x+3)(x-4)^2}$ is equal to 0 only if $x(x-2)$ is equal to 0 and $(x+3)(x-4)^2$ is not equal to 0. Note that the only values of x for which $x(x-2)=0$ are $x=0$ and $x=2$, and for these two values, $(x+3)(x-4)^2$ is not equal to 0. Therefore the only values of x for which the fraction $\dfrac{x(x-2)}{(x+3)(x-4)^2}$ is equal to 0 are $x=0$ and $x=2$. Since both 0 and 2 are greater than Quantity B, -2, the correct answer is **Choice A**.

This explanation uses the following strategy.
Strategy 8: Search for a Mathematical Relationship

$$x>0$$

	Quantity A	Quantity B	
2.	$\dfrac{1}{x}$	$\dfrac{x+1}{x^2}$	Ⓐ Ⓑ Ⓒ Ⓓ

Explanation

Note that Quantity B, $\dfrac{x+1}{x^2}$, can be expressed as $\dfrac{x}{x^2}+\dfrac{1}{x^2}$, which can be simplified to $\dfrac{1}{x}+\dfrac{1}{x^2}$. Note that Quantity A is $\dfrac{1}{x}$, and for all nonzero values of x, $\dfrac{1}{x^2}>0$. It follows that $\dfrac{1}{x}+\dfrac{1}{x^2}>\dfrac{1}{x}$; that is, Quantity B is greater than Quantity A. Thus the correct answer is **Choice B**.

This explanation uses the following strategy.
Strategy 8: Search for a Mathematical Relationship

	Quantity A	Quantity B	

3. $|m+25|$ $\qquad$ $25-m$

Explanation

To compare $|m+25|$ with $25-m$, first note that because the absolute value of any quantity is greater than or equal to 0, it must be true that $|m+25| \geq 0$ for all values of m. But you know that $25-m$ is less than 0 when m is greater than 25. So Quantity A is greater than Quantity B when $m > 25$.

   On the other hand, both $|m+25|$ and $25-m$ are equal to 25 when $m=0$. So in one case Quantity A is greater than Quantity B, and in the other case the two quantities are equal. Thus the correct answer is **Choice D**.

This explanation uses the following strategies.
Strategy 11: Divide into Cases
Strategy 13: Determine Whether a Conclusion Follows from the Information Given

---

During an experiment, the pressure of a fixed mass of gas increased from 40 pounds per square inch (psi) to 50 psi. Throughout the experiment, the pressure, P psi, and the volume, V cubic inches, of the gas varied in such a way that the value of the product PV was constant.

	Quantity A	Quantity B	

4. The volume of the gas when the pressure was 40 psi   1.2 times the volume of the gas when the pressure was 50 psi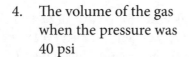

Explanation

You are given that the relationship between the pressure and volume of the gas throughout the experiment was $PV = C$, where C is a positive constant.

   Quantity A is the volume of the gas when the pressure was 40 psi. At this pressure, the equation $PV = C$ becomes $40V = C$. Solving this equation for V, you get $V = \dfrac{C}{40} = 0.025C$; that is, the volume of the gas was $0.025C$ cubic inches.

   Quantity B is 1.2 times the volume of the gas when the pressure was 50 psi. At this pressure, the equation $PV = C$ becomes $50V = C$, or $V = \dfrac{C}{50} = 0.02C$. Therefore $(1.2)V = (1.2)(0.02C) = 0.024C$; that is, Quantity B is $0.024C$ cubic inches. Thus the correct answer is **Choice A**.

This explanation uses the following strategies.
Strategy 1: Translate from Words to an Arithmetic or Algebraic Representation
Strategy 8: Search for a Mathematical Relationship

$$x > 0$$

	Quantity A	Quantity B	
5.	x percent of $100x$	x^2	Ⓐ Ⓑ Ⓒ Ⓓ

Explanation

Note that Quantity A can be expressed algebraically as $\left(\dfrac{x}{100}\right)(100x)$. Simplifying this algebraic expression gives x^2, which is Quantity B. The correct answer is therefore **Choice C**.

This explanation uses the following strategy.
Strategy 1: Translate from Words to an Arithmetic or Algebraic Representation

---

$$(4x - 2y)(6x + 3y) = 18$$

	Quantity A	Quantity B	
6.	$4x^2 - y^2$	6	Ⓐ Ⓑ Ⓒ Ⓓ

Explanation

The given equation $(4x - 2y)(6x + 3y) = 18$ can be simplified as follows.

Step 1: Note that $(4x - 2y) = 2(2x - y)$ and $(6x + 3y) = 3(2x + y)$, so the given equation can be rewritten as $(2)(2x - y)(3)(2x + y) = 18$.
Step 2: Dividing both sides of the rewritten equation by 6 gives $(2x - y)(2x + y) = 3$.
Step 3: Multiplying out the left side of the equation in Step 2 gives $4x^2 - y^2 = 3$.

Since Quantity A is $4x^2 - y^2$, it follows that Quantity A is equal to 3. Since Quantity B is 6, the correct answer is **Choice B**.

This explanation uses the following strategy.
Strategy 8: Search for a Mathematical Relationship

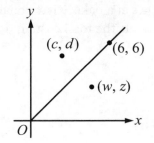

	Quantity A	Quantity B	

7. $w + d$ $c + z$

Explanation

The line in the xy-plane passes through the origin and the point with coordinates $(6, 6)$, so the equation of the line is $y = x$. Since the point with coordinates (c, d) is above the line, it follows that $d > c$, and since the point with coordinates (w, z) is below the line, it follows that $w > z$. From the fact that $d > c$ and $w > z$, you get $w + d > c + z$; that is, Quantity A is greater than Quantity B. Thus the correct answer is **Choice A**.

This explanation uses the following strategy.
Strategy 8: Search for a Mathematical Relationship

---

8. If $xy^2 = 12$ and $xy = 4$, then $x =$

Ⓐ 1

Ⓑ 2

Ⓒ $\sqrt{3}$

Ⓓ $\dfrac{2}{3}$

Ⓔ $\dfrac{4}{3}$

Explanation

From the given equations $xy^2 = 12$ and $xy = 4$, it follows that $12 = xy^2 = (xy)y = 4y$, and so $y = 3$. Substituting $y = 3$ in the equation $xy = 4$ gives $3x = 4$, or $x = \dfrac{4}{3}$. Thus the correct answer is Choice E.

This explanation uses the following strategy.
Strategy 8: Search for a Mathematical Relationship

9. The total cost of 8 bagels at a bakery is x dollars. At this cost per bagel, which of the following represents the total cost, in dollars, of y bagels?

    (A) $\dfrac{8}{xy}$

    (B) $\dfrac{8x}{y}$

    (C) $\dfrac{8y}{x}$

    (D) $\dfrac{xy}{8}$

    (E) $\dfrac{x}{8y}$

Explanation

The total cost of 8 bagels is x dollars, so one bagel costs $\dfrac{x}{8}$ dollars. Therefore the total cost of y bagels is $y\left(\dfrac{x}{8}\right)$, or $\dfrac{xy}{8}$ dollars. Thus the correct answer is **Choice D**.

This explanation uses the following strategy.
Strategy 1: Translate from Words to an Arithmetic or Algebraic Representation

---

10. Which of the following is equal to $\dfrac{2^{x-y}}{2^{x+y}}$ for all integers x and y ?

    (A) 4^{-x}

    (B) 4^{-y}

    (C) 2^{xy}

    (D) 4^{x}

    (E) 4^{y}

Explanation

Simplifying the fraction $\dfrac{2^{x-y}}{2^{x+y}}$ yields $\dfrac{2^{x-y}}{2^{x+y}} = 2^{x-y-(x+y)} = 2^{x-y-x-y} = 2^{-2y}$. The only answer choice with 2 as the base is Choice C, 2^{xy}, which is clearly not the correct answer. Since all the other answer choices have 4 as the base, it is a good idea to rewrite 2^{-2y} as an expression with 4 as the base, as follows.

$$2^{-2y} = \dfrac{1}{2^{2y}} = \dfrac{1}{(2^2)^y} = \dfrac{1}{4^y} = 4^{-y}$$

Thus the correct answer is **Choice B**.

This explanation uses the following strategies.
Strategy 5: Simplify an Arithmetic or Algebraic Representation
Strategy 8: Search for a Mathematical Relationship

11. How many integers are in the solution set of the inequality $x^2 - 10 < 0$?

    (A) Two

    (B) Five

    (C) Six

    (D) Seven

    (E) Ten

Explanation

The inequality $x^2 - 10 < 0$ is equivalent to $x^2 < 10$. By inspection, the positive integers that satisfy this inequality are 1, 2, and 3. Note that 0 and the negative integers −1, −2, and −3 also satisfy the inequality, and there are no other integer solutions. So there are seven integers in the solution set: −3, −2, −1, 0, 1, 2, and 3. Thus the correct answer is **Choice D**.

This explanation uses the following strategy.
Strategy 8: Search for a Mathematical Relationship

---

12. A group of 5,000 investors responded to a survey asking whether they owned stocks and whether they owned bonds. Of the group, 20 percent responded that they owned only one of the two types of investments. If r is the number of investors in the group who owned stocks but not bonds, which of the following represents the number of investors in the group who owned bonds but not stocks, in terms of r ?

    (A) $5,000 - r$

    (B) $1,000 - r$

    (C) $r - 1,000$

    (D) $1,000r$

    (E) $(0.2)(5,000 - r)$

Explanation

Twenty percent of the 5,000 investors that responded to the survey said they owned either stocks or bonds, but not both. So the number of investors in that group is $(0.20)(5,000)$, or 1,000. Given that r members of that group owned stocks but not bonds, the number of investors in that group who owned bonds but not stocks is $1,000 - r$. Thus the correct answer is **Choice B**.

This explanation uses the following strategies.
Strategy 1: Translate from Words to an Arithmetic or Algebraic Representation
Strategy 8: Search for a Mathematical Relationship

13. If $\dfrac{m+n}{4+5} = \dfrac{m}{4} + \dfrac{n}{5}$, which of the following statements must be true?

(A) $m = n$

(B) $5m = 4n$

(C) $5m = -4n$

(D) $25m = 16n$

(E) $25m = -16n$

Explanation

You can simplify each side of the equation $\dfrac{m+n}{4+5} = \dfrac{m}{4} + \dfrac{n}{5}$ as follows.

$$\dfrac{m+n}{4+5} = \dfrac{m+n}{9}$$

$$\dfrac{m}{4} + \dfrac{n}{5} = \dfrac{5m+4n}{20}$$

So the equation $\dfrac{m+n}{4+5} = \dfrac{m}{4} + \dfrac{n}{5}$ can be rewritten as $\dfrac{m+n}{9} = \dfrac{5m+4n}{20}$.

Cross multiplying in the rewritten equation gives $20(m + n) = 9(5m + 4n)$, which simplifies to $20m + 20n = 45m + 36n$, or $-16n = 25m$. Thus the correct answer is **Choice E**.

This explanation uses the following strategy.
Strategy 5: Simplify an Arithmetic or Algebraic Representation

14. In the *xy*-plane, triangular region *R* is bounded by the lines $x = 0$, $y = 0$, and $4x + 3y = 60$. Which of the following points lie inside region *R* ?

Indicate <u>all</u> such points.

A (2, 18)

B (5, 12)

C (10, 7)

D (12, 3)

E (15, 2)

Explanation

Consider the three lines that bound triangular region *R*. The line $x = 0$ is the *y*-axis, and the line $y = 0$ is the *x*-axis. The line $4x + 3y = 60$ intersects the *x*-axis at (15, 0) and intersects the *y*-axis at (0, 20). The figure below shows region *R*.

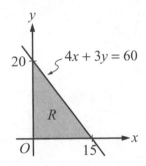

From the figure, you can see that all points inside region *R* have positive coordinates and lie below the line $4x + 3y = 60$. Note that the equation $4x + 3y = 60$ can be rewritten in the form $y = 20 - \frac{4}{3}x$. In this form, you can see that points inside region *R* satisfy the inequality $y < 20 - \frac{4}{3}x$. Since all of the answer choices have positive coordinates, you need only to check whether the coordinates in each answer choice satisfy the inequality $y < 20 - \frac{4}{3}x$, or equivalently $4x + 3y < 60$.

Choice A, (2, 18): $4x + 3y = 4(2) + 3(18) = 62 > 60$. So Choice A is not in region *R*.
Choice B, (5, 12): $4x + 3y = 4(5) + 3(12) = 56 < 60$. So Choice B is in region *R*.
Choice C, (10, 7): $4x + 3y = 4(10) + 3(7) = 61 > 60$. So Choice C is not in region *R*.
Choice D, (12, 3): $4x + 3y = 4(12) + 3(3) = 57 < 60$. So Choice D is in region *R*.
Choice E, (15, 2): $4x + 3y = 4(15) + 3(2) = 66 > 60$. So Choice E is not in region *R*.

Thus the correct answer consists of **Choices B and D**.

This explanation uses the following strategies.
Strategy 3: Translate from an Algebraic to a Graphical Representation
Strategy 8: Search for a Mathematical Relationship

15. At the beginning of a trip, the tank of Diana's car was filled with gasoline to half of its capacity. During the trip, Diana used 30 percent of the gasoline in the tank. At the end of the trip, Diana added 8 gallons of gasoline to the tank. The capacity of the tank of Diana's car was x gallons. Which of the following expressions represent the number of gallons of gasoline in the tank after Diana added gasoline to the tank at the end of the trip?

Indicate <u>all</u> such expressions.

A $\dfrac{x}{2} - \dfrac{3x}{20} + 8$

B $\dfrac{7x}{20} + 8$

C $\dfrac{3x}{20} + 8$

D $\dfrac{x}{2} + \dfrac{3x}{20} - 8$

E $\dfrac{7x}{20} - 8$

Explanation

The capacity of the car's tank was x gallons of gasoline. Before the trip, the tank was half full and therefore contained $\dfrac{x}{2}$ gallons of gasoline. During the trip, 30 percent of the gasoline in the tank was used, so the number of gallons left was 70 percent of $\dfrac{x}{2}$, or $\left(\dfrac{7}{10}\right)\left(\dfrac{x}{2}\right) = \dfrac{7x}{20}$. After Diana added 8 gallons of gasoline to the tank, the total number of gallons in the tank was $\dfrac{7x}{20} + 8$. Thus one correct choice is Choice B, $\dfrac{7x}{20} + 8$.

However, the question asks you to find <u>all</u> of the answer choices that represent the number of gallons of gasoline in the tank at the end of the trip. So you need to determine whether any of the other choices are equivalent to $\dfrac{7x}{20} + 8$. Of the answer choices, only Choices A and C have the same constant term as Choice B: 8. So these are the only choices that need to be checked. Choice A, $\dfrac{x}{2} - \dfrac{3x}{20} + 8$, can be simplified as follows.

$$\frac{x}{2} - \frac{3x}{20} + 8 = \frac{10x}{20} - \frac{3x}{20} + 8 = \frac{7x}{20} + 8$$

So Choice A is equivalent to $\dfrac{7x}{20}+8$. Choice C, $\dfrac{3x}{20}+8$, is clearly not equivalent to $\dfrac{7x}{20}+8$. Thus the correct answer consists of **Choices A and B**.

This explanation uses the following strategies.
Strategy 1: Translate from Words to an Arithmetic or Algebraic Representation
Strategy 5: Simplify an Arithmetic or Algebraic Representation
Strategy 8: Search for a Mathematical Relationship

---

16. Machine A, working alone at its constant rate, produces x pounds of peanut butter in 12 minutes. Machine B, working alone at its constant rate, produces x pounds of peanut butter in 18 minutes. How many minutes will it take machines A and B, working simultaneously at their respective constant rates, to produce x pounds of peanut butter?

$$\boxed{}\text{ minutes}$$

Explanation

Translating the given information into an algebraic expression, you see that machine A produces $\dfrac{x}{12}$ pounds of peanut butter in 1 minute, and machine B produces $\dfrac{x}{18}$ pounds of peanut butter in 1 minute. Therefore, working simultaneously, machine A and machine B produce $\dfrac{x}{12}+\dfrac{x}{18}$ pounds of peanut butter in 1 minute.

Letting t be the number of minutes it takes machines A and B, working simultaneously, to produce x pounds of peanut butter, you can set up the following equation.

$$\left(\frac{x}{12}+\frac{x}{18}\right)t = x$$

Solving for t, you get

$$\left(\frac{1}{12}+\frac{1}{18}\right)t = 1$$

$$\frac{5}{36}t = 1$$

$$t = \frac{36}{5} = 7.2$$

The correct answer is **7.2**.

This explanation uses the following strategies.
Strategy 1: Translate from Words to an Arithmetic or Algebraic Representation
Strategy 8: Search for a Mathematical Relationship

17. The function f has the property that $f(x) = f(x+1)$ for all numbers x. If $f(4) = 17$, what is the value of $f(8)$?

$$\boxed{}$$

Explanation

The property that $f(x) = f(x+1)$ for all numbers x implies that $f(4) = f(5)$, $f(5) = f(6)$, $f(6) = f(7)$, and $f(7) = f(8)$. Therefore, since $f(4) = 17$, it follows that $f(8) = 17$. Thus the correct answer is **17**.

This explanation uses the following strategy.
Strategy 7: Find a Pattern

5 Geometry

Your goals for this chapter	⇨ Practice answering *GRE*® questions in geometry ⇨ Review answers and explanations, particularly for questions you answered incorrectly

This chapter contains GRE Quantitative Reasoning practice questions that involve geometry.

Geometry topics include parallel and perpendicular lines, circles, triangles—including isosceles, equilateral, and 30°-60°-90° triangles—quadrilaterals, other polygons, congruent and similar figures, three-dimensional figures, area, perimeter, volume, the Pythagorean theorem, and angle measurement in degrees. The ability to construct proofs is not tested.

The questions are arranged by question type: Quantitative Comparison questions, followed by both types of Multiple-choice questions, and then Numeric Entry questions.

Following the questions is an answer key for quick reference. Then, at the end of the chapter, you will find complete explanations for every question. Each explanation is presented with the corresponding question for easy reference.

Review the answers and explanations carefully, paying particular attention to explanations for questions that you answered incorrectly.

Before answering the practice questions, read the Quantitative Reasoning section directions that begin on the following page. Also, review the directions that precede each question type to make sure you understand how to answer the questions.

Quantitative Reasoning Section Directions

For each question, indicate the best answer, using the directions given.

Notes: All numbers used are real numbers.

All figures are assumed to lie in a plane unless otherwise indicated.

Geometric figures, such as lines, circles, triangles, and quadrilaterals, **are not necessarily** drawn to scale. That is, you should **not** assume that quantities such as lengths and angle measures are as they appear in a figure. You should assume, however, that lines shown as straight are actually straight, points on a line are in the order shown, and more generally, all geometric objects are in the relative positions shown. For questions with geometric figures, you should base your answers on geometric reasoning, not on estimating or comparing quantities by sight or by measurement.

Coordinate systems, such as xy-planes and number lines, **are** drawn to scale; therefore, you can read, estimate, or compare quantities in such figures by sight or by measurement.

Graphical data presentations, such as bar graphs, circle graphs, and line graphs, **are** drawn to scale; therefore, you can read, estimate, or compare data values by sight or by measurement.

Quantitative Comparison Questions

For Questions 1 to 5, compare Quantity A and Quantity B, using additional information centered above the two quantities if such information is given. Select one of the following four answer choices and fill in the corresponding oval to the right of the question.

Ⓐ **Quantity A is greater.**

Ⓑ **Quantity B is greater.**

Ⓒ **The two quantities are equal.**

Ⓓ **The relationship cannot be determined from the information given.**

A symbol that appears more than once in a question has the same meaning throughout the question.

	Quantity A	Quantity B	Correct Answer
Example 1:	(2)(6)	2 + 6	● Ⓑ Ⓒ Ⓓ

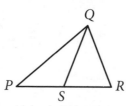

	Quantity A	Quantity B	Correct Answer
Example 2:	PS	SR	Ⓐ Ⓑ Ⓒ ●

(since equal lengths cannot be assumed, even though *PS* and *SR* appear equal)

In the *xy*-plane, one of the vertices of square *S* is the point (2, 2). The diagonals of *S* intersect at the point (6, 6).

	Quantity A	Quantity B	
1.	The area of *S*	64	Ⓐ Ⓑ Ⓒ Ⓓ

	Quantity A	Quantity B	

2. The length of a side of a regular pentagon with a perimeter of 12.5 | The length of a side of a regular hexagon with a perimeter of 15 | Ⓐ Ⓑ Ⓒ Ⓓ

A line in the *xy*-plane contains the points (5, 4) and (2, −1).

	Quantity A	Quantity B	

3. The slope of the line | 0 | Ⓐ Ⓑ Ⓒ Ⓓ

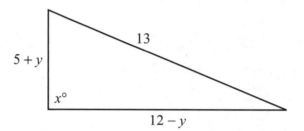

Quantity A	Quantity B

4. x | 90 | Ⓐ Ⓑ Ⓒ Ⓓ

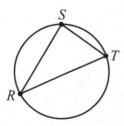

In the figure above, triangle *RST* is inscribed in a circle. The measure of angle *RST* is greater than 90°, and the area of the circle is 25π.

Quantity A	Quantity B

5. The length of line segment *RT* | 10 | Ⓐ Ⓑ Ⓒ Ⓓ

Multiple-choice Questions—Select One Answer Choice

For Questions 6 to 10, select a single answer choice.

6. A construction company will produce identical metal supports in the shape of a right triangle with legs of length 3 feet and 4 feet. The three sides of each triangular support are to be constructed of metal stripping. If the company has a total of 6,000 feet of metal stripping and there is no waste of material in the construction of the supports, what is the greatest possible number of supports that the company can produce?

   (A) 428
   (B) 500
   (C) 545
   (D) 600
   (E) 1,000

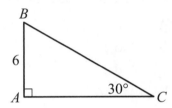

7. What is the area of triangle *ABC* shown above?

   (A) 18
   (B) 20
   (C) $12\sqrt{3}$
   (D) $18\sqrt{3}$
   (E) 36

8. The volume *V* of a right circular cylinder is $V = \pi r^2 h$, where *r* is the radius of the base and *h* is the height of the cylinder. If the volume of a right circular cylinder is 45π and its height is 5, what is the circumference of its base?

   (A) 3
   (B) 9
   (C) 3π
   (D) 6π
   (E) 9π

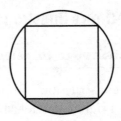

9. In the figure above, if the square inscribed in the circle has an area of 16, what is the area of the shaded region?

    (A) $2\pi - 1$
    (B) $2\pi - 4$
    (C) $4\pi - 2$
    (D) $4\pi - 4$
    (E) $8\pi - 4$

10. The radius of circle A is r, and the radius of circle B is $\dfrac{3}{4}r$. What is the ratio of the area of circle A to the area of circle B ?

    (A) 1 to 4
    (B) 3 to 4
    (C) 4 to 3
    (D) 9 to 16
    (E) 16 to 9

Multiple-choice Questions—Select One or More Answer Choices

For Questions 11 to 12, select all the answer choices that apply.

11. A flat, rectangular flower bed with an area of 2,400 square feet is bordered by a fence on three sides and by a walkway on the fourth side. If the entire length of the fence is 140 feet, which of the following could be the length, in feet, of one of the sides of the flower bed?

Indicate <u>all</u> such lengths.

- A 20
- B 30
- C 40
- D 50
- E 60
- F 70
- G 80
- H 90

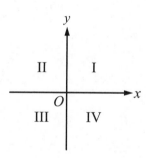

12. The quadrants of the *xy*-plane are shown in the figure above. In the *xy*-plane, line *m* (not shown) has a positive slope and a positive *x*-intercept. Line *m* intersects which of the quadrants?

Indicate <u>all</u> such quadrants.

- A Quadrant I
- B Quadrant II
- C Quadrant III
- D Quadrant IV

Numeric Entry Questions

For Question 13, enter your answer in the answer box(es) below the question.

- Your answer may be an integer, a decimal, or a fraction, and it may be negative.
- If a question asks for a fraction, there will be two boxes—one for the numerator and one for the denominator. A decimal point cannot be used in a fraction.
- Equivalent forms of the correct answer, such as 2.5 and 2.50, are all correct. Fractions do not need to be reduced to lowest terms, though you may need to reduce your fraction to fit in the boxes.
- Enter the exact answer unless the question asks you to round your answer.

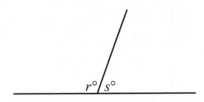

13. In the figure above, if $\dfrac{r}{r+s} = \dfrac{5}{8}$, what is the value of r?

$$r = \boxed{}$$

ANSWER KEY

1. **Choice C**: The two quantities are equal.
2. **Choice C**: The two quantities are equal.
3. **Choice A**: Quantity A is greater.
4. **Choice D**: The relationship cannot be determined from the information given.
5. **Choice B**: Quantity B is greater.
6. **Choice B**: 500
7. **Choice D**: $18\sqrt{3}$
8. **Choice D**: 6π
9. **Choice B**: $2\pi - 4$
10. **Choice E**: 16 to 9
11. **Choice B**: 30

    AND

    Choice C: 40

    AND

    Choice E: 60

    AND

    Choice G: 80
12. **Choice A**: Quadrant I

    AND

    Choice C: Quadrant III

    AND

    Choice D: Quadrant IV
13. **112.5**

Answers and Explanations

In the xy-plane, one of the vertices of square S is the point (2, 2). The diagonals of S intersect at the point (6, 6).

Quantity A	Quantity B	
1. The area of S	64	Ⓐ Ⓑ Ⓒ Ⓓ

Explanation

Since the point (2, 2) is a vertex of square S and the point (6, 6) is the midpoint of the diagonals, it follows that the point (10, 10) is also a vertex of the square. Using this information you can sketch square S in the xy-plane, labeling the points (2, 2), (6, 6), and (10, 10) as shown in the figure below.

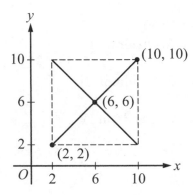

From the figure, you can see that S has sides of length 8. Therefore the area of S is $8^2 = 64$. Hence Quantity A is equal to Quantity B, and the correct answer is **Choice C**.

This explanation uses the following strategies.
Strategy 2: Translate from Words to a Figure or Diagram
Strategy 4: Translate from a Figure to an Arithmetic or Algebraic Representation

	Quantity A	Quantity B	

2. The length of a side of a regular pentagon with a perimeter of 12.5

The length of a side of a regular hexagon with a perimeter of 15

Explanation

A regular pentagon has 5 sides of equal length, so the length of a side of a regular pentagon is $\frac{1}{5}$ of its perimeter. Thus Quantity A is $\frac{12.5}{5}$, or 2.5. A regular hexagon has 6 sides of equal length, so the length of a side of a regular hexagon is $\frac{1}{6}$ of its perimeter.

Thus Quantity B is $\frac{15}{6}$, or 2.5. So Quantity A and Quantity B are both equal to 2.5, and the correct answer is **Choice C**.

This explanation uses the following strategy.
Strategy 1: Translate from Words to an Arithmetic or Algebraic Representation

---

A line in the xy-plane contains the points (5, 4) and (2, −1).

	Quantity A	Quantity B	

3. The slope of the line

0

Ⓐ Ⓑ Ⓒ Ⓓ

Explanation

You can begin by sketching the line in the xy-plane and labeling the points (5, 4) and (2, −1) on the line, as shown below.

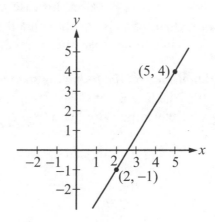

From the figure, you can see that the line through the two points slants upward and to the right. So the slope of the line is greater than 0; that is, Quantity A is greater than Quantity B. The correct answer is **Choice A**. (Note that it is not necessary to calculate the slope of the line.)

This explanation uses the following strategy.
Strategy 2: Translate from Words to a Figure or Diagram

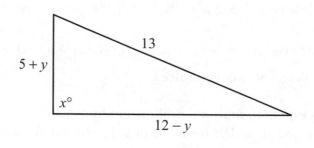

	Quantity A		Quantity B	

4. x 90   Ⓐ   Ⓑ   Ⓒ   Ⓓ

Explanation

The figure looks like a right triangle with legs of length $5 + y$ and $12 - y$ and hypotenuse of length 13. If $y = 0$, then the sides of the triangle have lengths 5, 12, and 13. This triangle is in fact a right triangle because $5^2 + 12^2 = 13^2$. So the angle labeled $x°$ is a right angle; that is, $x = 90$. In this case, Quantity A is equal to Quantity B.

Now consider another value of y, say $y = 1$, to see if the triangle is still a right triangle in this case. If $y = 1$, then the sides of the triangle have lengths 6, 11, and 13. This triangle is <u>not</u> a right triangle because $6^2 + 11^2 \neq 13^2$. So the angle labeled $x°$ is not a right angle; that is, $x \neq 90$. In this case, Quantity A is not equal to Quantity B.

Because Quantity A is equal to Quantity B in one case and Quantity A is not equal to Quantity B in another case, the correct answer is **Choice D**.

This explanation uses the following strategies.
Strategy 10: Trial and Error
Strategy 13: Determine Whether a Conclusion Follows from the Information Given

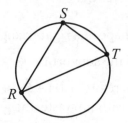

In the figure above, triangle *RST* is inscribed in a circle. The measure of angle *RST* is greater than 90°, and the area of the circle is 25π.

	Quantity A	Quantity B	
5.	The length of line segment *RT*	10	Ⓐ Ⓑ Ⓒ Ⓓ

Explanation

Since the area of the circle is 25π, it follows that the radius of the circle is 5 and the diameter is 10. Line segment *RT* is a diameter of the circle if and only if angle *RST* is a right angle. Since you are given that the measure of angle *RST* is greater than 90°, it follows that angle *RST* is not a right angle and that line segment *RT* is a chord but not a diameter. Therefore the length of line segment *RT* is less than 10, and the correct answer is **Choice B**.

This explanation uses the following strategy.
Strategy 8: Search for a Mathematical Relationship

---

6. A construction company will produce identical metal supports in the shape of a right triangle with legs of length 3 feet and 4 feet. The three sides of each triangular support are to be constructed of metal stripping. If the company has a total of 6,000 feet of metal stripping and there is no waste of material in the construction of the supports, what is the greatest possible number of supports that the company can produce?

Ⓐ 428
Ⓑ 500
Ⓒ 545
Ⓓ 600
Ⓔ 1,000

Explanation

Since each support is in the shape of a right triangle with legs of length 3 feet and 4 feet, the length of the third side of the support is $\sqrt{3^2 + 4^2}$, or 5 feet. The total length of the stripping of each support is therefore $3 + 4 + 5$, or 12 feet. The company has 6,000 feet of metal stripping available. So, with no waste, the greatest possible number of supports that can be produced is $\dfrac{6{,}000}{12}$, or 500. The correct answer is **Choice B**.

This explanation uses the following strategy.
Strategy 1: Translate from Words to an Arithmetic or Algebraic Representation

---

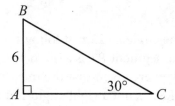

7. What is the area of triangle *ABC* shown above?

    (A) 18

    (B) 20

    (C) $12\sqrt{3}$

    (D) $18\sqrt{3}$

    (E) 36

Explanation

The triangle is a 30°-60°-90° triangle, so the ratio of the lengths of the legs is 1 to $\sqrt{3}$. Since the length of the shorter leg, *AB*, is 6, it follows that the length of the longer leg, *AC*, is $6\sqrt{3}$. The area of the triangle is therefore $\dfrac{1}{2}(6)\left(6\sqrt{3}\right)$, or $18\sqrt{3}$. The correct answer is **Choice D**.

This explanation uses the following strategies.
Strategy 4: Translate from a Figure to an Arithmetic or Algebraic Representation
Strategy 8: Search for a Mathematical Relationship

8. The volume V of a right circular cylinder is $V = \pi r^2 h$, where r is the radius of the base and h is the height of the cylinder. If the volume of a right circular cylinder is 45π and its height is 5, what is the circumference of its base?

Ⓐ 3

Ⓑ 9

Ⓒ 3π

Ⓓ 6π

Ⓔ 9π

Explanation

You are given that the volume of the right circular cylinder is 45π and the height is 5. It follows that $\pi r^2 h = 45\pi$, or $r^2 h = 45$. Since $h = 5$ and $r^2 h = 45$, it follows that $r^2 = 9$, or $r = 3$. Therefore the circumference of the circular base is $2\pi r = 2\pi(3) = 6\pi$, and the correct answer is **Choice D**.

This explanation uses the following strategy.
Strategy 1: Translate from Words to an Arithmetic or Algebraic Representation

---

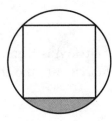

9. In the figure above, if the square inscribed in the circle has an area of 16, what is the area of the shaded region?

Ⓐ $2\pi - 1$

Ⓑ $2\pi - 4$

Ⓒ $4\pi - 2$

Ⓓ $4\pi - 4$

Ⓔ $8\pi - 4$

Explanation

It is clear from the figure that the area of the shaded region is $\dfrac{1}{4}$ of the difference between the area of the circle and the area of the square. You are given that the area of the square is 16, so each side has length 4.

You can find the area of the circle if you know the radius of the circle. If you draw a diagonal of the square, as shown in the figure below, you can see that the diagonal is also a diameter of the circle.

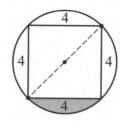

Note that the diagonal divides the square into two isosceles right triangles with legs of length 4. By the Pythagorean theorem applied to one of the right triangles, the length of the diagonal is equal to $\sqrt{4^2 + 4^2}$, or $4\sqrt{2}$. Thus the radius of the circle is $r = \dfrac{4\sqrt{2}}{2} = 2\sqrt{2}$, and the area of the circle is $\pi r^2 = \pi\left(2\sqrt{2}\right)^2 = 8\pi$. Therefore the area of the shaded region is $\dfrac{8\pi - 16}{4}$, or $2\pi - 4$. The correct answer is **Choice B**.

This explanation uses the following strategies.
Strategy 4: Translate from a Figure to an Arithmetic or Algebraic Representation
Strategy 6: Add to a Geometric Figure
Strategy 8: Search for a Mathematical Relationship

---

10. The radius of circle A is r, and the radius of circle B is $\dfrac{3}{4}r$. What is the ratio of the area of circle A to the area of circle B ?

　(A)　1 to 4

　(B)　3 to 4

　(C)　4 to 3

　(D)　9 to 16

　(E)　16 to 9

Explanation

Circle A has radius r, so its area is πr^2. Circle B has radius $\dfrac{3r}{4}$, so its area is $\pi\left(\dfrac{3r}{4}\right)^2 = \dfrac{9\pi r^2}{16}$. Therefore the ratio of the area of circle A to the area of circle B is πr^2 to $\dfrac{9\pi r^2}{16}$, which is the same as the ratio 1 to $\dfrac{9}{16}$, which is the same as the ratio 16 to 9. The correct answer is **Choice E**.

This explanation uses the following strategy.
Strategy 1: Translate from Words to an Arithmetic or Algebraic Representation

11. A flat, rectangular flower bed with an area of 2,400 square feet is bordered by a fence on three sides and by a walkway on the fourth side. If the entire length of the fence is 140 feet, which of the following could be the length, in feet, of one of the sides of the flower bed?

Indicate <u>all</u> such lengths.

- [A] 20
- [B] 30
- [C] 40
- [D] 50
- [E] 60
- [F] 70
- [G] 80
- [H] 90

Explanation

You know that the area of the rectangular flower bed is 2,400 square feet. So if the flower bed is a feet long and b feet wide, then $ab = 2{,}400$. If the side of the flower bed that is bordered by the walkway is one of the sides that are b feet long, then the total length of the three sides of the flower bed bordered by the fence is $2a + b$ feet. Since you are given that the total length of the fence is 140 feet, it follows that $2a + b = 140$. Since $ab = 2{,}400$,

you can substitute $\dfrac{2{,}400}{a}$ for b in the equation $2a + b = 140$ to get the equation

$2a + \dfrac{2{,}400}{a} = 140$. It follows that $2a^2 + 2{,}400 = 140a$, or $a^2 - 70a + 1{,}200 = 0$.

When you solve this equation for a (either by factoring or by using the quadratic formula), you get $a = 30$ or $a = 40$. If $a = 30$, then $b = \dfrac{2{,}400}{30} = 80$; if $a = 40$, then

$b = \dfrac{2{,}400}{40} = 60$. So the possible lengths of the sides are 30, 40, 60, and 80. Thus the correct answer consists of **Choices B, C, E, and G**.

This explanation uses the following strategies.
Strategy 1: Translate from Words to an Arithmetic or Algebraic Representation
Strategy 8: Search for a Mathematical Relationship

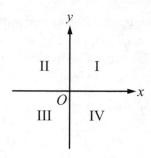

12. The quadrants of the *xy*-plane are shown in the figure above. In the *xy*-plane, line *m* (not shown) has a positive slope and a positive *x*-intercept. Line *m* intersects which of the quadrants?

    Indicate <u>all</u> such quadrants.

    $\boxed{A}$ Quadrant I
    $\boxed{B}$ Quadrant II
    $\boxed{C}$ Quadrant III
    $\boxed{D}$ Quadrant IV

Explanation

Since line *m* has a positive *x*-intercept, it must cross the *x*-axis to the right of the origin; and since the slope of line *m* is positive, the line must slant upward and to the right. Consequently, the line must have a negative *y*-intercept. The figure below shows a typical line that satisfies these conditions.

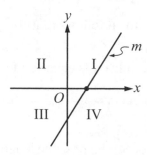

In the figure, the line intersects quadrants I, III, and IV. Thus the correct answer consists of **Choices A, C, and D**.

This explanation uses the following strategy.
Strategy 6: Add to a Geometric Figure

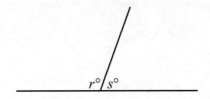

13. In the figure above, if $\dfrac{r}{r+s} = \dfrac{5}{8}$, what is the value of r ?

$$r = \boxed{}$$

Explanation

From the figure, note that $r° + s°$ must equal $180°$. Therefore $\dfrac{r}{r+s} = \dfrac{r}{180}$. Since you

are also given in the question that $\dfrac{r}{r+s} = \dfrac{5}{8}$, you can conclude that $\dfrac{r}{180} = \dfrac{5}{8}$. Thus

$r = \dfrac{5(180)}{8} = 112.5$, and the correct answer is **112.5**.

This explanation uses the following strategy.
Strategy 4: Translate from a Figure to an Arithmetic or Algebraic Representation

Data Analysis

⇨ Practice answering *GRE*® questions in data analysis
⇨ Review answers and explanations, particularly for questions you answered incorrectly

This chapter contains GRE Quantitative Reasoning practice questions that involve data analysis.

Data analysis topics include basic descriptive statistics, such as mean, median, mode, range, standard deviation, interquartile range, quartiles, and percentiles; interpretation of data in tables and graphs, such as line graphs, bar graphs, circle graphs, boxplots, scatterplots, and frequency distributions; elementary probability, such as probabilities of compound events and independent events; random variables and probability distributions, including normal distributions; and counting methods, such as combinations, permutations, and Venn diagrams. These topics are typically taught in high school algebra courses or introductory statistics courses. Inferential statistics is not tested.

The questions are arranged by question type: Quantitative Comparison questions, followed by both types of Multiple-choice questions, followed by Numeric Entry questions, and finally Data Interpretation sets.

Following the questions is an answer key for quick reference. Then, at the end of the chapter, you will find complete explanations for every question. Each explanation is presented with the corresponding question for easy reference.

Review the answers and explanations carefully, paying particular attention to explanations for questions that you answered incorrectly.

Before answering the practice questions, read the Quantitative Reasoning section directions that begin on the following page. Also, review the directions that precede each question type to make sure you understand how to answer the questions.

Quantitative Reasoning Section Directions

For each question, indicate the best answer, using the directions given.

Notes: All numbers used are real numbers.

All figures are assumed to lie in a plane unless otherwise indicated.

Geometric figures, such as lines, circles, triangles, and quadrilaterals, **are not necessarily** drawn to scale. That is, you should **not** assume that quantities such as lengths and angle measures are as they appear in a figure. You should assume, however, that lines shown as straight are actually straight, points on a line are in the order shown, and more generally, all geometric objects are in the relative positions shown. For questions with geometric figures, you should base your answers on geometric reasoning, not on estimating or comparing quantities by sight or by measurement.

Coordinate systems, such as xy-planes and number lines, **are** drawn to scale; therefore, you can read, estimate, or compare quantities in such figures by sight or by measurement.

Graphical data presentations, such as bar graphs, circle graphs, and line graphs, **are** drawn to scale; therefore, you can read, estimate, or compare data values by sight or by measurement.

Quantitative Comparison Questions

For Questions 1 to 6, compare Quantity A and Quantity B, using additional information centered above the two quantities if such information is given. Select one of the following four answer choices and fill in the corresponding oval to the right of the question.

Ⓐ Quantity A is greater.

Ⓑ Quantity B is greater.

Ⓒ The two quantities are equal.

Ⓓ The relationship cannot be determined from the information given.

A symbol that appears more than once in a question has the same meaning throughout the question.

	Quantity A	Quantity B	Correct Answer
Example 1:	(2)(6)	2 + 6	Ⓐ Ⓑ Ⓒ Ⓓ

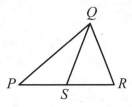

	Quantity A	Quantity B	Correct Answer
Example 2:	*PS*	*SR*	Ⓐ Ⓑ Ⓒ Ⓓ

(since equal lengths cannot be assumed, even though *PS* and *SR* appear equal)

The average (arithmetic mean) of 4 donations to a charity was $80. Two of the 4 donations were $90 and $60.

	Quantity A	Quantity B	
1.	The average of the other 2 donations	$80	Ⓐ Ⓑ Ⓒ Ⓓ

AGE DISTRIBUTION OF
EMPLOYEES OF A BUSINESS

Age Interval	Number of Employees
15–24	17
25–34	24
35–44	26
45–54	21
55–64	18
Total	106

	Quantity A	Quantity B	
2.	The range of the ages of the 20 oldest employees of the business	11 years	Ⓐ Ⓑ Ⓒ Ⓓ

	Quantity A	Quantity B	
3.	The sum of the first 7 positive integers	7 times the median of the first 7 positive integers	Ⓐ Ⓑ Ⓒ Ⓓ

	Quantity A	Quantity B	
4.	The number of two-digit positive integers for which the units digit is not equal to the tens digit	80	Ⓐ Ⓑ Ⓒ Ⓓ

In a probability experiment, G and H are independent events. The probability that G will occur is r, and the probability that H will occur is s, where both r and s are greater than 0.

	Quantity A	Quantity B	
5.	The probability that either G will occur or H will occur, but not both	$r + s - rs$	Ⓐ Ⓑ Ⓒ Ⓓ

$$S = \{1, 4, 7, 10\}$$
$$T = \{2, 3, 5, 8, 13\}$$

x is a number in set S, and y is a number in set T.

	Quantity A	Quantity B	
6.	The number of different possible values of the product xy	20	Ⓐ Ⓑ Ⓒ Ⓓ

Multiple-choice Questions—Select One Answer Choice

For Questions 7 to 12, select a single answer choice.

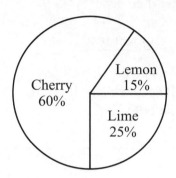

7. The graph above shows the distribution of three different flavors of hard candies—cherry, lemon, and lime—in a candy jar. If all the lemon candies are removed and no other candies are added or removed, what fraction of the remaining candies in the jar will be lime candies?

   (A) $\dfrac{1}{7}$

   (B) $\dfrac{2}{9}$

   (C) $\dfrac{1}{4}$

   (D) $\dfrac{5}{17}$

   (E) $\dfrac{5}{12}$

8. R is a list of 15 consecutive integers, and T is a list of 21 consecutive integers. The median of the integers in list R is equal to the least integer in list T. If the two lists are combined into one list of 36 integers, how many different integers are on the combined list?

   (A) 25
   (B) 27
   (C) 28
   (D) 32
   (E) 36

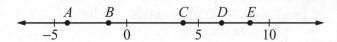

9. From the 5 points A, B, C, D, and E on the number line above, 3 different points are to be randomly selected. What is the probability that the coordinates of the 3 points selected will all be positive?

(A) $\dfrac{1}{10}$

(B) $\dfrac{1}{5}$

(C) $\dfrac{3}{10}$

(D) $\dfrac{2}{5}$

(E) $\dfrac{3}{5}$

10. In a distribution of 850 different measurements, x centimeters is at the 73rd percentile. If there are 68 measurements in the distribution that are greater than y centimeters but less than x centimeters, then y is approximately at what percentile in the distribution?

(A) 45th

(B) 50th

(C) 55th

(D) 60th

(E) 65th

11. Each of the following linear equations defines y as a function of x for all integers x from 1 to 100. For which of the following equations is the standard deviation of the y-values corresponding to all the x-values the greatest?

(A) $y = \dfrac{x}{3}$

(B) $y = \dfrac{x}{2} + 40$

(C) $y = x$

(D) $y = 2x + 50$

(E) $y = 3x - 20$

12. For a certain distribution, the measurement 12.1 is 1.5 standard deviations below the mean, and the measurement 17.5 is 3.0 standard deviations above the mean. What is the mean of the distribution?

    (A) 13.8

    (B) 13.9

    (C) 14.0

    (D) 14.1

    (E) 14.2

Multiple-choice Questions—Select One or More Answer Choices

> **For Question 13, select all the answer choices that apply.**

13. Set *A* has 50 members and set *B* has 53 members. At least 2 of the members in set *A* are not in set *B*. Which of the following could be the number of members in set *B* that are not in set *A* ?

    Indicate all such numbers.

    A   3

    B   5

    C   13

    D   25

    E   50

    F   53

Numeric Entry Questions

For Questions 14 to 15, enter your answer in the answer box(es) below the question.

- **Your answer may be an integer, a decimal, or a fraction, and it may be negative.**
- **If a question asks for a fraction, there will be two boxes—one for the numerator and one for the denominator. A decimal point cannot be used in a fraction.**
- **Equivalent forms of the correct answer, such as 2.5 and 2.50, are all correct. Fractions do not need to be reduced to lowest terms, though you may need to reduce your fraction to fit in the boxes.**
- **Enter the exact answer unless the question asks you to round your answer.**

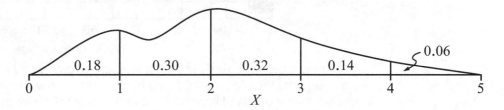

14. The figure above shows the probability distribution of a continuous random variable X. For each of the five intervals shown, the figure gives the probability that the value of X is in that interval. What is the probability that $1 < X < 4$?

FIVE MOST POPULOUS CITIES IN THE UNITED STATES
APRIL 2000

City	Population (in thousands)
New York	8,008
Los Angeles	3,695
Chicago	2,896
Houston	1,954
Philadelphia	1,518

15. The populations of the five most populous cities in the United States in April 2000 are listed in the table above. The total population of the United States in April 2000 was 281,422,000. Based on the data shown, the population of the three most populous cities combined was what percent of the total population of the United States in April 2000 ?

Give your answer to the <u>nearest whole percent</u>.

[   ] %

Data Interpretation Sets

Questions 16 to 19 are based on the following data. For these questions, select a single answer choice.

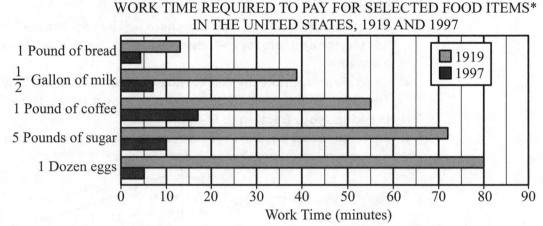

WORK TIME REQUIRED TO PAY FOR SELECTED FOOD ITEMS*
IN THE UNITED STATES, 1919 AND 1997

*For each year, the work time, in hours, required to pay for a food item is the average price of the food item divided by the average hourly wage for rank-and-file manufacturing workers. The work time in the graph is given in minutes.

16. In 1997, at the rates shown in the graph, the work time required to pay for which of the following food items was greatest?

   (A) 10 pounds of bread

   (B) 5 gallons of milk

   (C) 3 pounds of coffee

   (D) 20 pounds of sugar

   (E) 5 dozen eggs

17. If the average hourly wage of the rank-and-file manufacturing worker in 1919 was $0.55, which of the following is closest to the average price of $\frac{1}{2}$ gallon of milk in 1919 ?

   (A) $0.80

   (B) $0.65

   (C) $0.50

   (D) $0.35

   (E) $0.20

18. At the rates shown in the graph, which of the following is closest to the number of hours of work time that was required to pay for 20 kilograms of sugar in 1919 ? (1 kilogram equals 2.2 pounds, rounded to the nearest 0.1 pound.)

Ⓐ 11

Ⓑ 14

Ⓒ 20

Ⓓ 31

Ⓔ 53

19. Eight hours of work time paid for approximately how many more dozen eggs in 1997 than it did in 1919 ?

Ⓐ 50

Ⓑ 70

Ⓒ 90

Ⓓ 110

Ⓔ 130

Questions 20 to 23 are based on the following data. For these questions, select a single answer choice unless otherwise directed.

HOMES SOLD IN COUNTY *T*, 2009–2013

Number of
Homes Sold

Year	Number
2009	503
2010	351
2011	390
2012	410
2013	290

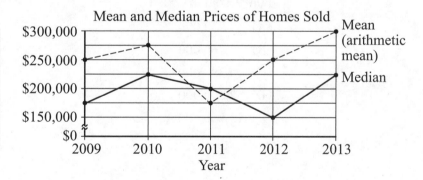

20. Which of the following is closest to the mean of the prices of the 700 homes sold in 2012 and 2013 combined?

Ⓐ $265,000

Ⓑ $270,000

Ⓒ $275,000

Ⓓ $280,000

Ⓔ $285,000

21. By approximately what percent did the median price of homes sold in County *T* decrease from 2011 to 2012 ?

    Ⓐ 10%

    Ⓑ 15%

    Ⓒ 25%

    Ⓓ 33%

    Ⓔ 50%

For Question 22, select all the answer choices that apply.

---

22. Based on the information given, which of the following statements about the sum of the prices of all the homes sold in a given year must be true?

    Indicate <u>all</u> such statements.

    Ⓐ The sum of the prices for 2010 was greater than the sum for 2009.

    Ⓑ The sum of the prices for 2010 was greater than the sum for 2011.

    Ⓒ The sum of the prices for 2009 was greater than the sum for 2011.

23. County *T* collected a tax equal to 3 percent of the price of each home sold in the county in 2009. Approximately how much did County *T* collect in taxes from all homes sold in 2009 ?

    Ⓐ $38,000

    Ⓑ $260,000

    Ⓒ $380,000

    Ⓓ $2,600,000

    Ⓔ $3,800,000

PERSONAL INCOME AND
PUBLIC EDUCATION REVENUE
IN COUNTRY X
(in constant 1998 dollars)

Year	Per Capita Income	Revenue per Student
1930	$6,610	$710
1940	6,960	950
1950	9,540	1,330
1960	12,780	2,020
1970	17,340	3,440
1980	20,150	4,400
1990	24,230	5,890

24. From 1930 to 1990, approximately what was the average increase per year in per capita income?

   (A) $150

   (B) $200

   (C) $250

   (D) $300

   (E) $350

25. In 1950 the revenue per student was approximately what percent of the per capita income?

   (A) 8%

   (B) 11%

   (C) 14%

   (D) 17%

   (E) 20%

26. For how many of the seven years shown was the revenue per student less than $\frac{1}{5}$ of the per capita income for the year?

   (A) One

   (B) Two

   (C) Three

   (D) Four

   (E) Five

ANSWER KEY

1. **Choice A**: Quantity A is greater.
2. **Choice D**: The relationship cannot be determined from the information given.
3. **Choice C**: The two quantities are equal.
4. **Choice A**: Quantity A is greater.
5. **Choice B**: Quantity B is greater.
6. **Choice B**: Quantity B is greater.
7. **Choice D**: $\dfrac{5}{17}$
8. **Choice C**: 28
9. **Choice A**: $\dfrac{1}{10}$
10. **Choice E**: 65th
11. **Choice E**: $y = 3x - 20$
12. **Choice B**: 13.9
13. **Choice B**: 5
    AND
    Choice C: 13
    AND
    Choice D: 25
    AND
    Choice E: 50
    AND
    Choice F: 53
14. **0.76**
15. **5**
16. **Choice B**: 5 gallons of milk
17. **Choice D**: $0.35
18. **Choice A**: 11
19. **Choice C**: 90
20. **Choice B**: $270,000
21. **Choice C**: 25%
22. **Choice B**: The sum of the prices for 2010 was greater than the sum for 2011.
    AND
    Choice C: The sum of the prices for 2009 was greater than the sum for 2011.
23. **Choice E**: $3,800,000
24. **Choice D**: $300
25. **Choice C**: 14%
26. **Choice E**: Five

Answers and Explanations

The average (arithmetic mean) of 4 donations to a charity was $80. Two of the 4 donations were $90 and $60.

	Quantity A	Quantity B	
1.	The average of the other 2 donations	$80	Ⓐ Ⓑ Ⓒ Ⓓ

Explanation

Note that Quantity B, $80, is the average of the 4 donations. The average of 2 of the 4 donations, $90 and $60, is $75. Since $75 is less than $80, it follows that Quantity A, the average of the other 2 donations, is greater than Quantity B. Therefore the correct answer is **Choice A**.

This explanation uses the following strategy.
Strategy 8: Search for a Mathematical Relationship

AGE DISTRIBUTION OF
EMPLOYEES OF A BUSINESS

Age Interval	Number of Employees
15–24	17
25–34	24
35–44	26
45–54	21
55–64	18
Total	106

	Quantity A	Quantity B	
2.	The range of the ages of the 20 oldest employees of the business	11 years	Ⓐ Ⓑ Ⓒ Ⓓ

Explanation

Of the 20 oldest employees, 18 are in the 55–64 age-group, and 2 are in the 45–54 age-group. Therefore the youngest of the 20 employees is in the 45–54 age-group, and the oldest is in the 55–64 age-group. The youngest of the 20 employees could be 45 years old and the oldest could be 64 years old. In this case, the range of their ages would be 64 − 45, or 19 years.

On the other hand, the youngest could be 54 years old and the oldest could be 55 years old, so the range of their ages would be 1 year. Because there are cases where the range is greater than 11 years and cases where it is less than 11 years, the correct answer is **Choice D**.

This explanation uses the following strategies.
Strategy 11: Divide into Cases
Strategy 13: Determine Whether a Conclusion Follows from the Information Given

---

Quantity A	Quantity B	
3. The sum of the first 7 positive integers	7 times the median of the first 7 positive integers	

Explanation

Quantity A is $1 + 2 + 3 + 4 + 5 + 6 + 7$, or 28. The median of the first 7 positive integers is the middle number when they are listed in order from least to greatest, which is 4. So Quantity B is $(7)(4)$, or 28. Thus the correct answer is **Choice C**.

This explanation uses the following strategy.
Strategy 8: Search for a Mathematical Relationship

Quantity A	Quantity B	
4. The number of two-digit positive integers for which the units digit is not equal to the tens digit	80	

Explanation

The two-digit positive integers are the integers from 10 to 99. There are 90 such integers. In 9 of these integers, namely, 11, 22, 33, . . . , 99, the units digit and tens digit are equal. Hence, Quantity A, the number of two-digit positive integers for which the units digit is not equal to the tens digit, is $90 - 9$, or 81. Since Quantity B is 80, the correct answer is **Choice A**.

This explanation uses the following strategy.
Strategy 11: Divide into Cases

In a probability experiment, *G* and *H* are independent events. The probability that *G* will occur is *r*, and the probability that *H* will occur is *s*, where both *r* and *s* are greater than 0.

Quantity A	Quantity B	
5. The probability that either *G* will occur or *H* will occur, but not both	$r + s - rs$	Ⓐ Ⓑ Ⓒ Ⓓ

Explanation

By the rules of probability, you can conclude that the probability that event *H* will not occur is $1 - s$. Also, the fact that *G* and *H* are independent events implies that *G* and "not *H*" are independent events. Therefore the probability that *G* will occur and *H* will not occur is $r(1 - s)$. Similarly, the probability that *H* will occur and *G* will not occur is $s(1 - r)$. So Quantity A, the probability that either *G* will occur or *H* will occur, but not both, is $r(1 - s) + s(1 - r) = r + s - 2rs$, which is less than Quantity B, $r + s - rs$. Thus the correct answer is **Choice B**.

This explanation uses the following strategy.
Strategy 1: Translate from Words to an Arithmetic or Algebraic Representation

---

$$S = \{1, 4, 7, 10\}$$
$$T = \{2, 3, 5, 8, 13\}$$

x is a number in set *S*, and *y* is a number in set *T*.

Quantity A	Quantity B	
6. The number of different possible values of the product *xy*	20	Ⓐ Ⓑ Ⓒ Ⓓ

Explanation

There are 4 numbers in *S* and 5 numbers in *T*, so the total number of possible products that can be formed using one number in each set is $(4)(5)$, or 20. However, some of these products have the same value; for example, $(1)(8) = (4)(2)$. Therefore, Quantity A, the number of different possible values of the product *xy*, is less than Quantity B, 20. Thus the correct answer is **Choice B**.

This explanation uses the following strategy.
Strategy 8: Search for a Mathematical Relationship

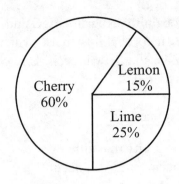

7. The graph above shows the distribution of three different flavors of hard candies—cherry, lemon, and lime—in a candy jar. If all the lemon candies are removed and no other candies are added or removed, what fraction of the remaining candies in the jar will be lime candies?

(A) $\dfrac{1}{7}$

(B) $\dfrac{2}{9}$

(C) $\dfrac{1}{4}$

(D) $\dfrac{5}{17}$

(E) $\dfrac{5}{12}$

Explanation

If the lemon candies are removed, then 85% of the original number of candies will remain. Of these, the fraction of lime candies will be $\dfrac{25}{85}$, or $\dfrac{5}{17}$. The correct answer is **Choice D**.

This explanation uses the following strategy.
Strategy 4: Translate from a Figure to an Arithmetic or Algebraic Representation

8. *R* is a list of 15 consecutive integers, and *T* is a list of 21 consecutive integers. The median of the integers in list *R* is equal to the least integer in list *T*. If the two lists are combined into one list of 36 integers, how many different integers are on the combined list?

(A) 25

(B) 27

(C) 28

(D) 32

(E) 36

Explanation

The median of the numbers in list *R* is the middle number when the numbers are listed in order from least to greatest, that is, the 8th number. Since the median of the numbers in list *R* is equal to the least integer in list *T*, the 8 greatest integers in *R* are the 8 least integers in *T*, and the number of different integers in the combined list is $15 + 21 - 8$, or 28. The correct answer is **Choice C**.

This explanation uses the following strategy.
Strategy 8: Search for a Mathematical Relationship

9. From the 5 points *A*, *B*, *C*, *D*, and *E* on the number line above, 3 different points are to be randomly selected. What is the probability that the coordinates of the 3 points selected will all be positive?

(A) $\dfrac{1}{10}$

(B) $\dfrac{1}{5}$

(C) $\dfrac{3}{10}$

(D) $\dfrac{2}{5}$

(E) $\dfrac{3}{5}$

Explanation

Of the 5 points, 3 have positive coordinates, points *C*, *D*, and *E*. The probability that the first point selected will have a positive coordinate is $\dfrac{3}{5}$. Since the second point selected must be different from the first point, there are 4 remaining points to select from, of which 2 are points with positive coordinates. Therefore, if the coordinate of the first point selected is positive, then the probability that the second point selected will have a positive coordinate is $\frac{2}{4}$.

Similarly, if the coordinates of the first 2 points selected are positive, then the probability that the third point selected will have a positive coordinate is $\frac{1}{3}$.

The probability that the coordinates of the 3 points selected will all be positive is the product of the three probabilities, $\left(\frac{3}{5}\right)\left(\frac{2}{4}\right)\left(\frac{1}{3}\right)$, or $\frac{1}{10}$. The correct answer is **Choice A**.

Alternatively, you can compute the probability as the following fraction.

$$\frac{\text{number of ways to select 3 points with positive coordinates}}{\text{number of ways to select 3 points from 5 points}}$$

Since there are only 3 points with positive coordinates, there is only 1 way to select them, so the numerator is 1. The denominator of the fraction is equal to the number of combinations of 5 objects taken 3 at a time, or "5 choose 3," which is $\frac{5!}{3!(5-3)!} = \frac{(5)(4)}{(2)(1)} = 10$. Therefore the probability is $\frac{1}{10}$, which is **Choice A**.

This explanation uses the following strategy.
Strategy 12: Adapt Solutions to Related Problems

---

10. In a distribution of 850 different measurements, x centimeters is at the 73rd percentile. If there are 68 measurements in the distribution that are greater than y centimeters but less than x centimeters, then y is approximately at what percentile in the distribution?

   (A) 45th
   (B) 50th
   (C) 55th
   (D) 60th
   (E) 65th

Explanation

If x centimeters is at the 73rd percentile, then approximately 73% of the measurements in the distribution are less than or equal to x centimeters. The 68 measurements that are greater than y centimeters but less than x centimeters are $\left(\frac{68}{850}\right)(100\%)$, or 8%, of the distribution. Thus approximately $73\% - 8\%$, or 65%, of the measurements are less than or equal to y centimeters, that is, y is approximately at the 65th percentile in the distribution. The correct answer is **Choice E**.

This explanation uses the following strategy.
Strategy 8: Search for a Mathematical Relationship

11. Each of the following linear equations defines y as a function of x for all integers x from 1 to 100. For which of the following equations is the standard deviation of the y-values corresponding to all the x-values the greatest?

    (A) $y = \dfrac{x}{3}$

    (B) $y = \dfrac{x}{2} + 40$

    (C) $y = x$

    (D) $y = 2x + 50$

    (E) $y = 3x - 20$

Explanation

Recall that the standard deviation of the numbers in a data set is a measure of the spread of the numbers about the mean of the numbers. The standard deviation is directly related to the distances between the mean and each of the numbers when the mean and the numbers are considered on a number line. Note that each of the answer choices is an equation of the form $y = ax + b$, where a and b are constants. For every value of x in a data set, the corresponding value of y is $ax + b$, and if m is the mean of the values of x, then $am + b$ is the mean of the corresponding values of y.

In the question, the set of values of x consists of the integers from 1 to 100, and each answer choice gives a set of 100 values of y corresponding to the 100 values of x. For each value of x in the data set,

(1)   the distance between x and the mean m is $|x - m|$, and

(2)   the distance between the corresponding y-value, $ax + b$, and the mean, $am + b$, of the corresponding y-values is $|ax + b - am - b|$, which is equal to $|ax - am|$, or $|a||x - m|$.

Therefore the greater the absolute value of a in the equation $y = ax + b$, the greater the distance between each y-value and the mean of the y-values; hence, the greater the spread. Note that the value of b is irrelevant. Scanning the choices, you can see that the equation in which the absolute value of a is greatest is $y = 3x - 20$. Thus the correct answer is **Choice E**.

This explanation uses the following strategy.
Strategy 8: Search for a Mathematical Relationship

12. For a certain distribution, the measurement 12.1 is 1.5 standard deviations below the mean, and the measurement 17.5 is 3.0 standard deviations above the mean. What is the mean of the distribution?

    Ⓐ 13.8

    Ⓑ 13.9

    Ⓒ 14.0

    Ⓓ 14.1

    Ⓔ 14.2

Explanation

If m represents the mean of the distribution and s represents the standard deviation, then the statement "the measurement 12.1 is 1.5 standard deviations below the mean" can be represented by the equation $12.1 = m - 1.5s$. Similarly, the statement "the measurement 17.5 is 3.0 standard deviations above the mean" can be represented by the equation $17.5 = m + 3.0s$.

One way to solve the two linear equations for m is to eliminate the s. To do this, you can multiply the equation $12.1 = m - 1.5s$ by 2 and then add the result to the equation $17.5 = m + 3.0s$ to get $41.7 = 3m$. Solving this equation for m gives the mean 13.9. Thus the correct answer is **Choice B**.

This explanation uses the following strategy.
Strategy 1: Translate from Words to an Arithmetic or Algebraic Representation

13. Set *A* has 50 members and set *B* has 53 members. At least 2 of the members in set *A* are <u>not</u> in set *B*. Which of the following could be the number of members in set *B* that are <u>not</u> in set *A* ?

Indicate <u>all</u> such numbers.

A 3
B 5
C 13
D 25
E 50
F 53

Explanation

Let *x* be the number of members in the intersection of set *A* and set *B*. Then the distribution of the members of *A* and *B* can be represented by the following Venn diagram.

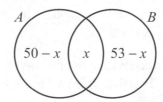

The question asks you to indicate which of the answer choices could be the number of members in set *B* that are <u>not</u> in set *A*. This is equivalent to determining which of the answer choices are possible values of $53 - x$.

You are given that the number of members in set *A* that are <u>not</u> in set *B* is at least 2, and clearly the number of members in set *A* that are <u>not</u> in set *B* is at most all 50 members of *A*; that is, $2 \leq 50 - x \leq 50$. Note that $53 - x$ is 3 more than $50 - x$. So by adding 3 to each part of $2 \leq 50 - x \leq 50$, you get the equivalent inequality $5 \leq 53 - x \leq 53$. Thus the number of members in set *B* that are <u>not</u> in set *A* can be any integer from 5 to 53. The correct answer consists of **Choices B, C, D, E, and F.**

This explanation uses the following strategies.
Strategy 1: Translate from Words to an Arithmetic or Algebraic Representation
Strategy 2: Translate from Words to a Figure or Diagram

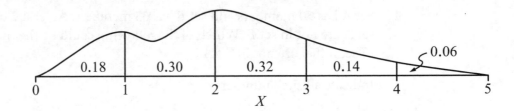

14. The figure above shows the probability distribution of a continuous random variable X. For each of the five intervals shown, the figure gives the probability that the value of X is in that interval. What is the probability that $1 < X < 4$?

Explanation

In the distribution shown, the interval from 1 to 4 is divided into the three intervals—the interval from 1 to 2, the interval from 2 to 3, and the interval from 3 to 4. The probability that $1 < X < 4$ is the sum of the probability that $1 < X < 2$, the probability that $2 < X < 3$, and the probability that $3 < X < 4$, that is, $0.30 + 0.32 + 0.14 = 0.76$. The correct answer is **0.76**.

This explanation uses the following strategy.
Strategy 4: Translate from a Figure to an Arithmetic or Algebraic Representation

FIVE MOST POPULOUS CITIES IN THE UNITED STATES
APRIL 2000

City	Population (in thousands)
New York	8,008
Los Angeles	3,695
Chicago	2,896
Houston	1,954
Philadelphia	1,518

15. The populations of the five most populous cities in the United States in April 2000 are listed in the table above. The total population of the United States in April 2000 was 281,422,000. Based on the data shown, the population of the three most populous cities combined was what percent of the total population of the United States in April 2000 ?

Give your answer to the nearest whole percent.

[   ] %

Explanation

From the data given, the three most populous cities were New York, Los Angeles, and Chicago, and the population of the three cities combined was $8,008,000 + 3,695,000 + 2,896,000,$ or 14,599,000. As a percent of the total population of the United States, this is $\left(\dfrac{14,599,000}{281,422,000}\right)(100\%) \approx 5.19\%,$ which, rounded to the nearest whole percent, is 5%.

The correct answer is **5**.

This explanation uses the following strategy.
Strategy 4: Translate from a Figure to an Arithmetic or Algebraic Representation

WORK TIME REQUIRED TO PAY FOR SELECTED FOOD ITEMS*
IN THE UNITED STATES, 1919 AND 1997

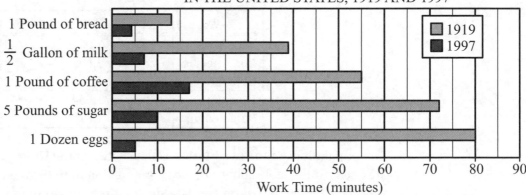

*For each year, the work time, in hours, required to pay for a food item is the
average price of the food item divided by the average hourly wage for rank-and-file
manufacturing workers. The work time in the graph is given in minutes.

16. In 1997, at the rates shown in the graph, the work time required to pay for which
of the following food items was greatest?

   Ⓐ 10 pounds of bread

   Ⓑ 5 gallons of milk

   Ⓒ 3 pounds of coffee

   Ⓓ 20 pounds of sugar

   Ⓔ 5 dozen eggs

Explanation

Reading from the graph, you can compute the approximate work times for the quantities
listed in the choices.

     Choice A: The approximate work time required to pay for 1 pound of bread was
4 minutes, so the approximate work time to pay for 10 pounds of bread was (10)(4), or
40 minutes.

     Choice B: The approximate work time required to pay for $\frac{1}{2}$ gallon of milk was

7 minutes, so the approximate work time to pay for 5 gallons of milk was (10)(7), or
70 minutes.

     Choice C: The approximate work time required to pay for 1 pound of coffee was
17 minutes, so the approximate work time to pay for 3 pounds of coffee was (3)(17), or
51 minutes.

     Choice D: The approximate work time required to pay for 5 pounds of sugar was
10 minutes, so the approximate work time to pay for 20 pounds of sugar was (4)(10),
or 40 minutes.

     Choice E: The approximate work time required to pay for 1 dozen eggs was 5 minutes,
so the approximate work time to pay for 5 dozen eggs was (5)(5), or 25 minutes.

     Of these times, the greatest is 70 minutes for 5 gallons of milk. The correct answer
is **Choice B**.

This explanation uses the following strategies.

Strategy 4: Translate from a Figure to an Arithmetic or Algebraic Representation
Strategy 5: Simplify an Arithmetic or Algebraic Representation
Strategy 9: Estimate

17. If the average hourly wage of the rank-and-file manufacturing worker in 1919 was $0.55, which of the following is closest to the average price of $\frac{1}{2}$ gallon of milk in 1919?

    Ⓐ $0.80

    Ⓑ $0.65

    Ⓒ $0.50

    Ⓓ $0.35

    Ⓔ $0.20

Explanation

From the graph, you see that in 1919 the work time required to pay for $\frac{1}{2}$ gallon of milk was approximately 38 minutes. Given an hourly wage of $0.55, the wage for 38 minutes is $\left(\frac{38}{60}\right)(\$0.55)$, or about $0.35. The correct answer is **Choice D**.

This explanation uses the following strategies.
Strategy 4: Translate from a Figure to an Arithmetic or Algebraic Representation
Strategy 5: Simplify an Arithmetic or Algebraic Representation
Strategy 9: Estimate

---

18. At the rates shown in the graph, which of the following is closest to the number of hours of work time that was required to pay for 20 kilograms of sugar in 1919?
(1 kilogram equals 2.2 pounds, rounded to the nearest 0.1 pound.)

    Ⓐ 11

    Ⓑ 14

    Ⓒ 20

    Ⓓ 31

    Ⓔ 53

Explanation

If 1 kilogram equals 2.2 pounds, then 20 kilograms equals 44 pounds.

According to the graph, in 1919 the work time required to pay for 5 pounds of sugar was approximately 72 minutes, so the work time required to pay for 44 pounds of sugar was $\left(\frac{72}{5}\right)(44)$, or 633.6 minutes, which is approximately 10.6 hours. Of the given choices, the one closest to this number is 11 hours. The correct answer is **Choice A**.

This explanation uses the following strategies.
Strategy 4: Translate from a Figure to an Arithmetic or Algebraic Representation
Strategy 5: Simplify an Arithmetic or Algebraic Representation
Strategy 9: Estimate

19. Eight hours of work time paid for approximately how many more dozen eggs in 1997 than it did in 1919 ?

(A) 50

(B) 70

(C) 90

(D) 110

(E) 130

Explanation

Since the work times are given in minutes, first convert 8 hours to 480 minutes.

In 1919, the work time that paid for 1 dozen eggs was approximately 80 minutes, so 480 minutes paid for $\dfrac{480}{80}$, or 6 dozen eggs.

In 1997, the work time that paid for 1 dozen eggs was approximately 5 minutes, so 480 minutes paid for $\dfrac{480}{5}$, or 96 dozen eggs.

Thus 8 hours of work time paid for 90 dozen more eggs in 1997 than it paid for in 1919. The correct answer is **Choice C**.

This explanation uses the following strategies.

Strategy 4: Translate from a Figure to an Arithmetic or Algebraic Representation
Strategy 5: Simplify an Arithmetic or Algebraic Representation
Strategy 9: Estimate

HOMES SOLD IN COUNTY *T*, 2009–2013

Number of
Homes Sold

Year	Number
2009	503
2010	351
2011	390
2012	410
2013	290

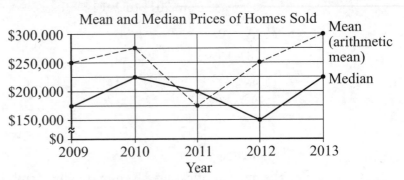

20. Which of the following is closest to the mean of the prices of the 700 homes sold in 2012 and 2013 combined?

Ⓐ $265,000

Ⓑ $270,000

Ⓒ $275,000

Ⓓ $280,000

Ⓔ $285,000

Explanation

The number of homes sold is given in the table, and the mean of the prices is given in the line graph.

The mean price of the 700 homes sold in 2012 and 2013 is the weighted average of the mean price of the 410 homes sold in 2012, which is $250,000, and the mean price of the 290 homes sold in 2013, which is $300,000:

$$\frac{(410)(\$250,000) + (290)(\$300,000)}{700} \approx \$270,714$$

Of the choices given, the closest is $270,000. The correct answer is **Choice B**.

This explanation uses the following strategies.
Strategy 4: Translate from a Figure to an Arithmetic or Algebraic Representation
Strategy 9: Estimate

21. By approximately what percent did the median price of homes sold in County T decrease from 2011 to 2012 ?

  (A) 10%

  (B) 15%

  (C) 25%

  (D) 33%

  (E) 50%

Explanation

The median prices are given in the line graph. The median price decreased from $200,000 in 2011 to $150,000 in 2012, which is a decrease of $50,000. As a percent of the 2011 price, this is $\left(\dfrac{50,000}{200,000}\right)(100\%)$, or 25%. The correct answer is **Choice C**.

This explanation uses the following strategy.
Strategy 4: Translate from a Figure to an Arithmetic or Algebraic Representation

---

22. Based on the information given, which of the following statements about the sum of the prices of all the homes sold in a given year must be true?

  Indicate all such statements.

  [A] The sum of the prices for 2010 was greater than the sum for 2009.

  [B] The sum of the prices for 2010 was greater than the sum for 2011.

  [C] The sum of the prices for 2009 was greater than the sum for 2011.

Explanation

For each year, the sum of the prices is equal to the number of homes sold times the mean price of the homes sold.

  For 2010, the sum is equal to (351)($275,000), or $96,525,000.

  For 2009, the sum is (503)($250,000), or $125,750,000, which is greater than the sum for 2010. So statement A is false.

  For 2011, the sum is (390)($175,000), or $68,250,000, which is less than the sum for 2010. So statement B is true.

  Since the sum for 2009 is greater than the sum for 2011, statement C is true.

  The correct answer consists of **Choices B and C**.

This explanation uses the following strategy.
Strategy 4: Translate from a Figure to an Arithmetic or Algebraic Representation

23. County T collected a tax equal to 3 percent of the price of each home sold in the county in 2009. Approximately how much did County T collect in taxes from all homes sold in 2009 ?

(A) $38,000

(B) $260,000

(C) $380,000

(D) $2,600,000

(E) $3,800,000

Explanation

The total price of all the homes sold in 2009 is equal to the number of homes sold times the mean price of the homes sold. The tax is 3% of this amount. Since the choices given are far apart, there is no need for accurate computations. Using estimation, you get a total price of about (500)($250,000), or $125 million. The tax of 3% is (0.03)($125 million), or approximately $3.75 million. Of the choices given, $3,800,000 is closest to this amount. The correct answer is **Choice E.**

This explanation uses the following strategies.
Strategy 4: Translate from a Figure to an Arithmetic or Algebraic Representation
Strategy 9: Estimate

PERSONAL INCOME AND
PUBLIC EDUCATION REVENUE
IN COUNTRY X
(in constant 1998 dollars)

Year	Per Capita Income	Revenue per Student
1930	$6,610	$710
1940	6,960	950
1950	9,540	1,330
1960	12,780	2,020
1970	17,340	3,440
1980	20,150	4,400
1990	24,230	5,890

24. From 1930 to 1990, approximately what was the average increase per year in per capita income?

(A) $150

(B) $200

(C) $250

(D) $300

(E) $350

Explanation

For the 60-year period from 1930 to 1990, the per capita income increased by

$24,230 − $6,610, or $17,620. The average annual increase is $\dfrac{\$17,620}{60}$, which is

approximately $\dfrac{\$18,000}{60}$, or $300. (Since the choices are quite far apart, there is no need

for an accurate calculation.) The correct answer is **Choice D**.

This explanation uses the following strategies.
Strategy 4: Translate from a Figure to an Arithmetic or Algebraic Representation
Strategy 9: Estimate

---

25. In 1950 the revenue per student was approximately what percent of the per capita
    income?

   (A) 8%

   (B) 11%

   (C) 14%

   (D) 17%

   (E) 20%

Explanation

The table shows that in 1950 the revenue per student was $1,330. As a percent of the

per capita income of $9,540, this is $\left(\dfrac{1,330}{9,540}\right)(100\%)$, which is approximately 13.9%.

Of the given choices, the closest is 14%. The correct answer is **Choice C**.

This explanation uses the following strategies.
Strategy 4: Translate from a Figure to an Arithmetic or Algebraic Representation
Strategy 9: Estimate

26. For how many of the seven years shown was the revenue per student less than $\frac{1}{5}$ of the per capita income for the year?

(A) One

(B) Two

(C) Three

(D) Four

(E) Five

Explanation

For most of the years, a rough estimate of $\frac{1}{5}$ of the per capita income is sufficient for the comparison to the revenue per student. For the years 1930, 1940, 1950, and 1960, you might estimate $\frac{1}{5}$ of the per capita incomes as $1,300, $1,400, $2,000, and $2,500, respectively, which are clearly greater than the corresponding revenues per student.

For 1980 and 1990, your estimates might be $4,000 and $5,000, which are less than the corresponding revenues per student.

For 1970, you do have to calculate $\frac{\$17,340}{5} = \$3,468$, which is greater than $3,440.

So the revenue per student was less than $\frac{1}{5}$ of the per capita income for the five years 1930, 1940, 1950, 1960, and 1970. The correct answer is **Choice E**.

This explanation uses the following strategies.
Strategy 4: Translate from a Figure to an Arithmetic or Algebraic Representation
Strategy 9: Estimate

Your goals for this chapter	⇨ Practice answering *GRE*® Quantitative Reasoning questions in all four content areas ⇨ Review answers and explanations, particularly for questions you answered incorrectly

This chapter contains three sets of practice questions. Each set has 25 questions, with a mixture of content and question types.

In each set, the questions are arranged by question type: Quantitative Comparison questions, followed by both types of Multiple-choice questions, then by Numeric Entry questions, and ending with a Data Interpretation set.

After each set of questions, there is an answer key for quick reference, followed by explanations for every question. Each explanation is presented with the corresponding question for easy reference. Review the answers and explanations carefully, paying particular attention to explanations for questions that you answered incorrectly.

Before answering the practice questions, read the Quantitative Reasoning section directions on the next page. Also, review the directions that precede each question type to make sure you understand how to answer the questions.

Note that each set of 25 practice questions has about the same number of questions of each type as the individual Quantitative Reasoning sections in the paper-delivered GRE revised General Test, with 25 questions per 40-minute section. Therefore, to help you gauge the timed aspect of the Quantitative Reasoning measure, it may be useful to set aside a 40-minute block of time for each set of 25 questions.

If you are taking the computer-delivered GRE revised General Test, note that each Quantitative Reasoning section will contain 20 questions and you will have 35 minutes to answer them. If you can successfully complete each practice set in this chapter in 40 minutes, you should be able to answer 20 questions in 35 minutes. However, for a more realistic experience of taking the computer-delivered test under timed conditions, you should use the practice tests in the free *POWERPREP II* software.

Quantitative Reasoning Section Directions

For each question, indicate the best answer, using the directions given.

Notes: All numbers used are real numbers.

All figures are assumed to lie in a plane unless otherwise indicated.

Geometric figures, such as lines, circles, triangles, and quadrilaterals, **are not necessarily** drawn to scale. That is, you should **not** assume that quantities such as lengths and angle measures are as they appear in a figure. You should assume, however, that lines shown as straight are actually straight, points on a line are in the order shown, and more generally, all geometric objects are in the relative positions shown. For questions with geometric figures, you should base your answers on geometric reasoning, not on estimating or comparing quantities by sight or by measurement.

Coordinate systems, such as *xy*-planes and number lines, **are** drawn to scale; therefore, you can read, estimate, or compare quantities in such figures by sight or by measurement.

Graphical data presentations, such as bar graphs, circle graphs, and line graphs, **are** drawn to scale; therefore, you can read, estimate, or compare data values by sight or by measurement.

PRACTICE SET 1

Quantitative Comparison Questions

For Questions 1 to 9, compare Quantity A and Quantity B, using additional information centered above the two quantities if such information is given. Select one of the following four answer choices and fill in the corresponding oval to the right of the question.

(A) **Quantity A is greater.**

(B) **Quantity B is greater.**

(C) **The two quantities are equal.**

(D) **The relationship cannot be determined from the information given.**

A symbol that appears more than once in a question has the same meaning throughout the question.

	Quantity A	Quantity B	Correct Answer
Example 1:	(2)(6)	2 + 6	Ⓐ Ⓑ Ⓒ Ⓓ

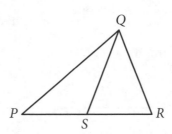

	Quantity A	Quantity B	Correct Answer
Example 2:	PS	SR	Ⓐ Ⓑ Ⓒ Ⓓ

(since equal lengths cannot
be assumed, even though
PS and *SR* appear equal)

Points *R*, *S*, and *T* lie on a number line, where *S* is between *R* and *T*. The distance between *R* and *S* is 6, and the distance between *R* and *T* is 15.

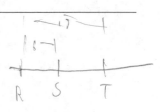

	Quantity A	Quantity B	
1.	The distance between the midpoints of line segments *RS* and *ST*	The distance between *S* and *T*	Ⓐ Ⓑ Ⓒ Ⓓ

S is a set of 8 numbers, of which 4 are negative and 4 are positive.

	Quantity A	Quantity B	
2.	The average (arithmetic mean) of the numbers in S	The median of the numbers in S	Ⓐ Ⓑ Ⓒ ⑩

The length of each side of rectangle R is an integer, and the area of R is 36.

	Quantity A	Quantity B	
3.	The number of possible values of the perimeter of R	6	Ⓐ Ⓑ Ⓒ Ⓓ

1×36
2×18
3×12
4×9
6×6

$$x = (z-1)^2$$
$$y = (z+1)^2$$

	Quantity A	Quantity B	
4.	The average (arithmetic mean) of x and y	z^2	Ⓐ Ⓑ Ⓒ Ⓓ

x, y, and z are the lengths of the sides of a triangle.

	Quantity A	Quantity B	
5.	$x + y + z$	$2z$	Ⓐ Ⓑ Ⓒ Ⓓ

At a club meeting, there are 10 more club members than nonmembers. The number of club members at the meeting is c.

$c = n + 10$

$m = n + c$

	Quantity A	Quantity B	
6.	The total number of people at the club meeting	$2c - 10$	Ⓐ Ⓑ Ⓒ Ⓓ

$2n + 20 \; ? \; n + n + 10$
$2n + 20 \; ? \; 2n + 10$

n is a positive integer that is greater than 3 and has
d positive divisors.

	Quantity A	Quantity B	
7.	n	2^{d-1}	Ⓐ Ⓑ Ⓒ Ⓓ

$$m = 10^{32} + 2$$

When *m* is divided by 11, the remainder is *r*.

	Quantity A	Quantity B	
8.	r	3	Ⓐ Ⓑ Ⓒ Ⓓ

$xy = 8$ and $x = y - 2$.

	Quantity A	Quantity B	
9.	y	0	Ⓐ Ⓑ Ⓒ Ⓓ

Multiple-choice Questions—Select One Answer Choice

For Questions 10 to 17, select a single answer choice.

10. The area of circle W is 16π and the area of circle Z is 4π. What is the ratio of the circumference of W to the circumference of Z?

    (A) 2 to 1

    (B) 4 to 1

    (C) 8 to 1

    (D) 16 to 1

    (E) 32 to 1

[handwritten: $C = 2\pi r$, $\pi r^2 = 16\pi$, $W_r = 4$, $W_z = 2$]

11. In the xy-plane, a quadrilateral has vertices at $(-1, 4), (7, 4), (7, -5)$, and $(-1, -5)$. What is the perimeter of the quadrilateral?

    (A) 17

    (B) 18

    (C) 19

    (D) 32

    (E) 34

[handwritten diagram with coordinates: $-1,4$; 8; $7,4$; $16 + 18 = 34$; $-1,-5$; 8; $7,-5$]

DISTRIBUTION OF THE
HEIGHTS OF 80 STUDENTS

Height (centimeters)	Number of Students
140–144	6
145–149	26
150–154	32
155–159	12
160–164	4
Total	80

12. The table above shows the frequency distribution of the heights of 80 students, where the heights are recorded to the nearest centimeter. What is the least possible range of the recorded heights of the 80 students?

    (A) 15

    (B) 16

    (C) 20

    (D) 24

    (E) 28

13. Which of the following functions f defined for all numbers x has the property that $f(-x) = -f(x)$ for all numbers x?

(A) $f(x) = \dfrac{x^3}{x^2+1}$

(B) $f(x) = \dfrac{x^2-1}{x^2+1}$

(C) $f(x) = x^2(x^2-1)$

(D) $f(x) = x(x^3-1)$

(E) $f(x) = x^2(x^3-1)$

14. If 10^x equals 0.1 percent of 10^y, where x and y are integers, which of the following must be true?

(A) $y = x + 2$

(B) $y = x + 3$

(C) $x = y + 3$

(D) $y = 1{,}000x$

(E) $x = 1{,}000y$

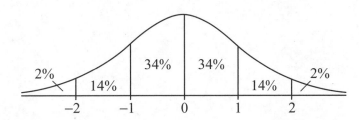

$$10^x = 0.1\left(10^Y\right)$$
$$10^x = \frac{1}{1000}\left(10^Y\right)$$
$$10^x = \frac{10^Y}{10^3}$$
$$10^x = 10^{Y-3} \qquad x = Y-3$$
$$y = x+3$$

15. The figure above shows the standard normal distribution, with mean 0 and standard deviation 1, including approximate percents of the distribution corresponding to the six regions shown.

The random variable Y is normally distributed with a mean of 470, and the value $Y = 340$ is at the 15th percentile of the distribution. Of the following, which is the best estimate of the standard deviation of the distribution?

(A) 125

(B) 135

(C) 145

(D) 155

(E) 165

16. A car dealer received a shipment of cars, half of which were black, with the remainder consisting of equal numbers of blue, silver, and white cars. During the next month, 70 percent of the black cars, 80 percent of the blue cars, 30 percent of the silver cars, and 40 percent of the white cars were sold. What percent of the cars in the shipment were sold during that month?

(A) 36%

(B) 50%

(C) 55%

(D) 60%

(E) 72%

17. If an investment of P dollars is made today and the value of the investment doubles every 7 years, what will be the value of the investment, in dollars, 28 years from today?

(A) $8P^4$

(B) P^4

(C) $16P$

(D) $8P$

(E) $4P$

Multiple-choice Questions—Select One or More Answer Choices

For Questions 18 to 19, select all the answer choices that apply.

18. The distribution of the numbers of hours that students at a certain college studied for final exams has a mean of 12 hours and a standard deviation of 3 hours. Which of the following numbers of hours are within 2 standard deviations of the mean of the distribution?

    Indicate all such numbers.

    [A] 2
    [B] 5
    [C] 10
    [D] 14
    [E] 16
    [F] 20

19. In a certain sequence of numbers, each term after the first term is found by multiplying the preceding term by 2 and then subtracting 3 from the product. If the 4th term in the sequence is 19, which of the following numbers are in the sequence?

    Indicate all such numbers.

    [A] 5
    [B] 8
    [C] 11
    [D] 16
    [E] 22
    [F] 35

Numeric Entry Questions

> **For Questions 20 to 21, enter your answer in the answer box(es) below the question.**
>
> - Your answer may be an integer, a decimal, or a fraction, and it may be negative.
> - If a question asks for a fraction, there will be two boxes—one for the numerator and one for the denominator. A decimal point cannot be used in a fraction.
> - Equivalent forms of the correct answer, such as 2.5 and 2.50, are all correct. Fractions do not need to be reduced to lowest terms, though you may need to reduce your fraction to fit in the boxes.
> - Enter the exact answer unless the question asks you to round your answer.

20. In a single line of people waiting to purchase tickets for a movie, there are currently 10 people behind Shandra. If 3 of the people who are currently in line ahead of Shandra purchase tickets and leave the line, and no one else leaves the line, there will be 8 people ahead of Shandra in line. How many people are in the line currently?

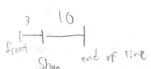

$$\boxed{18} \text{ people}$$

21. When the decimal point of a certain positive decimal number is moved six places to the right, the resulting number is 9 times the reciprocal of the original number. What is the original number?

$$\boxed{0.000009}$$

$$x \cdot 10^6 = 9\frac{1}{x}$$

$$x 10^6 = 9/x$$

$$x^2 = \frac{9}{10^6}$$

$$x = 0$$

Data Interpretation Set

Questions 22 to 25 are based on the following data. For these questions, select a single answer choice unless otherwise directed.

SELECTED DATA FOR GREETING CARD SALES

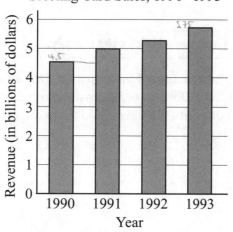

Annual Revenue from All
Greeting Card Sales, 1990–1993

Number of Greeting Cards Sold
for Ten Occasions in 1993

Occasion	Number of Cards
Christmas	2.4 billion
Valentine's Day	900 million
Easter	158 million
Mother's Day	155 million
Father's Day	102 million
Graduation	81 million
Thanksgiving	42 million
Halloween	32 million
St. Patrick's Day	18 million
Jewish New Year	12 million
Total	3.9 billion

Note: 1 billion = 1,000,000,000

22. In 1993 the number of Valentine's Day cards sold was approximately how many times the number of Thanksgiving cards sold?

   (A) 20
   (B) 30
   (C) 40
   (D) 50
   (E) 60

23. In 1993 a card company that sold 40 percent of the Mother's Day cards that year priced its cards for that occasion between $1.00 and $8.00 each. If the revenue from sales of the company's Mother's Day cards in 1993 was r million dollars, which of the following indicates all possible values of r?

   (A) $155 < r < 1,240$
   (B) $93 < r < 496$
   (C) $93 < r < 326$
   (D) $62 < r < 744$
   (E) $62 < r < 496$

24. Approximately what was the percent increase in the annual revenue from all greeting card sales from 1990 to 1993 ?

   (A) 50%

   (B) 45%

   (C) 39%

   (D) 28%

   (E) 20%

For Question 25, select all the answer choices that apply.

---

25. In 1993 the average (arithmetic mean) price per card for all greeting cards sold was $1.25. For which of the following occasions was the number of cards sold in 1993 less than the total number of cards sold that year for occasions other than the ten occasions shown?

   Indicate <u>all</u> such occasions.

   [A] Christmas
   [B] Valentine's Day
   [C] Easter
   [D] Mother's Day
   [E] Father's Day
   [F] Graduation
   [G] Thanksgiving
   [H] Halloween

ANSWER KEY

1. **Choice B**: Quantity B is greater.
2. **Choice D**: The relationship cannot be determined from the information given.
3. **Choice B**: Quantity B is greater.
4. **Choice A**: Quantity A is greater.
5. **Choice A**: Quantity A is greater.
6. **Choice C**: The two quantities are equal.
7. **Choice D**: The relationship cannot be determined from the information given.
8. **Choice C**: The two quantities are equal.
9. **Choice D**: The relationship cannot be determined from the information given.
10. **Choice A**: 2 to 1
11. **Choice E**: 34
12. **Choice B**: 16
13. **Choice A**: $f(x) = \dfrac{x^3}{x^2 + 1}$
14. **Choice B**: $y = x + 3$
15. **Choice A**: 125
16. **Choice D**: 60%
17. **Choice C**: $16P$
18. **Choice C**: 10

    AND

    Choice D: 14

    AND

    Choice E: 16
19. **Choice A**: 5

    AND

    Choice C: 11

    AND

    Choice F: 35
20. **22**
21. **0.003**
22. **Choice A**: 20
23. **Choice E**: $62 < r < 496$
24. **Choice D**: 28%
25. **Choice C**: Easter

    AND

    Choice D: Mother's Day

    AND

    Choice E: Father's Day

    AND

    Choice F: Graduation

    AND

    Choice G: Thanksgiving

    AND

    Choice H: Halloween

Answers and Explanations

Points R, S, and T lie on a number line, where S is between R and T. The distance between R and S is 6, and the distance between R and T is 15.

Quantity A	Quantity B	
1. The distance between the midpoints of line segments RS and ST	The distance between S and T	Ⓐ Ⓑ Ⓒ Ⓓ

Explanation

The figure below shows points R, S, and T on the number line.

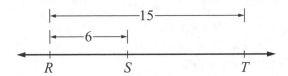

From the figure, you can see that the distance between S and T is $15 - 6$, or 9, which is Quantity B. You can also see that Quantity A, the distance between the midpoints of line segments RS and ST, is equal to one-half of the distance between R and S plus one-half of the distance between S and T. So Quantity A is $\frac{6}{2} + \frac{9}{2}$, or 7.5. Since 7.5 is less than 9, the correct answer is **Choice B**.

This explanation uses the following strategy.
Strategy 2: Translate from Words to a Figure or Diagram

S is a set of 8 numbers, of which 4 are negative and 4 are positive.

Quantity A	Quantity B	
2. The average (arithmetic mean) of the numbers in S	The median of the numbers in S	Ⓐ Ⓑ Ⓒ Ⓓ

Explanation

In the question, the only information you are given about the 8 numbers in set S is that 4 are negative and 4 are positive. Sets with 4 negative and 4 positive numbers can vary greatly, so it is likely that the relationship between Quantity A, the average of the numbers in *S*, and Quantity B, the median of the numbers in *S*, cannot be determined from the information given. To explore this by trial and error, consider some different sets with 4 negative and 4 positive numbers. Here are some examples.

Example 1: $\{-4, -3, -2, -1, 1, 2, 3, 4\}$. In this case, the average of the numbers in the set is 0, and the median is also 0, so Quantity A is equal to Quantity B.

Example 2: $\{-100, -3, -2, -1, 1, 2, 3, 4\}$. In this case, the median of the numbers is 0, but the average of the numbers is less than 0, so Quantity B is greater than Quantity A.

Example 3: $\{-4, -3, -2, -1, 1, 2, 3, 100\}$. In this case, the median of the numbers is 0, but the average of the numbers is greater than 0, so Quantity A is greater than Quantity B.

From the three examples, you can see that the correct answer is **Choice D**.

This explanation uses the following strategies.
Strategy 10: Trial and Error
Strategy 13: Determine Whether a Conclusion Follows from the Information Given

---

The length of each side of rectangle *R* is an integer, and the area of *R* is 36.

Quantity A	Quantity B
3. The number of possible values of the perimeter of *R*	6

 (A) (B) (C) (D)

Explanation

Because the length of each side of rectangle *R* is an integer and each length is a factor of the area 36, there are 5 possible rectangles: a 1×36 rectangle, a 2×18 rectangle, a 3×12 rectangle, a 4×9 rectangle, and a 6×6 rectangle.

The perimeter of the 1×36 rectangle is $2(1 + 36)$, or 74.
The perimeter of the 2×18 rectangle is $2(2 + 18)$, or 40.
The perimeter of the 3×12 rectangle is $2(3 + 12)$, or 30.
The perimeter of the 4×9 rectangle is $2(4 + 9)$, or 26.
The perimeter of the 6×6 rectangle is $2(6 + 6)$, or 24.

Since each of the 5 possible rectangles has a different perimeter, Quantity A, the number of possible values of the perimeter, is 5. Since Quantity B is 6, the correct answer is **Choice B**.

This explanation uses the following strategy.
Strategy 11: Divide into Cases

$$x = (z-1)^2$$
$$y = (z+1)^2$$

Quantity A	Quantity B	
4. The average (arithmetic mean) of x and y	z^2	Ⓐ Ⓑ Ⓒ Ⓓ

Explanation

The average of x and y is $\dfrac{x+y}{2}$. Since you are given that $x = (z-1)^2$ and $y = (z+1)^2$, you can express Quantity A in terms of z as follows.

$$\frac{x+y}{2} = \frac{(z-1)^2 + (z+1)^2}{2}$$

This expression can be simplified as follows.

$$\frac{(z-1)^2 + (z+1)^2}{2} = \frac{z^2 - 2z + 1 + z^2 + 2z + 1}{2}$$
$$= \frac{2z^2 + 2}{2}$$
$$= z^2 + 1$$

In terms of z, Quantity A is $z^2 + 1$. Since $z^2 + 1$ is greater than z^2 for all values of z, the correct answer is **Choice A**.

This explanation uses the following strategies.
Strategy 1: Translate from Words to an Arithmetic or Algebraic Representation
Strategy 5: Simplify an Arithmetic or Algebraic Representation

x, *y*, and *z* are the lengths of the sides of a triangle.

	Quantity A	Quantity B	
5.	$x + y + z$	$2z$	Ⓐ Ⓑ Ⓒ Ⓓ

Explanation

In this question, you are comparing $x + y + z$ with $2z$. By subtracting z from both quantities, you can see that this is the same as comparing $x + y$ with z. Since x, y, and z are the lengths of the sides of a triangle, and in all triangles the length of each side must be less than the sum of the lengths of the other two sides, it follows that $z < x + y$. Thus the correct answer is **Choice A**.

This explanation uses the following strategies.
Strategy 1: Translate from Words to an Arithmetic or Algebraic Representation
Strategy 8: Search for a Mathematical Relationship

At a club meeting, there are 10 more club members than nonmembers. The number of club members at the meeting is *c*.

	Quantity A	Quantity B	
6.	The total number of people at the club meeting	$2c - 10$	Ⓐ Ⓑ Ⓒ Ⓓ

Explanation

Since the number of club members is *c* and there are 10 more members than nonmembers, the number of nonmembers is $c - 10$. Therefore Quantity A, the total number of people at the meeting, is $c + (c - 10)$, or $2c - 10$. Since Quantity B is also $2c - 10$, the correct answer is **Choice C**.

This explanation uses the following strategy.
Strategy 1: Translate from Words to an Arithmetic or Algebraic Representation

n is a positive integer that is greater than 3 and has
d positive divisors.

Quantity A	Quantity B	

7. n 2^{d-1}

Explanation

Since there is no obvious relationship between the quantities n and 2^{d-1}, it is a good idea to try a few values of n to see what happens. Note that you are given that n is an integer greater than 3, so you can start comparing the quantities for the case $n = 4$ and proceed from there.

Case 1: $n = 4$. The integer 4 has three positive divisors, 1, 2, and 4. So in this case, $d = 3$. Therefore $2^{d-1} = 2^{3-1} = 4$, and the two quantities are equal.

Case 2: $n = 5$. The integer 5 has two positive divisors, 1 and 5. So in this case, $d = 2$. Therefore $2^{d-1} = 2^{2-1} = 2$, and Quantity A is greater than Quantity B.

In one case the two quantities are equal, and in the other case Quantity A is greater than Quantity B. Therefore the correct answer is **Choice D**.

This explanation uses the following strategies.
Strategy 10: Trial and Error
Strategy 13: Determine Whether a Conclusion Follows from the Information Given

$$m = 10^{32} + 2$$

When m is divided by 11, the remainder is r.

| Quantity A | Quantity B |

8. r 3   Ⓐ Ⓑ Ⓒ Ⓓ

Explanation

Actually dividing $10^{32} + 2$ by 11 would be very time consuming, so it is worth trying to compare the quantities without actually doing the division.

A good approach would be to compute the remainders when $10^1 + 2$, $10^2 + 2$, $10^3 + 2$, $10^4 + 2$, etc., are divided by 11 to see if there is a pattern that can help you determine the remainder when $10^{32} + 2$ is divided by 11. The following table shows the first few cases.

n	Value of $10^n + 2$	Remainder When Divided by 11
1	$10^1 + 2 = 12 = 11 + 1$	1
2	$10^2 + 2 = 102 = 99 + 3 = 9(11) + 3$	3
3	$10^3 + 2 = 1{,}002 = 1{,}001 + 1 = 91(11) + 1$	1
4	$10^4 + 2 = 10{,}002 = 9{,}999 + 3 = 909(11) + 3$	3

Note that the remainder is 1 when 10 is raised to an odd power, and the remainder is 3 when 10 is raised to an even power. This pattern suggests that since 32 is even, the remainder when $10^{32} + 2$ is divided by 11 is 3.

To see that this is true, note that the integers 99 and 9,999 in the rows for $n = 2$ and $n = 4$, respectively, are multiples of 11. That is because they each consist of an even number of consecutive digits of 9. Also, these multiples of 11 are each 3 less than $10^2 + 2$ and $10^4 + 2$, respectively, so that is why the remainders are 3 when $10^2 + 2$ and $10^4 + 2$ are divided by 11. Similarly, for $n = 32$, the integer with 32 consecutive digits of 9 is a multiple of 11 because 32 is even. Also, that multiple of 11 is 3 less than $10^{32} + 2$, so the remainder is 3 when $10^{32} + 2$ is divided by 11. Thus the correct answer is **Choice C**.

An alternative approach is to rewrite the expression $10^{32} + 2$ using the factoring technique $x^2 - 1 = (x - 1)(x + 1)$ repeatedly, as follows.

$$10^{32} + 2 = (10^{32} - 1) + 3$$

$$= (10^{16} - 1)(10^{16} + 1) + 3$$

$$= (10^8 - 1)(10^8 + 1)(10^{16} + 1) + 3$$

$$= (10^4 - 1)(10^4 + 1)(10^8 + 1)(10^{16} + 1) + 3$$

$$= (10^2 - 1)(10^2 + 1)(10^4 + 1)(10^8 + 1)(10^{16} + 1) + 3$$

$$= (10 + 1)(10 - 1)(10^2 + 1)(10^4 + 1)(10^8 + 1)(10^{16} + 1) + 3$$

$$= 11((10 - 1)(10^2 + 1)(10^4 + 1)(10^8 + 1)(10^{16} + 1)) + 3$$

$$= 11k + 3$$

where $k = (10 - 1)(10^2 + 1)(10^4 + 1)(10^8 + 1)(10^{16} + 1)$ is an integer. Since $10^{32} + 2$ is of the form $11k + 3$, where k is an integer, it follows that when $10^{32} + 2$ is divided by 11, the remainder is 3. The correct answer is **Choice C**.

This explanation uses the following strategies.
Strategy 5: Simplify an Arithmetic or Algebraic Representation
Strategy 7: Find a Pattern
Strategy 11: Divide into Cases

$$xy = 8 \text{ and } x = y - 2.$$

Quantity A	Quantity B
9. y	0 Ⓐ Ⓑ Ⓒ Ⓓ

Explanation

In order to compare y and 0, you can try to determine the value of y from the two equations $xy = 8$ and $x = y - 2$. Substituting $y - 2$ for x in the equation $xy = 8$ gives $(y - 2)y = 8$, or $y^2 - 2y - 8 = 0$. Factoring this quadratic equation yields $(y - 4)(y + 2) = 0$. Therefore y can be either 4 or -2, so Quantity A can be greater than 0 or less than 0. Thus the correct answer is **Choice D**.

This explanation uses the following strategies.
Strategy 5: Simplify an Arithmetic or Algebraic Representation
Strategy 13: Determine Whether a Conclusion Follows from the Information Given

10. The area of circle W is 16π and the area of circle Z is 4π. What is the ratio of the circumference of W to the circumference of Z ?

(A) 2 to 1

(B) 4 to 1

(C) 8 to 1

(D) 16 to 1

(E) 32 to 1

Explanation

Recall that if a circle has radius r, then the area of the circle is πr^2 and the circumference is $2\pi r$. Since the area of circle W is 16π, it follows that $\pi r^2 = 16\pi$, so $r^2 = 16$ and $r = 4$. Therefore the circumference of circle W is $2\pi(4)$, or 8π. Similarly, since the area of circle Z is 4π, it follows that $\pi r^2 = 4\pi$, so $r^2 = 4$ and $r = 2$. Therefore the circumference of circle Z is $2\pi(2)$, or 4π. Thus the ratio of the circumference of W to the circumference of Z is 8π to 4π, or 2 to 1. The correct answer is **Choice A**.

This explanation uses the following strategies.
Strategy 1: Translate from Words to an Arithmetic or Algebraic Representation
Strategy 5: Simplify an Arithmetic or Algebraic Representation

11. In the *xy*-plane, a quadrilateral has vertices at $(-1, 4)$, $(7, 4)$, $(7, -5)$, and $(-1, -5)$. What is the perimeter of the quadrilateral?

(A) 17

(B) 18

(C) 19

(D) 32

(E) 34

Explanation

A sketch of the quadrilateral with vertices at $(-1, 4)$, $(7, 4)$, $(7, -5)$, and $(-1, -5)$ is shown in the *xy*-plane below.

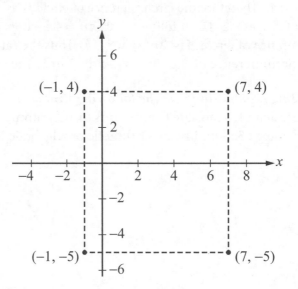

From the figure you can see that two of the sides of the quadrilateral are horizontal and two are vertical. Therefore the quadrilateral is a rectangle. Since the points $(-1, -5)$ and $(7, -5)$ are endpoints of one of the horizontal sides, the length of each horizontal side is $7 - (-1)$, or 8. Since the points $(-1, 4)$ and $(-1, -5)$ are endpoints of one of the vertical sides, the length of each vertical side is $4 - (-5)$, or 9. Therefore the perimeter of the rectangle is $2(8 + 9)$, or 34. The correct answer is **Choice E.**

This explanation uses the following strategies.
Strategy 2: Translate from Words to a Figure or Diagram
Strategy 4: Translate from a Figure to an Arithmetic or Algebraic Representation

DISTRIBUTION OF THE
HEIGHTS OF 80 STUDENTS

Height (centimeters)	Number of Students
140–144	6
145–149	26
150–154	32
155–159	12
160–164	4
Total	80

12. The table above shows the frequency distribution of the heights of 80 students, where the heights are recorded to the nearest centimeter. What is the least possible range of the recorded heights of the 80 students?

Ⓐ 15

Ⓑ 16

Ⓒ 20

Ⓓ 24

Ⓔ 28

Explanation

Recall that the range of the numbers in a group of data is the greatest number in the group minus the least number in the group. The table shows that the minimum recorded height of the 80 students can vary from 140 to 144 centimeters, and the maximum recorded height can vary from 160 to 164 centimeters. Thus the least possible range of the recorded heights is $160 - 144$, or 16 centimeters. The correct answer is **Choice B**.

This explanation uses the following strategy.
Strategy 4: Translate from a Figure to an Arithmetic or Algebraic Representation

13. Which of the following functions f defined for all numbers x has the property that $f(-x) = -f(x)$ for all numbers x?

(A) $f(x) = \dfrac{x^3}{x^2 + 1}$

(B) $f(x) = \dfrac{x^2 - 1}{x^2 + 1}$

(C) $f(x) = x^2(x^2 - 1)$

(D) $f(x) = x(x^3 - 1)$

(E) $f(x) = x^2(x^3 - 1)$

Explanation

To determine which of the functions among the five choices has the property that $f(-x) = -f(x)$ for all numbers x, you need to check each choice until you find one that has the property. In Choice A, $f(x) = \dfrac{x^3}{x^2 + 1}$:

$$f(-x) = \frac{(-x)^3}{(-x)^2 + 1} = \frac{-x^3}{x^2 + 1} \quad \text{and} \quad -f(x) = -\left(\frac{x^3}{x^2 + 1}\right) = \frac{-x^3}{x^2 + 1}.$$

Therefore Choice A has the property $f(-x) = -f(x)$, and since only one of the five choices can be the correct answer, the correct answer is **Choice A**.

This explanation uses the following strategies.
Strategy 5: Simplify an Arithmetic or Algebraic Representation
Strategy 8: Search for a Mathematical Relationship

14. If 10^x equals 0.1 percent of 10^y, where x and y are integers, which of the following must be true?

    (A) $y = x + 2$

    (B) $y = x + 3$

    (C) $x = y + 3$

    (D) $y = 1{,}000x$

    (E) $x = 1{,}000y$

Explanation

The quantity 0.1 percent of m can be expressed as $\dfrac{0.1}{100}m$, which is equal to $\dfrac{1}{1{,}000}m$, or $\dfrac{1}{10^3}m$. Given that 10^x equals 0.1 percent of 10^y, it follows that

$$10^x = \left(\frac{1}{10^3}\right)(10^y) = \frac{10^y}{10^3} = 10^{y-3},$$

or $10^x = 10^{y-3}$. Therefore $x = y - 3$, or $y = x + 3$. The correct answer is **Choice B**.

This explanation uses the following strategies.

Strategy 1: Translate from Words to an Arithmetic or Algebraic Representation

Strategy 5: Simplify an Arithmetic or Algebraic Representation

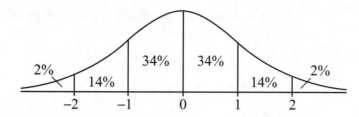

15. The figure above shows the standard normal distribution, with mean 0 and standard deviation 1, including approximate percents of the distribution corresponding to the six regions shown.

The random variable Y is normally distributed with a mean of 470, and the value $Y = 340$ is at the 15th percentile of the distribution. Of the following, which is the best estimate of the standard deviation of the distribution?

Ⓐ 125

Ⓑ 135

Ⓒ 145

Ⓓ 155

Ⓔ 165

Explanation

Since you know that the distribution of the random variable Y is normal with a mean of 470 and that the value 340 is at the 15th percentile of the distribution, you can estimate the standard deviation of the distribution of Y using the standard normal distribution. You can do this because the percent distributions of all normal distributions are the same in the following respect: The percentiles of every normal distribution are related to its standard deviation in exactly the same way as the percentiles of the standard normal distribution are related to its standard deviation. For example, approximately 14% of every normal distribution is between 1 and 2 standard deviations above the mean, just as the figure above illustrates for the standard normal distribution.

From the figure, approximately $2\% + 14\%$, or 16%, of the standard normal distribution is less than -1. Since $15\% < 16\%$, the 15th percentile of the distribution is at a value slightly below -1. For the standard normal distribution, the value -1 represents 1 standard deviation below the mean of 0. You can conclude that the 15th percentile of every normal distribution is at a value slightly below 1 standard deviation below the mean.

For the normal distribution of Y, the 15th percentile is 340, which is slightly below 1 standard deviation below the mean of 470. Consequently, the difference $470 - 340$, or 130, is a little greater than 1 standard deviation of Y; that is, the standard deviation of Y is a little less than 130. Of the answer choices given, the best estimate is 125, since it is close to, but a little less than, 130. The correct answer is **Choice A**.

This explanation uses the following strategies.
Strategy 4: Translate from a Figure to an Arithmetic or Algebraic Representation
Strategy 9: Estimate
Strategy 12: Adapt Solutions to Related Problems

16. A car dealer received a shipment of cars, half of which were black, with the remainder consisting of equal numbers of blue, silver, and white cars. During the next month, 70 percent of the black cars, 80 percent of the blue cars, 30 percent of the silver cars, and 40 percent of the white cars were sold. What percent of the cars in the shipment were sold during that month?

Ⓐ 36%

Ⓑ 50%

Ⓒ 55%

Ⓓ 60%

Ⓔ 72%

Explanation

In the shipment, $\frac{1}{2}$ of the cars were black. Since the remainder of the cars consisted of equal numbers of blue, silver, and white cars, it follows that $\left(\frac{1}{3}\right)\left(\frac{1}{2}\right)$, or $\frac{1}{6}$, of the cars were blue, $\frac{1}{6}$ were silver, and $\frac{1}{6}$ were white. Based on the percents of the cars of each color that were sold during the next month, the percent of the cars in the shipment that were sold during that month was

$$\left(\frac{1}{2}\right)(70\%) + \left(\frac{1}{6}\right)(80\%) + \left(\frac{1}{6}\right)(30\%) + \left(\frac{1}{6}\right)(40\%) = 60\%$$

The correct answer is **Choice D**.

This explanation uses the following strategy.
Strategy 1: Translate from Words to an Arithmetic or Algebraic Representation

17. If an investment of P dollars is made today and the value of the investment doubles every 7 years, what will be the value of the investment, in dollars, 28 years from today?

Ⓐ $8P^4$

Ⓑ P^4

Ⓒ $16P$

Ⓓ $8P$

Ⓔ $4P$

Explanation

The investment of P dollars doubles every 7 years. Therefore 7 years from today, the value of the investment will be $2P$ dollars; 14 years from today, the value of the investment will be $4P$ dollars; 21 years from today, the value of the investment will be $8P$ dollars; and 28 years from today, the value of the investment will be $16P$ dollars. The correct answer is **Choice C**.

This explanation uses the following strategies.
Strategy 1: Translate from Words to an Arithmetic or Algebraic Representation
Strategy 7: Find a Pattern

---

18. The distribution of the numbers of hours that students at a certain college studied for final exams has a mean of 12 hours and a standard deviation of 3 hours. Which of the following numbers of hours are within 2 standard deviations of the mean of the distribution?

Indicate <u>all</u> such numbers.

A   2

B   5

C   10

D   14

E   16

F   20

Explanation

Given that the mean of the distribution is 12 hours and the standard deviation is 3 hours, the numbers of hours within 2 standard deviations of the mean are all numbers of hours between $12 - 2(3)$, or 6, and $12 + 2(3)$, or 18. Thus the correct answer consists of **Choices C, D, and E**.

This explanation uses the following strategy.
Strategy 1: Translate from Words to an Arithmetic or Algebraic Representation

19. In a certain sequence of numbers, each term after the first term is found by multiplying the preceding term by 2 and then subtracting 3 from the product. If the 4th term in the sequence is 19, which of the following numbers are in the sequence?

Indicate all such numbers.

- A 5
- B 8
- C 11
- D 16
- E 22
- F 35

Explanation

Since the 4th term in the sequence is 19, it follows that the 5th term is $(19)(2) - 3$, or 35. Proceeding backwards in the sequence from the 4th term to determine each preceding term, you would add 3 and then divide the result by 2. So the 3rd term is $\frac{19+3}{2}$, or 11; the 2nd term is $\frac{11+3}{2}$, or 7; and the 1st term is $\frac{7+3}{2}$, or 5. Hence the first 5 terms of the sequence are 5, 7, 11, 19, and 35, of which 5, 11, and 35 are among the answer choices.

Can you show that the other three answer choices, 8, 16, and 22, are not in the sequence? Note that 8, 16, and 22 are not among the first 5 terms of the sequence, and the 5th term of the sequence is 35. If you can show that each successive term in the sequence is greater than the term before it, you can conclude that 8, 16 and 22 are not terms in the sequence. If b is any term in the sequence, then the successive term is $2b - 3$. Note that $b < 2b - 3$ is equivalent to $b > 3$, so the successive term, $2b - 3$, is greater than the term before it, b, if $b > 3$. Since the first term of the sequence is 5, which is greater than 3, each successive term is greater than the term before it.

Thus the correct answer consists of **Choices A, C, and F**.

This explanation uses the following strategies.
Strategy 1: Translate from Words to an Arithmetic or Algebraic Representation
Strategy 7: Find a Pattern

20. In a single line of people waiting to purchase tickets for a movie, there are currently 10 people behind Shandra. If 3 of the people who are currently in line ahead of Shandra purchase tickets and leave the line, and no one else leaves the line, there will be 8 people ahead of Shandra in line. How many people are in the line currently?

$\boxed{}$ people

Explanation

You are given that if 3 people currently ahead of Shandra leave the line and no one else leaves, there will be 8 people ahead of Shandra. This means that currently there are 11 people ahead of Shandra. In addition to the 11 people currently ahead of Shandra in line, Shandra herself is in line, and there are currently 10 people behind Shandra. Therefore the total number of people in line currently is $11 + 1 + 10$, or 22. The correct answer is **22**.

This explanation uses the following strategy.
Strategy 1: Translate from Words to an Arithmetic or Algebraic Representation

21. When the decimal point of a certain positive decimal number is moved six places to the right, the resulting number is 9 times the reciprocal of the original number. What is the original number?

$$\boxed{}$$

Explanation

Moving the decimal point of a positive decimal number, n, six places to the right is equivalent to multiplying n by 10^6. In the question, you are given that the result of such a change is 9 times the reciprocal of the original number, or $9\left(\dfrac{1}{n}\right)$. Therefore $n(10^6) = 9\left(\dfrac{1}{n}\right)$. You can solve this equation for n as follows.

$$n(10^6) = 9\left(\frac{1}{n}\right)$$

$$n^2 = \frac{9}{10^6}$$

$$n = \sqrt{\frac{9}{10^6}}$$

$$n = \frac{3}{10^3}$$

$$n = 0.003$$

The correct answer is **0.003**.

This explanation uses the following strategies.
Strategy 1: Translate from Words to an Arithmetic or Algebraic Representation
Strategy 5: Simplify an Arithmetic or Algebraic Representation

SELECTED DATA FOR GREETING CARD SALES

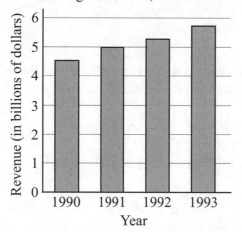

Annual Revenue from All
Greeting Card Sales, 1990–1993

Number of Greeting Cards Sold
for Ten Occasions in 1993

Occasion	Number of Cards
Christmas	2.4 billion
Valentine's Day	900 million
Easter	158 million
Mother's Day	155 million
Father's Day	102 million
Graduation	81 million
Thanksgiving	42 million
Halloween	32 million
St. Patrick's Day	18 million
Jewish New Year	12 million
Total	3.9 billion

Note: 1 billion = 1,000,000,000

22. In 1993 the number of Valentine's Day cards sold was approximately how many times the number of Thanksgiving cards sold?

(A) 20

(B) 30

(C) 40

(D) 50

(E) 60

Explanation

According to the table, the number of Valentine's Day cards sold in 1993 was 900 million, and the number of Thanksgiving cards sold was 42 million. Therefore the number of Valentine's Day cards sold was $\frac{900}{42}$, or approximately 21.4 times the number of Thanksgiving cards sold. Of the answer choices, the closest is 20. The correct answer is **Choice A**.

This explanation uses the following strategies.
Strategy 1: Translate from Words to an Arithmetic or Algebraic Representation
Strategy 4: Translate from a Figure to an Arithmetic or Algebraic Representation
Strategy 9: Estimate

23. In 1993 a card company that sold 40 percent of the Mother's Day cards that year priced its cards for that occasion between $1.00 and $8.00 each. If the revenue from sales of the company's Mother's Day cards in 1993 was r million dollars, which of the following indicates all possible values of r ?

(A) $155 < r < 1{,}240$

(B) $93 < r < 496$

(C) $93 < r < 326$

(D) $62 < r < 744$

(E) $62 < r < 496$

Explanation

According to the table, 155 million Mother's Day cards were sold in 1993. The card company that sold 40 percent of the Mother's Day cards sold $(0.4)(155)$ million, or 62 million cards. Since that company priced the cards between $1.00 and $8.00 each, the revenue, r million dollars, from selling the 62 million cards was between ($1.00)(62) million and ($8.00)(62) million, or between $62 million and $496 million; that is, $62 < r < 496$. Thus the correct answer is **Choice E.**

This explanation uses the following strategies.
Strategy 1: Translate from Words to an Arithmetic or Algebraic Representation
Strategy 4: Translate from a Figure to an Arithmetic or Algebraic Representation
Strategy 8: Search for a Mathematical Relationship

---

24. Approximately what was the percent increase in the annual revenue from all greeting card sales from 1990 to 1993 ?

(A) 50%

(B) 45%

(C) 39%

(D) 28%

(E) 20%

Explanation

According to the bar graph, the annual revenue from all greeting card sales in 1990 was approximately $4.5 billion, and the corresponding total in 1993 was approximately $5.75 billion. Therefore the percent increase from 1990 to 1993 was approximately $\left(\dfrac{5.75 - 4.5}{4.5} \right)(100\%)$, or approximately 28%. The correct answer is **Choice D.**

This explanation uses the following strategies.
Strategy 1: Translate from Words to an Arithmetic or Algebraic Representation
Strategy 4: Translate from a Figure to an Arithmetic or Algebraic Representation
Strategy 9: Estimate

25. In 1993 the average (arithmetic mean) price per card for all greeting cards sold was $1.25. For which of the following occasions was the number of cards sold in 1993 less than the total number of cards sold that year for occasions other than the ten occasions shown?

Indicate <u>all</u> such occasions.

A Christmas

B Valentine's Day

C Easter

D Mother's Day

E Father's Day

F Graduation

G Thanksgiving

H Halloween

Explanation

According to the bar graph, the total annual revenue in 1993 was approximately $5.75 billion. In the question, you are given that the average price per card for all greeting cards sold was $1.25. Therefore the total number of cards sold for all occasions was $\frac{5.75}{1.25}$ billion, or 4.6 billion.

According to the table, the total number of cards sold in 1993 for the ten occasions shown was 3.9 billion. So the number of cards sold for occasions other than the ten occasions shown, in billions, was $4.6 - 3.9$, or 0.7 billion. Note that 0.7 billion equals 700 million. From the table, you can see that less than 700 million cards were sold for each of six of the occasions in the answer choices: Easter, Mother's Day, Father's Day, Graduation, Thanksgiving, and Halloween. Thus the correct answer consists of **Choices C, D, E, F, G, and H**.

This explanation uses the following strategies.
Strategy 1: Translate from Words to an Arithmetic or Algebraic Representation
Strategy 4: Translate from a Figure to an Arithmetic or Algebraic Representation
Strategy 8: Search for a Mathematical Relationship
Strategy 9: Estimate

PRACTICE SET 2

Quantitative Comparison Questions

> For Questions 1 to 9, compare Quantity A and Quantity B, using additional information centered above the two quantities if such information is given. Select one of the following four answer choices and fill in the corresponding oval to the right of the question.
>
> (A) Quantity A is greater.
>
> (B) Quantity B is greater.
>
> (C) The two quantities are equal.
>
> (D) The relationship cannot be determined from the information given.
>
> A symbol that appears more than once in a question has the same meaning throughout the question.

	Quantity A	Quantity B	Correct Answer
Example 1:	$(2)(6)$	$2 + 6$	⊛ ⓑ ⓒ ⓓ

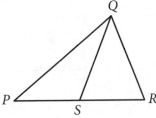

	Quantity A	Quantity B	Correct Answer
Example 2:	PS	SR	ⓐ ⓑ ⓒ ⊛

(since equal lengths cannot be assumed, even though PS and SR appear equal)

$$x < 0$$

	Quantity A	Quantity B	
1.	x^5	x^4	ⓐ ⊛ ⓒ ⓓ

Handwritten notes (left/top margin):
$xy + 3x + 4y + 12$
$3x + 4y + xy + 12$
$4y + 3y + xy + 12$

Handwritten note (above Quantity B, problem 2):
$xy + 4x + 3y + 12$

	Quantity A	Quantity B	
2.	$(x+4)(y+3)$	$(x+3)(y+4)$	Ⓐ Ⓑ Ⓒ Ⓓ

$0.\overline{b}$ represents the decimal in which the digit b is repeated without end.

	Quantity A	Quantity B	
3.	$0.\overline{3} + 0.\overline{7}$	1.0	Ⓐ Ⓑ Ⓒ Ⓓ

Handwritten note (left margin): $S = 2R - 0.05$

A company plans to manufacture two types of hammers, type R and type S. The cost of manufacturing each hammer of type S is $0.05 less than twice the cost of manufacturing each hammer of type R.

	Quantity A	Quantity B	
4.	The cost of manufacturing 1,000 hammers of type R and 1,000 hammers of type S	The cost of manufacturing 1,500 hammers of type S	Ⓐ Ⓑ Ⓒ Ⓓ

Handwritten notes (left margin):
$$\frac{4 + 16 + 16.4}{4}$$
$$1 + 4 + 16$$

	Quantity A	Quantity B	
5.	$\dfrac{\left(\dfrac{1}{4}\right)^{-1} + \left(\dfrac{1}{4}\right)^{-2} + \left(\dfrac{1}{4}\right)^{-3}}{4}$	21	Ⓐ Ⓑ Ⓒ Ⓓ

List X: 2, 5, s, t
List Y: 2, 5, t

Handwritten note (right):
$$\frac{2 + 5 + s + t}{2} = \frac{2 + 5 + t}{2}$$

The average (arithmetic mean) of the numbers in list X is equal to the average of the numbers in list Y.

	Quantity A	Quantity B	
6.	s	0	Ⓐ Ⓑ Ⓒ Ⓓ

The radius of circle A is 12 greater than the radius of circle B.

$r_A = r_B + 12$

$C = 2\pi r \quad c_A = 2\pi r_B + 24\pi$

	Quantity A	Quantity B	
7.	The circumference of circle A minus the circumference of circle B	72	Ⓐ Ⓑ Ⓒ Ⓓ

$24\pi > 72$

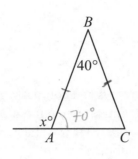

$180 - 40 = 140$

$180 - 70 = 110 = x$

$AB = BC$

	Quantity A	Quantity B	
8.	x	120	Ⓐ Ⓑ Ⓒ Ⓓ

$S = \{1, 2, 3, 4, 5, 6, 7, 8\}$

	Quantity A	Quantity B	
9.	The number of 4-member subsets of S	The number of 5-member subsets of S	Ⓐ Ⓑ Ⓒ Ⓓ

Multiple-choice Questions—Select One Answer Choice

For Questions 10 to 17, select a single answer choice.

10. In right triangle ABC, the ratio of the lengths of the two legs is 2 to 5. If the area of triangle ABC is 20, what is the length of the hypotenuse?

    (A) 7

    (B) 10

    (C) $4\sqrt{5}$

    (D) $\sqrt{29}$

    (E) $2\sqrt{29}$

11. According to surveys at a company, 20 percent of the employees owned cell phones in 1994, and 60 percent of the employees owned cell phones in 1998. From 1994 to 1998, what was the percent increase in the fraction of employees who owned cell phones?

    (A) 3%

    (B) 20%

    (C) 30%

    (D) 200%

    (E) 300%

12. If t is an integer and $8m = 16^t$, which of the following expresses m in terms of t?

    (A) 2^t

    (B) 2^{t-3}

    (C) $2^{3(t-3)}$

    (D) 2^{4t-3}

    (E) $2^{4(t-3)}$

13. Three pumps, P, R, and T, working simultaneously at their respective constant rates, can fill a tank in 5 hours. Pumps P and R, working simultaneously at their respective constant rates, can fill the tank in 7 hours. How many hours will it take pump T, working alone at its constant rate, to fill the tank?

    (A) 1.7

    (B) 10.0

    (C) 15.0

    (D) 17.5

    (E) 30.0

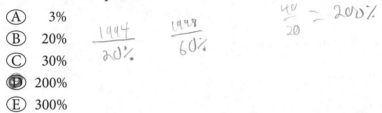

14. The perimeter of a flat rectangular lawn is 42 meters. The width of the lawn is 75 percent of its length. What is the area of the lawn, in square meters?

    (A) 40.5
    (B) 96
    (C) 108
    (D) 192
    (E) 432

    $2L + 1.5L = 42$

    $3.5L = 42$

    $L = 12$

    $W = 9$

15. The greatest of the 21 positive integers in a certain list is 16. The median of the 21 integers is 10. What is the least possible average (arithmetic mean) of the 21 integers?

    (A) 4
    (B) 5
    (C) 6
    (D) 7
    (E) 8

    $X = \dfrac{10 + 16 + [\quad]}{21}$

16. If x and y are integers and $x = \dfrac{(2)(3)(4)(5)(7)(11)(13)}{39 y}$, which of the following could be the value of y?

    (A) 15
    (B) 28
    (C) 38
    (D) 64
    (E) 143

17. Of the 40 specimens of bacteria in a dish, 3 specimens have a certain trait. If 5 specimens are to be selected from the dish at random and without replacement, which of the following represents the probability that only 1 of the 5 specimens selected will have the trait?

(A) $\dfrac{\dbinom{5}{1}}{\dbinom{40}{3}}$

$\dfrac{5}{40} \cdot \dfrac{4}{39} \cdot \dfrac{3}{38}$

(B) $\dfrac{\dbinom{5}{1}}{\dbinom{40}{5}}$

(C) $\dfrac{\dbinom{40}{3}}{\dbinom{40}{5}}$

(D) $\dfrac{\dbinom{3}{1}\dbinom{37}{4}}{\dbinom{40}{3}}$

(E) $\dfrac{\dbinom{3}{1}\dbinom{37}{4}}{\dbinom{40}{5}}$

Multiple-choice Questions—Select One or More Answer Choices

For Questions 18 to 19, select all the answer choices that apply.

18. Two different positive integers x and y are selected from the odd integers that are less than 10. If $z = x + y$ and z is less than 10, which of the following integers could be the sum of x, y, and z ?

    Indicate all such integers.

    [A] 8
    [B] 9
    [C] 10
    [D] 12
    [E] 14
    [F] 15
    [G] 16
    [H] 18

19. For a certain probability experiment, the probability that event A will occur is $\frac{1}{2}$ and the probability that event B will occur is $\frac{1}{3}$. Which of the following values could be the probability that the event $A \cup B$ (that is, the event A or B, or both) will occur?

    Indicate all such values.

    [A] $\frac{1}{3}$

    [B] $\frac{1}{2}$

    [C] $\frac{3}{4}$

Numeric Entry Questions

> **For Questions 20 to 21, enter your answer in the answer box(es) below the question.**
>
> - **Your answer may be an integer, a decimal, or a fraction, and it may be negative.**
> - **If a question asks for a fraction, there will be two boxes—one for the numerator and one for the denominator. A decimal point cannot be used in a fraction.**
> - **Equivalent forms of the correct answer, such as 2.5 and 2.50, are all correct. Fractions do not need to be reduced to lowest terms, though you may need to reduce your fraction to fit in the boxes.**
> - **Enter the exact answer unless the question asks you to round your answer.**

20. If a and b are the two solutions of the equation $x^2 - 5x + 4 = 0$, what is the value of $\left(\dfrac{1+a}{a}\right)\left(\dfrac{1+b}{b}\right)$?

    Give your answer as a fraction.

    $$\frac{5}{2}$$

21. From 2011 to 2012, Jack's annual salary increased by 10 percent and Arnie's annual salary decreased by 5 percent. If their annual salaries were equal in 2012, then Arnie's annual salary in 2011 was what percent greater than Jack's annual salary in 2011?

    Give your answer to the nearest 0.1 percent.

    ☐ %

Data Interpretation Set

Questions 22 to 25 are based on the following data. For these questions, select a single answer choice unless otherwise directed.

INTERNET USE IN YEAR *X*

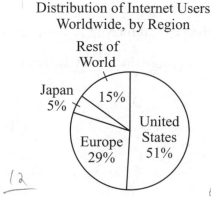

Distribution of Internet Users Worldwide, by Region

Rest of World 15%

Japan 5%

Europe 29%

United States 51%

$\dfrac{12}{27}$

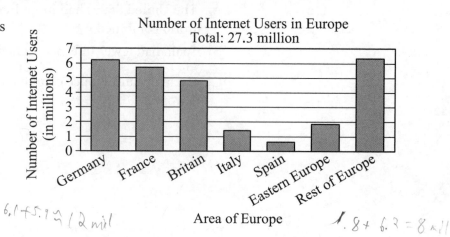

Number of Internet Users in Europe
Total: 27.3 million

Number of Internet Users (in millions)

Germany France Britain Italy Spain Eastern Europe Rest of Europe

Area of Europe

6.1+5.9 ≈ 12 mil

1.8 + 6.3 = 8 mil

22. Which of the following is closest to the percent of Internet users in Europe who were in countries other than Germany, France, Britain, Italy, and Spain?

   Ⓐ 30%

   Ⓑ 34%

   Ⓒ 38%

   Ⓓ 42%

   Ⓔ 46%

$\dfrac{27}{8} =$

23. Approximately what was the range of the numbers of Internet users in the seven areas of Europe shown in the bar graph?

   Ⓐ 6.5 million

   Ⓑ 5.5 million

   Ⓒ 3.5 million

   Ⓓ 3.0 million

   Ⓔ 2.5 million

0.5 — 6.2

24. The number of Internet users in the United States was approximately how many times the number of Internet users in Italy?

   Ⓐ 5

   Ⓑ 15

   Ⓒ 20

   Ⓓ 25

   Ⓔ 35

29% = 27.3 mill

51% × 27.3 + 5.6

51% × 33 mil USA

$\dfrac{0.2}{5.6}$

1.3 mil

For Question 25, select all the answer choices that apply.

25. Based on the information given, which of the following statements about Internet use in year X must be true?

Indicate <u>all</u> such statements.

☑ A The United States had more Internet users than all other countries in the world combined.

☑ B Spain had fewer Internet users than any country in Eastern Europe.

☐ C Germany and France combined had more than $\frac{1}{3}$ of the Internet users in Europe.

ANSWER KEY

1. **Choice B**: Quantity B is greater.
2. **Choice D**: The relationship cannot be determined from the information given.
3. **Choice A**: Quantity A is greater.
4. **Choice A**: Quantity A is greater.
5. **Choice C**: The two quantities are equal.
6. **Choice D**: The relationship cannot be determined from the information given.
7. **Choice A**: Quantity A is greater.
8. **Choice B**: Quantity B is greater.
9. **Choice A**: Quantity A is greater.
10. **Choice E**: $2\sqrt{29}$
11. **Choice D**: 200%
12. **Choice D**: 2^{4t-3}
13. **Choice D**: 17.5
14. **Choice C**: 108
15. **Choice C**: 6
16. **Choice B**: 28
17. **Choice E**: $\dfrac{\dbinom{3}{1}\dbinom{37}{4}}{\dbinom{40}{5}}$
18. **Choice A**: 8
    AND
    Choice D: 12
    AND
    Choice G: 16
19. **Choice B**: $\dfrac{1}{2}$
    AND
    Choice C: $\dfrac{3}{4}$
20. $\dfrac{5}{2}$
21. **15.8**
22. **Choice A**: 30%
23. **Choice B**: 5.5 million
24. **Choice E**: 35
25. **Choice A**: The United States had more Internet users than all other countries in the world combined.
    AND
    Choice C: Germany and France combined had more than $\dfrac{1}{3}$ of the Internet users in Europe.

Answers and Explanations

$$x < 0$$

	Quantity A	Quantity B	
1.	x^5	x^4	Ⓐ Ⓑ Ⓒ Ⓓ

Explanation

If $x < 0$, then $x^5 < 0$ and $x^4 > 0$. Thus $x^5 < x^4$, and the correct answer is **Choice B**.

This explanation uses the following strategy.
Strategy 8: Search for a Mathematical Relationship

	Quantity A	Quantity B	
2.	$(x + 4)(y + 3)$	$(x + 3)(y + 4)$	Ⓐ Ⓑ Ⓒ Ⓓ

Explanation

To compare $(x + 4)(y + 3)$ and $(x + 3)(y + 4)$, try plugging in a few values for x and y.

Case 1: $x = 0$ and $y = 0$. In this case, Quantity A is equal to $(4)(3)$, or 12, and Quantity B is equal to $(3)(4)$, or 12. So Quantity A is equal to Quantity B.

Case 2: $x = 0$ and $y = 1$. In this case, Quantity A is equal to $(4)(4)$, or 16, and Quantity B is equal to $(3)(5)$, or 15. So Quantity A is greater than Quantity B.

In one case, Quantity A is equal to Quantity B, and in the other case, Quantity A is greater than Quantity B. Therefore the correct answer is **Choice D**.

This explanation uses the following strategies.
Strategy 10: Trial and Error
Strategy 13: Determine Whether a Conclusion Follows from the Information Given

---

$0.\overline{b}$ represents the decimal in which the digit b is repeated without end.

	Quantity A	Quantity B	
3.	$0.\overline{3} + 0.\overline{7}$	1.0	Ⓐ Ⓑ Ⓒ Ⓓ

Explanation

By the definition given in the question, $0.\overline{3}$ represents the decimal in which the digit 3 is repeated without end; that is, $0.\overline{3} = 0.333\ldots$. It follows that $0.\overline{3}$ is greater than 0.3. Similarly, $0.\overline{7}$ is greater than 0.7. Therefore $0.\overline{3} + 0.\overline{7}$ is greater than 1; that is, Quantity A is greater than Quantity B. The correct answer is **Choice A**.

This explanation uses the following strategy.
Strategy 1: Translate from Words to an Arithmetic or Algebraic Representation

A company plans to manufacture two types of hammers, type R and type S. The cost of manufacturing each hammer of type S is $0.05 less than twice the cost of manufacturing each hammer of type R.

Quantity A	Quantity B	
4. The cost of manufacturing 1,000 hammers of type R and 1,000 hammers of type S	The cost of manufacturing 1,500 hammers of type S	

Explanation

Note that Quantity A and Quantity B both include the cost of manufacturing 1,000 hammers of type S. If you remove that cost from both quantities, the problem is reduced to comparing the cost of manufacturing 1,000 hammers of type R with the cost of manufacturing 500 hammers of type S. Since the cost of manufacturing each hammer of type S is $0.05 less than twice the cost of manufacturing each hammer of type R, it follows that the cost of manufacturing 1,000 hammers of type R is greater than the cost of manufacturing 500 hammers of type S. Thus the correct answer is **Choice A.**

This explanation uses the following strategies.
Strategy 8: Search for a Mathematical Relationship
Strategy 9: Estimate

Quantity A	Quantity B	
5. $\dfrac{\left(\dfrac{1}{4}\right)^{-1}+\left(\dfrac{1}{4}\right)^{-2}+\left(\dfrac{1}{4}\right)^{-3}}{4}$	21	

Explanation

Since $\left(\dfrac{1}{4}\right)^{-1}=4$, $\left(\dfrac{1}{4}\right)^{-2}=4^2$, and $\left(\dfrac{1}{4}\right)^{-3}=4^3$, you can simplify Quantity A as follows.

$$\frac{\left(\dfrac{1}{4}\right)^{-1}+\left(\dfrac{1}{4}\right)^{-2}+\left(\dfrac{1}{4}\right)^{-3}}{4}=\frac{4+4^2+4^3}{4}=1+4+4^2=21$$

Since Quantity B is also 21, the correct answer is **Choice C.**

This explanation uses the following strategy.
Strategy 5: Simplify an Arithmetic or Algebraic Representation

List X: 2, 5, s, t
List Y: 2, 5, t

The average (arithmetic mean) of the numbers in list X
is equal to the average of the numbers in list Y.

	Quantity A	Quantity B	
6.	s	0	Ⓐ Ⓑ Ⓒ Ⓓ

Explanation

Since you are given that the average of the 4 numbers in list X is equal to the average
of the 3 numbers in list Y, it follows that $\dfrac{2+5+s+t}{4} = \dfrac{2+5+t}{3}$. To make it easier to
compare Quantity A and Quantity B, you can simplify this equation as follows.

$$\frac{2+5+s+t}{4} = \frac{2+5+t}{3}$$

$$\frac{7+s+t}{4} = \frac{7+t}{3}$$

$$3(7+s+t) = 4(7+t)$$

$$21+3s+3t = 28+4t$$

$$3s = 7+t$$

From the equation $3s = 7+t$, if $t = -7$, then $s = 0$, but if $t = 0$, then $s > 0$. In one
case, the quantities are equal, and in the other case, Quantity A is greater. Therefore the
correct answer is **Choice D.**

This explanation uses the following strategies.
Strategy 1: Translate from Words to an Arithmetic or Algebraic Representation
Strategy 10: Trial and Error
Strategy 13: Determine Whether a Conclusion Follows from the Information Given

---

The radius of circle A is 12 greater than the radius of circle B.

	Quantity A	Quantity B	
7.	The circumference of circle A minus the circumference of circle B	72	Ⓐ Ⓑ Ⓒ Ⓓ

Explanation

Since the radius of circle A is 12 greater than the radius of circle B, if the radius of circle B
is r, then the radius of circle A is $r + 12$. The circumference of circle A minus the circumference of circle B is $2\pi(r + 12) - 2\pi r$, which simplifies to 24π. Since $\pi > 3$, it follows that
$24\pi > 24(3)$; that is, $24\pi > 72$. Since Quantity B is 72, the correct answer is **Choice A.**

This explanation uses the following strategies.
Strategy 8: Search for a Mathematical Relationship
Strategy 9: Estimate

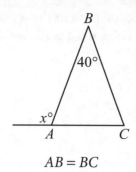

$$AB = BC$$

	Quantity A	Quantity B	
8.	x	120	Ⓐ Ⓑ Ⓒ Ⓓ

Explanation

Note that there are four angles in the figure: the three interior angles of triangle ABC and the exterior angle at vertex A. Since the measure of the exterior angle at vertex A is x degrees, it follows that the measure of interior angle A is $(180 - x)°$. Also, since $AB = BC$, it follows that triangle ABC is isosceles and the measures of interior angles A and C are equal. Therefore the measure of interior angle C is also $(180 - x)°$.

Since the sum of the measures of the interior angles of a triangle is $180°$ and you are given that the measure of interior angle B is $40°$, it follows that

$$40 + (180 - x) + (180 - x) = 180.$$

Solving the equation for x gives $x = 110$. Since Quantity B is 120, the correct answer is **Choice B**.

This explanation uses the following strategies.
Strategy 4: Translate from a Figure to an Arithmetic or Algebraic Representation
Strategy 8: Search for a Mathematical Relationship

$$S = \{1, 2, 3, 4, 5, 6, 7, 8\}$$

	Quantity A	Quantity B	
9.	The number of 4-member subsets of S	The number of 5-member subsets of S	Ⓐ Ⓑ Ⓒ Ⓓ

Explanation

Recall that the number of r-member subsets of a set with n members is equal to $\dfrac{n!}{r!(n-r)!}$. So Quantity A is equal to $\dfrac{8!}{4!\,4!} = \dfrac{(8)(7)(6)(5)}{(4)(3)(2)(1)} = 70$. Similarly, Quantity B is equal to $\dfrac{8!}{5!\,3!} = \dfrac{(8)(7)(6)}{(3)(2)(1)} = 56$. Thus the correct answer is **Choice A**.

This explanation uses the following strategy.
Strategy 1: Translate from Words to an Arithmetic or Algebraic Representation

10. In right triangle ABC, the ratio of the lengths of the two legs is 2 to 5. If the area of triangle ABC is 20, what is the length of the hypotenuse?

(A)   7

(B)   10

(C) $4\sqrt{5}$

(D) $\sqrt{29}$

(E) $2\sqrt{29}$

Explanation

The ratio of the lengths of the legs of right triangle ABC is 2 to 5, so you can represent the lengths as $2x$ and $5x$, respectively, where $x > 0$. Since the area of the triangle is 20, it follows that $\dfrac{(2x)(5x)}{2} = 20$. Solving this equation for x gives $x = 2$. So the lengths of the two legs are $2(2)$ and $2(5)$, or 4 and 10, respectively. Therefore, by the Pythagorean theorem, the length of the hypotenuse is $\sqrt{4^2 + 10^2}$. This square root can be simplified as follows.

$$\sqrt{4^2 + 10^2} = \sqrt{116}$$
$$= \sqrt{(4)(29)}$$
$$= 2\sqrt{29}$$

The correct answer is **Choice E**.

This explanation uses the following strategies.
Strategy 5: Simplify an Arithmetic or Algebraic Representation
Strategy 8: Search for a Mathematical Relationship

---

11. According to surveys at a company, 20 percent of the employees owned cell phones in 1994, and 60 percent of the employees owned cell phones in 1998. From 1994 to 1998, what was the percent increase in the fraction of employees who owned cell phones?

(A)   3%

(B)   20%

(C)   30%

(D)   200%

(E)   300%

Explanation

From 1994 to 1998, the percent of employees who owned cell phones increased from 20% to 60%. Thus the percent increase in the fraction of employees who owned cell phones was $\left(\dfrac{60\% - 20\%}{20\%}\right)(100\%)$, or 200%. The correct answer is **Choice D**.

This explanation uses the following strategy.
Strategy 1: Translate from Words to an Arithmetic or Algebraic Representation

12. If t is an integer and $8m = 16^t$, which of the following expresses m in terms of t?

  (A) 2^t

  (B) 2^{t-3}

  (C) $2^{3(t-3)}$

  (D) 2^{4t-3}

  (E) $2^{4(t-3)}$

Explanation

Note that all of the choices are expressions of the form 2 raised to a power. Expressing 8 and 16 as powers of 2, you can rewrite the given equation $8m = 16^t$ as $2^3m = (2^4)^t$, which is the same as $2^3m = 2^{4t}$. Solving for m and using the rules of exponents, you get $m = \dfrac{2^{4t}}{2^3} = 2^{4t-3}$. The correct answer is **Choice D**.

This explanation uses the following strategies.
Strategy 5: Simplify an Arithmetic or Algebraic Representation
Strategy 8: Search for a Mathematical Relationship

---

13. Three pumps, P, R, and T, working simultaneously at their respective constant rates, can fill a tank in 5 hours. Pumps P and R, working simultaneously at their respective constant rates, can fill the tank in 7 hours. How many hours will it take pump T, working alone at its constant rate, to fill the tank?

  (A) 1.7

  (B) 10.0

  (C) 15.0

  (D) 17.5

  (E) 30.0

Explanation

Working simultaneously, pumps P and R fill $\dfrac{1}{7}$ of the tank in 1 hour. Working simultaneously, the three pumps fill $\dfrac{1}{5}$ of the tank in 1 hour. Therefore, working alone, pump T fills $\dfrac{1}{5} - \dfrac{1}{7}$, or $\dfrac{2}{35}$, of the tank in 1 hour. Thus, working alone, pump T takes $\dfrac{35}{2}$ hours, or 17.5 hours, to fill the tank. The correct answer is **Choice D**.

This explanation uses the following strategies.
Strategy 1: Translate from Words to an Arithmetic or Algebraic Representation
Strategy 8: Search for a Mathematical Relationship

14. The perimeter of a flat rectangular lawn is 42 meters. The width of the lawn is 75 percent of its length. What is the area of the lawn, in square meters?

(A) 40.5

(B) 96

(C) 108

(D) 192

(E) 432

Explanation

Let s and t be the width and length, in meters, of the lawn, respectively. Then the perimeter is $2s + 2t$ meters, so that $2s + 2t = 42$. Also, the relationship between the width and the length can be translated as $s = 0.75t$. Substituting $0.75t$ for s in the equation for the perimeter yields $42 = 2(0.75t) + 2t = 3.5t$. So $t = \dfrac{42}{3.5} = 12$ and $s = (0.75)(12) = 9$. Since $st = 108$, the area of the lawn is 108 square meters. The correct answer is **Choice C**.

This explanation uses the following strategies.

Strategy 1: Translate from Words to an Arithmetic or Algebraic Representation

Strategy 8: Search for a Mathematical Relationship

---

15. The greatest of the 21 positive integers in a certain list is 16. The median of the 21 integers is 10. What is the least possible average (arithmetic mean) of the 21 integers?

(A) 4

(B) 5

(C) 6

(D) 7

(E) 8

Explanation

You are given that the median of the 21 positive integers is 10 and the greatest of the 21 integers is 16. This means that when the 21 integers are listed in order from least to greatest,

- the 1st through 10th integers are between 1 and 10, inclusive;
- the 11th integer is 10;
- the 12th through 20th integers are between 10 and 16, inclusive; and
- the 21st integer is 16.

The least possible average of the 21 integers would be achieved by using the least possible value of each integer as described above in the reordered list:

- the 1st through 10th integers would each be 1;
- the 11th integer would be 10;
- the 12th through 20th integers would each be 10; and
- the 21st integer would be 16.

For the least possible integers, the sum is $(10)(1) + 10 + (9)(10) + 16$, or 126. Therefore the least possible average is $\dfrac{126}{21}$, or 6. The correct answer is **Choice C**.

This explanation uses the following strategies.
Strategy 1: Translate from Words to an Arithmetic or Algebraic Representation
Strategy 8: Search for a Mathematical Relationship

---

16. If x and y are integers and $x = \dfrac{(2)(3)(4)(5)(7)(11)(13)}{39y}$, which of the following could be the value of y?

   (A) 15
   (B) 28
   (C) 38
   (D) 64
   (E) 143

Explanation

To simplify the equation $x = \dfrac{(2)(3)(4)(5)(7)(11)(13)}{39y}$, divide the numerator and

denominator of the fraction by 39 to get $x = \dfrac{(2)(4)(5)(7)(11)}{y}$. From the simplified

equation, you can see that x is an integer if and only if y is a factor of $(2)(4)(5)(7)(11)$. To answer the question, you need to check each of the answer choices until you find the one that is a factor of $(2)(4)(5)(7)(11)$.

   Choice A: 15. Since $15 = (3)(5)$ and 3 is not a factor of $(2)(4)(5)(7)(11)$, neither is 15.
   Choice B: 28. Since $28 = (4)(7)$ and both 4 and 7 are factors of $(2)(4)(5)(7)(11)$, so is 28.

   You can check the other choices to confirm that none of them is a factor of $(2)(4)(5)(7)(11)$. The correct answer is **Choice B**.

This explanation uses the following strategies.
Strategy 5: Simplify an Arithmetic or Algebraic Representation
Strategy 8: Search for a Mathematical Relationship

17. Of the 40 specimens of bacteria in a dish, 3 specimens have a certain trait. If 5 specimens are to be selected from the dish at random and without replacement, which of the following represents the probability that only 1 of the 5 specimens selected will have the trait?

(A) $\dfrac{\dbinom{5}{1}}{\dbinom{40}{3}}$

(B) $\dfrac{\dbinom{5}{1}}{\dbinom{40}{5}}$

(C) $\dfrac{\dbinom{40}{3}}{\dbinom{40}{5}}$

(D) $\dfrac{\dbinom{3}{1}\dbinom{37}{4}}{\dbinom{40}{3}}$

(E) $\dfrac{\dbinom{3}{1}\dbinom{37}{4}}{\dbinom{40}{5}}$

Explanation

In the context of this problem, $\dbinom{n}{r}$ represents the number of ways r specimens can be selected without replacement from n specimens.

The probability that only 1 of the 5 specimens selected from the 40 specimens will have the trait is equal to

$$\frac{\text{number of ways to select 5 specimens, only 1 of which has the trait}}{\text{number of ways to select 5 specimens}}.$$

The number of ways 5 specimens can be selected from the 40 specimens is $\dbinom{40}{5}$. To select 5 specimens, only 1 of which has the trait, you have to select 1 of the 3 specimens that have the trait and select 4 of the 37 specimens that do not have the trait. The number of such selections is the product $\binom{3}{1}\binom{37}{4}$. So the probability that only 1 of the 5

specimens selected will have the trait is represented by $\dfrac{\binom{3}{1}\binom{37}{4}}{\binom{40}{5}}$. The correct answer is **Choice E**.

This explanation uses the following strategies.
Strategy 1: Translate from Words to an Arithmetic or Algebraic Representation
Strategy 8: Search for a Mathematical Relationship

---

18. Two different positive integers x and y are selected from the odd integers that are less than 10. If $z = x + y$ and z is less than 10, which of the following integers could be the sum of x, y, and z?

    Indicate <u>all</u> such integers.

    - [A]   8
    - [B]   9
    - [C]   10
    - [D]   12
    - [E]   14
    - [F]   15
    - [G]   16
    - [H]   18

Explanation

The only pairs of positive odd integers x and y that are less than 10 and satisfy the condition $x + y < 10$ are the pair 1 and 3, the pair 1 and 5, the pair 1 and 7, and the pair 3 and 5. Since $z = x + y$, it follows that the sum of x, y, and z is equal to $2z$. The sum for each of the four possible pairs is found as follows.

- 1 and 3: $z = 4$, and the sum of x, y, and z is $2z$, or 8.
- 1 and 5: $z = 6$, and the sum of x, y, and z is 12.
- 1 and 7: $z = 8$, and the sum of x, y, and z is 16.
- 3 and 5: $z = 8$, and the sum of x, y, and z is 16.

Thus the only possible values of the sum of x, y, and z are 8, 12, and 16. The correct answer consists of **Choices A, D, and G**.

This explanation uses the following strategies.
Strategy 1: Translate from Words to an Arithmetic or Algebraic Representation
Strategy 8: Search for a Mathematical Relationship
Strategy 11: Divide into Cases

19. For a certain probability experiment, the probability that event A will occur is $\frac{1}{2}$ and the probability that event B will occur is $\frac{1}{3}$. Which of the following values could be the probability that the event $A \cup B$ (that is, the event A or B, or both) will occur?

Indicate <u>all</u> such values.

A. $\frac{1}{3}$

B. $\frac{1}{2}$

C. $\frac{3}{4}$

Explanation

Since you know that the probability of event A is $\frac{1}{2}$ and the probability of event B is $\frac{1}{3}$ but you are not given any information about the relationship between events A and B, you can compute only the minimum possible value and the maximum possible value of the probability of the event $A \cup B$.

The probability of $A \cup B$ is least if B is a subset of A; in that case, the probability of $A \cup B$ is just the probability of A, or $\frac{1}{2}$.

The probability of $A \cup B$ is greatest if A and B do not intersect at all; in that case, the probability of $A \cup B$ is the sum of the probabilities of A and B, or $\frac{1}{2} + \frac{1}{3} = \frac{5}{6}$.

With no further information about A and B, the probability that A or B, or both, will occur could be any number from $\frac{1}{2}$ to $\frac{5}{6}$. Of the answer choices given, only $\frac{1}{2}$ and $\frac{3}{4}$ are in this interval. The correct answer consists of **Choices B and C**.

This explanation uses the following strategies.
Strategy 8: Search for a Mathematical Relationship
Strategy 11: Divide into Cases

20. If a and b are the two solutions of the equation $x^2 - 5x + 4 = 0$, what is the value of $\left(\dfrac{1+a}{a}\right)\left(\dfrac{1+b}{b}\right)$?

Give your answer as a fraction.

Explanation

Factoring the quadratic equation $x^2 - 5x + 4 = 0$, you get $(x-1)(x-4) = 0$, so the two solutions are either $a = 1$ and $b = 4$ or $a = 4$ and $b = 1$. Note that a and b are interchangeable in the expression $\left(\dfrac{1+a}{a}\right)\left(\dfrac{1+b}{b}\right)$ so the value of the expression will be the same regardless of the choices of a and b. Thus

$$\left(\frac{1+a}{a}\right)\left(\frac{1+b}{b}\right) = \left(\frac{1+1}{1}\right)\left(\frac{1+4}{4}\right) = (2)\left(\frac{5}{4}\right) = \frac{5}{2},$$

and the correct answer is $\dfrac{5}{2}$.

This explanation uses the following strategies.
Strategy 5: Simplify an Arithmetic or Algebraic Representation
Strategy 8: Search for a Mathematical Relationship

---

21. From 2011 to 2012, Jack's annual salary increased by 10 percent and Arnie's annual salary decreased by 5 percent. If their annual salaries were equal in 2012, then Arnie's annual salary in 2011 was what percent greater than Jack's annual salary in 2011 ?

Give your answer to the nearest 0.1 percent.

 %

Explanation

Let k be Jack's annual salary in 2011, and let r be Arnie's annual salary in 2011. Then Jack's annual salary in 2012 was $1.1k$, and Arnie's was $0.95r$. Since their salaries in 2012 were equal to each other, you have $0.95r = 1.1k$. Solving the equation for r, you get $r = \dfrac{1.1}{0.95}k$. Since $\dfrac{1.1}{0.95} = 1.1578\ldots$, it follows that, rounded to the nearest 0.1%, Arnie's annual salary in 2011 was 15.8% greater than Jack's annual salary in 2011. The correct answer is **15.8**.

This explanation uses the following strategies.
Strategy 1: Translate from Words to an Arithmetic or Algebraic Representation
Strategy 5: Simplify an Arithmetic or Algebraic Representation

INTERNET USE IN YEAR X

Distribution of Internet Users
Worldwide, by Region

Number of Internet Users in Europe
Total: 27.3 million

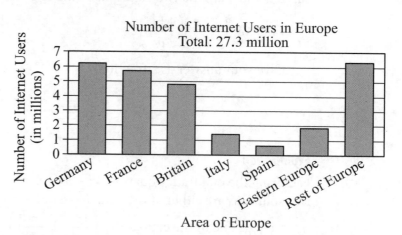

22. Which of the following is closest to the percent of Internet users in Europe who were in countries other than Germany, France, Britain, Italy, and Spain?

Ⓐ 30%

Ⓑ 34%

Ⓒ 38%

Ⓓ 42%

Ⓔ 46%

Explanation

The distribution of Internet users in Europe is given in the bar graph. In the graph, the countries in Europe other than Germany, France, Britain, Italy, and Spain are grouped into two areas: Eastern Europe and Rest of Europe. According to the graph, there were approximately 1.9 million users in Eastern Europe and 6.3 million users in Rest of Europe. Thus the number of users in these two areas combined was approximately $1.9 + 6.3$, or 8.2 million.

From the title of the bar graph, the total number of Internet users in Europe was 27.3 million. Therefore the number of users in the two areas combined, expressed as a percent of all users in Europe, is about $\left(\dfrac{8.2}{27.3}\right)(100\%)$, or approximately 30%.

The answer choice that is closest is 30%. The correct answer is **Choice A.**

This explanation uses the following strategies.

Strategy 4: Translate from a Figure to an Arithmetic or Algebraic Representation
Strategy 5: Simplify an Arithmetic or Algebraic Representation
Strategy 9: Estimate

23. Approximately what was the range of the numbers of Internet users in the seven areas of Europe shown in the bar graph?

    Ⓐ 6.5 million

    Ⓑ 5.5 million

    Ⓒ 3.5 million

    Ⓓ 3.0 million

    Ⓔ 2.5 million

Explanation

The range of the numbers of Internet users in the seven areas of Europe shown in the bar graph is equal to the greatest of the seven numbers minus the least of the seven numbers. Of the seven areas, Rest of Europe had the greatest number of users, approximately 6.3 million, and Spain had the least number of users, approximately 0.7 million. So the range was approximately $6.3 - 0.7$, or 5.6 million. The answer choice that is closest is 5.5 million. The correct answer is **Choice B**.

This explanation uses the following strategies.
Strategy 4: Translate from a Figure to an Arithmetic or Algebraic Representation
Strategy 9: Estimate

---

24. The number of Internet users in the United States was approximately how many times the number of Internet users in Italy?

    Ⓐ 5

    Ⓑ 15

    Ⓒ 20

    Ⓓ 25

    Ⓔ 35

Explanation

According to the bar graph, the number of Internet users in Italy was approximately 1.4 million. The number of Internet users in the United States is not explicitly given, but you know from the circle graph that it was equal to 51% of the number of Internet users worldwide.

From the bar graph, the number of Internet users in Europe was 27.3 million, and from the circle graph this number was 29% of Internet users worldwide. It follows that the number of users worldwide was $\dfrac{27.3}{0.29}$ million, which is approximately 94 million.

Thus the number of users in the United States was 51% of 94 million, or approximately 48 million.

Since the numbers of Internet users in the United States and in Italy were about 48 million and 1.4 million, respectively, it follows that the number in the United States was approximately $\frac{48}{1.4}$ times the number in Italy. Since $\frac{48}{1.4}$ is approximately 34, and the answer choice closest to 34 is 35, the correct answer is **Choice E**.

This explanation uses the following strategies.
Strategy 4: Translate from a Figure to an Arithmetic or Algebraic Representation
Strategy 8: Search for a Mathematical Relationship
Strategy 9: Estimate
Strategy 14: Determine What Additional Information Is Sufficient to Solve a Problem

---

25. Based on the information given, which of the following statements about Internet use in year X must be true?

    Indicate all such statements.

    A The United States had more Internet users than all other countries in the world combined.

    B Spain had fewer Internet users than any country in Eastern Europe.

    C Germany and France combined had more than $\frac{1}{3}$ of the Internet users in Europe.

Explanation

Each statement needs to be evaluated separately.

Statement A. According to the circle graph, 51% of Internet users worldwide were in the United States. Since 51% is greater than $\frac{1}{2}$, Statement A must be true.

Statement B. According to the bar graph, the number of Internet users in Eastern Europe, approximately 1.9 million, was greater than the number in Spain, approximately 0.7 million. However, since the bar graph does not give any information about the distribution of users in the individual countries in Eastern Europe, Statement B may or may not be true.

Statement C. According to the bar graph, Germany and France together had about 12 million Internet users. Since there were 27.3 million users in Europe and 12 is greater than $\frac{1}{3}$ of 27.3, Statement C must be true.

The correct answer consists of **Choices A and C**.

This explanation uses the following strategies.
Strategy 4: Translate from a Figure to an Arithmetic or Algebraic Representation
Strategy 13: Determine Whether a Conclusion Follows from the Information Given
Strategy 14: Determine What Additional Information Is Sufficient to Solve a Problem

PRACTICE SET 3

Quantitative Comparison Questions

For Questions 1 to 9, compare Quantity A and Quantity B, using additional information centered above the two quantities if such information is given. Select one of the following four answer choices and fill in the corresponding oval to the right of the question.

Ⓐ Quantity A is greater.

Ⓑ Quantity B is greater.

Ⓒ The two quantities are equal.

Ⓓ The relationship cannot be determined from the information given.

A symbol that appears more than once in a question has the same meaning throughout the question.

	Quantity A	Quantity B	Correct Answer
Example 1:	(2)(6)	2 + 6	**Ⓐ** Ⓑ Ⓒ Ⓓ

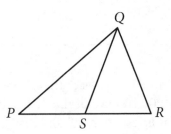

	Quantity A	Quantity B	Correct Answer
Example 2:	PS	SR	Ⓐ Ⓑ Ⓒ **Ⓓ**

(since equal lengths cannot be assumed, even though PS and SR appear equal)

$y < -6$

	Quantity A	Quantity B	
1.	y	-5	Ⓐ **Ⓑ** Ⓒ Ⓓ

x is an integer and 23 < x < 27.

	Quantity A	Quantity B	
2.	The median of the five integers 23, 24, 26, 27, and x	25	Ⓐ Ⓑ Ⓒ Ⓓ

---

r and t are consecutive integers and $p = r^2 + t$.

	Quantity A	Quantity B	
3.	$(-1)^p$	-1	Ⓐ Ⓑ Ⓒ Ⓓ

The function f is defined by $f\left(\dfrac{x+3}{2}\right) = 3x^2 - x + 5$ for all numbers x.

	Quantity A	Quantity B	
4.	$f(4)$	75	Ⓐ Ⓑ Ⓒ Ⓓ

The sum of the annual salaries of the 21 teachers at School X is $781,200. Twelve of the 21 teachers have an annual salary that is less than $37,000.

	Quantity A	Quantity B	
5.	The average (arithmetic mean) of the annual salaries of the teachers at School X	The median of the annual salaries of the teachers at School X	Ⓐ Ⓑ Ⓒ Ⓓ

37,200

37,000

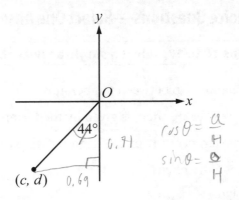

(c, d)   0.69

~0.69, ~0.71

$\cos\theta = \dfrac{a}{H}$

$\sin\theta = \dfrac{o}{H}$

	Quantity A	Quantity B	
6.	*c*	*d*	Ⓐ Ⓑ Ⓒ Ⓓ

$N = 824^x$, where x is a positive integer.

	Quantity A	Quantity B	
7.	The number of possible values of the units digit of N	4	Ⓐ Ⓑ Ⓒ Ⓓ

$x > 0$ and $x \neq 1$. $1 < x > 0$ $x > 1$

	Quantity A	Quantity B	
8.	$(2x^{-4})(3x^2)$ $\quad 6x^{-2} = \dfrac{6}{x^2}$	$\dfrac{24x}{4x^2} = \dfrac{6}{x}$	Ⓐ Ⓑ Ⓒ Ⓓ

	Quantity A	Quantity B	
9.	The length of a leg of an isosceles right triangle with area R	The length of a side of a square with area R	Ⓐ Ⓑ Ⓒ Ⓓ

$A_R = \frac{1}{2} b \cdot h$

$\frac{1}{2} b^2$

$\frac{1}{2} b_1{}^2 = b_2{}^2$

Multiple-choice Questions—Select One Answer Choice

For Questions 10 to 17, select a single answer choice.

10. The relationship between temperature C, in degrees Celsius, and temperature F, in degrees Fahrenheit, is given by the formula $F = \dfrac{9}{5}C + 32$. If a recipe calls for an oven temperature of 210 degrees Celsius, what is the oven temperature in degrees Fahrenheit?

    (A) 320

    (B) 350

    (C) 410

    (D) 420

    (E) 500

11. Of the students in a school, 20 percent are in the science club and 30 percent are in the band. If 25 percent of the students in the school are in the band but are <u>not</u> in the science club, what percent of the students who are in the science club are <u>not</u> in the band?

    (A) 5%

    (B) 20%

    (C) 25%

    (D) 60%

    (E) 75%

12. Each year, the members of a book club select novels and nonfiction books to read. The club meets 3 times to discuss each novel and 5 times to discuss each nonfiction book they select. Last year, the club met 52 times and discussed 12 books. How many novels did the club discuss last year?

    (A) 2

    (B) 4

    (C) 5

    (D) 7

    (E) 14

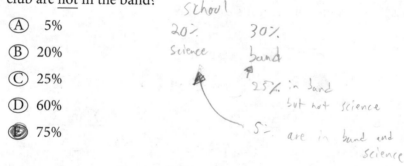

13. If $-1 < x < y < 0$, which of the following shows the expressions xy, x^2y, and xy^2 listed in order from least to greatest?

   (A) xy, x^2y, xy^2

   (B) xy, xy^2, x^2y

   (C) xy^2, xy, x^2y

   (D) xy^2, x^2y, xy

   (E) x^2y, xy^2, xy

14. The 5 letters in the list G, H, I, J, K are to be rearranged so that G is the 3rd letter in the list and H is not next to G. How many such rearrangements are there?

   (A) 60

   (B) 36

   (C) 24

   (D) 12

   (E) 6

15. If j and k are even integers and $j < k$, which of the following equals the number of even integers that are greater than j and less than k?

   (A) $\dfrac{k-j-2}{2}$

   (B) $\dfrac{k-j-1}{2}$

   (C) $\dfrac{k-j}{2}$

   (D) $k-j$

   (E) $k-j-1$

16. Which of the following is closest to $\sqrt{2.3 \times 10^9}$?

   $(10^4)^2 = 10^8$

   (A) 50,000

   (B) 150,000

   (C) 500,000

   (D) 1,500,000

   (E) 5,000,000

   $10^4 \sqrt{2.3 \times 10} = 10^4 \sqrt{23}$

   $\approx 10^4 \cdot 5$

   $5 \cdot 5 = 25$
   $4 \cdot 4 = 16$

   50,000

17. The interior dimensions of a rectangular tank are as follows: length 110 centimeters, width 90 centimeters, and height 270 centimeters. The tank rests on level ground. Based on the assumption that the volume of water increases by 10 percent when it freezes, which of the following is closest to the maximum height, in centimeters, to which the tank can be filled with water so that when the water freezes, the ice would not rise above the top of the tank?

   (A) 230

   (B) 235

   (C) 240

   (D) 245

   (E) 250

   $V_{max} = ? = b \cdot h \cdot w$

   $1.1 V_x = V_{max}$

   $b \cdot w \cdot h_x =$

   270 cm   90 cm   110 cm

   $1.1 = 1 + \frac{1}{10}$

   $1.1 (b \cdot w \cdot h_x) = b \cdot h \cdot w$

   $1.1 \overline{)270}$
   -1.1
   0.9

   $\frac{270}{\left(\frac{11}{10}\right)} = \frac{2700}{11}$

   $h_x = \frac{h}{1.1}$

   $h_x = \frac{270}{1.1}$

   $245.\overline{45}$
   $11\overline{)2700}$
   -22
   50
   -44
   60
   -55
   5

Multiple-choice Questions—Select One or More Answer Choices

For Questions 18 to 19, select all the answer choices that apply.

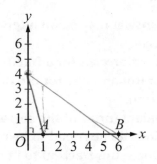

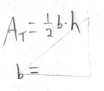

18. Points A and B are shown in the xy-plane above. Point C (not shown) is above the x-axis so that the area of triangle ABC is 10. Which of the following could be the coordinates of C?

    Indicate all such coordinates.

    A (0, 4)

    B (1, 3)

    C (2, 5)

    D (3, 4)

    E (4, 5)

19. In a factory, machine A operates on a cycle of 20 hours of work followed by 4 hours of rest, and machine B operates on a cycle of 40 hours of work followed by 8 hours of rest. Last week, the two machines began their respective cycles at 12 noon on Monday and continued until 12 noon on the following Saturday. On which days during that time period was there a time when both machines were at rest?

    Indicate all such days.

    A Monday

    B Tuesday

    C Wednesday

    D Thursday

    E Friday

    F Saturday

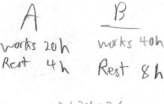

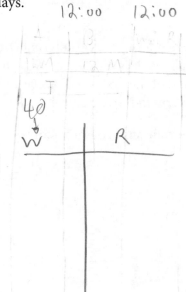

Numeric Entry Questions

For Questions 20 to 21, enter your answer in the answer box(es) below the question.

- **Your answer may be an integer, a decimal, or a fraction, and it may be negative.**
- **If a question asks for a fraction, there will be two boxes—one for the numerator and one for the denominator. A decimal point cannot be used in a fraction.**
- **Equivalent forms of the correct answer, such as 2.5 and 2.50, are all correct. Fractions do not need to be reduced to lowest terms, though you may need to reduce your fraction to fit in the boxes.**
- **Enter the exact answer unless the question asks you to round your answer.**

AVERAGE RATING OF PRODUCT X
GIVEN BY THREE GROUPS OF PEOPLE

Group	Number of People in Group	Average Rating
A	45	3.8
B	25	4.6
C	30	4.2

20. Each of the people in three groups gave a rating of Product X on a scale from 1 through 5. For each of the groups, the table above shows the number of people in the group and the average (arithmetic mean) of their ratings. What is the average of the ratings of the product given by the 100 people in the three groups combined?

    Give your answer to the nearest 0.1.

4.2

21. The first term in a certain sequence is 1, the 2nd term in the sequence is 2, and, for all integers $n \geq 3$, the nth term in the sequence is the average (arithmetic mean) of the first $n-1$ terms in the sequence. What is the value of the 6th term in the sequence?

    Give your answer as a fraction.

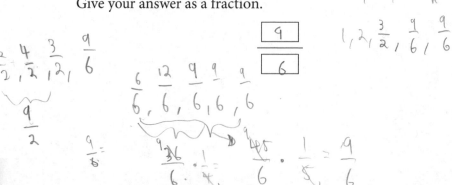

Data Interpretation Set

Questions 22 to 25 are based on the following data. For these questions, select a single answer choice unless otherwise directed.

SIGHTINGS OF SELECTED BIRD SPECIES
IN PARK *H* IN 1999, BY SEASON

Species	Number of Sightings			
	Winter	Spring	Summer	Fall
Cardinal	30	18	11	20
Goldfinch	6	12	6	9
Junco	12	0	0	6
Nuthatch	8	2	0	4
Robin	6	12	28	18
Sparrow	20	19	23	22
Wren	0	18	30	12

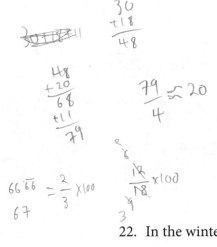

22. In the winter, $\frac{2}{3}$ of the cardinal sightings, $\frac{1}{2}$ of the junco sightings, and $\frac{1}{4}$ of the sparrow sightings were in January. What fraction of the total number of sightings of these three bird species in the winter were in January?

  (A) $\frac{1}{4}$

  (B) $\frac{1}{3}$

  (C) $\frac{1}{2}$

  (D) $\frac{2}{3}$

  (E) $\frac{3}{4}$

23. For which of the following bird species is the standard deviation of the numbers of sightings shown for the four seasons least?

  (A) Cardinal

  (B) Junco

  (C) Robin

  (D) Sparrow

  (E) Wren

24. Which of the following is closest to the average (arithmetic mean) number of cardinal sightings for the 4 seasons?

(A) 12

(B) 14

(C) 16

(D) 18

(E) 20

For Question 25, use the directions for Numeric Entry questions.

25. By what percent did the number of wren sightings increase from spring to summer?

Give your answer to the <u>nearest whole percent.</u>

67 %

ANSWER KEY

1. **Choice B**: Quantity B is greater.
2. **Choice D**: The relationship cannot be determined from the information given.
3. **Choice C**: The two quantities are equal.
4. **Choice C**: The two quantities are equal.
5. **Choice A**: Quantity A is greater.
6. **Choice A**: Quantity A is greater.
7. **Choice B**: Quantity B is greater.
8. **Choice D**: The relationship cannot be determined from the information given.
9. **Choice A**: Quantity A is greater.
10. **Choice C**: 410
11. **Choice E**: 75%
12. **Choice B**: 4
13. **Choice E**: $x^2y,\ xy^2,\ xy$
14. **Choice D**: 12
15. **Choice A**: $\dfrac{k-j-2}{2}$
16. **Choice A**: 50,000
17. **Choice D**: 245
18. **Choice A**: (0, 4)

    AND

    Choice D: (3, 4)
19. **Choice C**: Wednesday

    AND

    Choice E: Friday
20. **4.1**
21. $\dfrac{3}{2}$
22. **Choice C**: $\dfrac{1}{2}$
23. **Choice D**: Sparrow
24. **Choice E**: 20
25. **67**

Answers and Explanations

$$y < -6$$

	Quantity A	Quantity B	
1.	y	-5	Ⓐ Ⓑ Ⓒ Ⓓ

Explanation

You are given that y is a number that is less than -6. Since -6 is less than -5, it follows that y is less than -5. Thus the correct answer is **Choice B**.

This explanation uses the following strategy.
Strategy 8: Search for a Mathematical Relationship

---

x is an integer and $23 < x < 27$.

	Quantity A	Quantity B	
2.	The median of the five integers 23, 24, 26, 27, and x	25	Ⓐ Ⓑ Ⓒ Ⓓ

Explanation

You are given that x is an integer that is greater than 23 and less than 27. So x could be 24, 25, or 26. If $x = 24$, the median of the five integers 23, 24, 26, 27, and x is 24. Similarly, if $x = 25$, the median of the five integers is 25, and if $x = 26$, the median of the five integers is 26. So the median of the five integers is 24, 25, or 26. Thus the median of the five integers could be less than, equal to, or greater than 25. The correct answer is **Choice D**.

This explanation uses the following strategies.
Strategy 11: Divide into Cases
Strategy 13: Determine Whether a Conclusion Follows from the Information Given

r and *t* are consecutive integers and $p = r^2 + t$.

	Quantity A	Quantity B	
3.	$(-1)^p$	-1	Ⓐ Ⓑ Ⓒ Ⓓ

Explanation

Recall that

$$(-1)^p = \begin{cases} 1 & \text{if } p \text{ is an even integer} \\ -1 & \text{if } p \text{ is an odd integer} \end{cases}$$

Since $p = r^2 + t$, the value of $(-1)^p$ depends on whether $r^2 + t$ is odd or even.

If *r* is an odd integer, then r^2 is an odd integer and, since *r* and *t* are consecutive integers, *t* is an even integer. In this case, *p* is the sum of an odd integer and an even integer and is therefore an odd integer.

Similarly, if *r* is an even integer, then r^2 is an even integer and *t* is an odd integer. In this case, *p* is the sum of an even integer and an odd integer and is therefore an odd integer.

In both cases, *p* is an odd integer. It follows that $(-1)^p = -1$, and the correct answer is **Choice C**.

This explanation uses the following strategies.
Strategy 1: Translate from Words to an Arithmetic or Algebraic Representation
Strategy 11: Divide into Cases

The function *f* is defined by $f\left(\dfrac{x+3}{2}\right) = 3x^2 - x + 5$ for all numbers *x*.

	Quantity A	Quantity B	
4.	$f(4)$	75	Ⓐ Ⓑ Ⓒ Ⓓ

Explanation
The function *f* is defined by $f\left(\dfrac{x+3}{2}\right) = 3x^2 - x + 5$. To find the value of $f(4)$, you first need to find the value of *x* for which $\dfrac{x+3}{2} = 4$, and then you can plug that value of *x* into $f\left(\dfrac{x+3}{2}\right) = 3x^2 - x + 5$. Solving the equation $\dfrac{x+3}{2} = 4$ for *x* yields $x = 5$. Plugging $x = 5$ into $f\left(\dfrac{x+3}{2}\right) = 3x^2 - x + 5$, you get $f(4) = 3(5)^2 - 5 + 5$, or 75. Since Quantity B is 75, the correct answer is **Choice C**.

This explanation uses the following strategy.
Strategy 8: Search for a Mathematical Relationship

The sum of the annual salaries of the 21 teachers at School X is $781,200. Twelve of the 21 teachers have an annual salary that is less than $37,000.

	Quantity A	Quantity B	

5. The average (arithmetic mean) of the annual salaries of the teachers at School X

The median of the annual salaries of the teachers at School X

Explanation

The average of the annual salaries of the 21 teachers is $\dfrac{\$781,200}{21}$, or $37,200. By definition, the median of the 21 annual salaries is the 11th salary when the 21 salaries are listed in increasing order. Note that in the question you are given that 12 of the 21 salaries are less than $37,000. Thus, when the 21 salaries are listed in increasing order, the first 12 salaries in the list are less than $37,000. Thus the median of the salaries, which is the 11th salary in the list, is less than $37,000, which is less than the average salary of $37,200. The correct answer is **Choice A**.

This explanation uses the following strategy.
Strategy 8: Search for a Mathematical Relationship

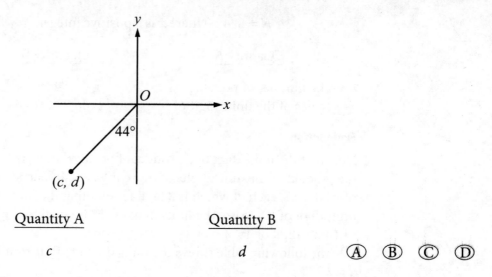

Quantity A	Quantity B
6. c	d Ⓐ Ⓑ Ⓒ Ⓓ

Explanation

Note that if you draw a horizontal line segment from the point (c, d) to the y-axis, you form a 44°-46°-90° right triangle, with a horizontal leg of length $|c|$ and a vertical leg of length $|d|$, as shown in the figure below.

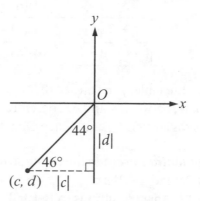

In the triangle, the horizontal leg is opposite the 44° angle and the vertical leg is opposite the 46° angle. Since the 44° angle is smaller than the 46° angle, the length of the horizontal leg is less than the length of the vertical leg; that is, $|c| < |d|$. Since c and d are both negative, it follows that $c > d$. The correct answer is **Choice A**.

This explanation uses the following strategies.
Strategy 4: Translate from a Figure to an Arithmetic or Algebraic Representation
Strategy 6: Add to a Geometric Figure
Strategy 8: Search for a Mathematical Relationship

$N = 824^x$, where x is a positive integer.

Quantity A	Quantity B	

7. The number of possible values of the units digit of N — 4 —

Explanation

Note that the units digit of a product of positive integers is equal to the units digit of the product of the units digits of those integers. In particular, since 824^x is a product of x integers, each of which is 824, it follows that the units digit of 824^x is equal to the units digit of 4^x. Also, the units digit of 4^x is equal to the units digit of the product $(4)(\text{units digit of } 4^{x-1})$.

The following table shows the units digit of 4^x for some values of x, beginning with $x = 2$.

x	(4)(units digit of 4^{x-1})	Units Digit of 4^x
2	$(4)(4) = 16$	6
3	$(4)(6) = 24$	4
4	$(4)(4) = 16$	6
5	$(4)(6) = 24$	4

From the table, you can see that the units digit of 4^x alternates, and will continue to alternate, between 4 and 6. Therefore, Quantity A, the number of possible values of the units digit of 824^x, is 2. Since Quantity B is 4, the correct answer is **Choice B**.

This explanation uses the following strategies.
Strategy 7: Find a Pattern
Strategy 12: Adapt Solutions to Related Problems

$x > 0$ and $x \neq 1$.

Quantity A	Quantity B	

8. $(2x^{-4})(3x^2)$ — $\dfrac{24x}{4x^2}$ —

Explanation

The two quantities can be simplified as follows.

Quantity A: $(2x^{-4})(3x^2) = \dfrac{6}{x^2}$

Quantity B: $\dfrac{24x}{4x^2} = \dfrac{6}{x}$

So comparing Quantity A with Quantity B is the same as comparing $\dfrac{6}{x^2}$ with $\dfrac{6}{x}$.

Since you are given that $x > 0$ and $x \neq 1$, and the quantities to be compared involve fractions and exponents, it is reasonable to consider two cases: $0 < x < 1$ and $x > 1$.

Case 1: $0 < x < 1$. If x is a number that satisfies $0 < x < 1$, then $x^2 < x$. Therefore $\dfrac{6}{x^2} > \dfrac{6}{x}$, and Quantity A is greater than Quantity B.

Case 2: $x > 1$. If x is a number that satisfies $x > 1$, then $x^2 > x$. Therefore $\dfrac{6}{x^2} < \dfrac{6}{x}$, and Quantity B is greater than Quantity A.

In one case Quantity A is greater, and in the other case Quantity B is greater. Thus the correct answer is **Choice D**.

This explanation uses the following strategies.
Strategy 5: Simplify an Arithmetic or Algebraic Representation
Strategy 8: Search for a Mathematical Relationship
Strategy 11: Divide into Cases
Strategy 13: Determine Whether a Conclusion Follows from the Information Given

---

Quantity A	Quantity B	
9. The length of a leg of an isosceles right triangle with area R	The length of a side of a square with area R	

Explanation

In an isosceles right triangle, both legs have the same length. The area of an isosceles right triangle with legs of length x is equal to $\dfrac{x^2}{2}$. The area of a square with sides of length s is s^2. Since you are given that an isosceles right triangle and a square have the same area R, it follows that $\dfrac{x^2}{2} = s^2$, and so $x = \sqrt{2}s$.

Since $\sqrt{2}$ is greater than 1, the length of a leg of the triangle is greater than the length of a side of the square. The correct answer is **Choice A**.

This explanation uses the following strategies.
Strategy 1: Translate from Words to an Arithmetic or Algebraic Representation
Strategy 5: Simplify an Arithmetic or Algebraic Representation
Strategy 8: Search for a Mathematical Relationship

10. The relationship between temperature C, in degrees Celsius, and temperature F, in degrees Fahrenheit, is given by the formula $F = \dfrac{9}{5}C + 32$. If a recipe calls for an oven temperature of 210 degrees Celsius, what is the oven temperature in degrees Fahrenheit?

    (A) 320

    (B) 350

    (C) 410

    (D) 420

    (E) 500

Explanation

You are given the relationship $F = \dfrac{9}{5}C + 32$. If the temperature is 210 degrees Celsius, then $C = 210$ and the temperature F, in degrees Fahrenheit, is $\dfrac{9}{5}(210) + 32$, or 410. Thus the correct answer is **Choice C**.

This explanation uses the following strategy.
Strategy 5: Simplify an Arithmetic or Algebraic Representation

---

11. Of the students in a school, 20 percent are in the science club and 30 percent are in the band. If 25 percent of the students in the school are in the band but are not in the science club, what percent of the students who are in the science club are not in the band?

    (A) 5%

    (B) 20%

    (C) 25%

    (D) 60%

    (E) 75%

Explanation

You are given that 20% of the students are in the science club, 30% are in the band, and 25% are in the band but are not in the science club. You need to determine what percent of the students who are in the science club are not in the band. The information can be represented in a Venn diagram as follows.

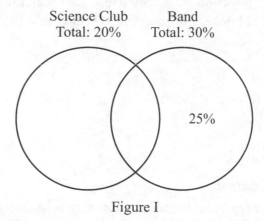

Figure I

From the Venn Diagram, you can see that the 30% who are in the band consists of 25% who are in the band but not in the science club, and 5% who are in both the band and the science club. Then you can see that the 20% who are in the science club consists of 5% who are in both the science club and the band, and 15% who are in the science club but not in the band, as shown in the revised Venn diagram below.

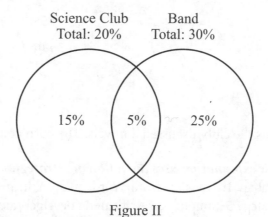

Figure II

Thus $\frac{15\%}{20\%}(100\%)$, or 75%, of the students in the science club are not in the band. The correct answer is **Choice E.**

This explanation uses the following strategies.
Strategy 1: Translate from Words to an Arithmetic or Algebraic Representation
Strategy 2: Translate from Words to a Figure or Diagram

12. Each year, the members of a book club select novels and nonfiction books to read. The club meets 3 times to discuss each novel and 5 times to discuss each nonfiction book they select. Last year, the club met 52 times and discussed 12 books. How many novels did the club discuss last year?

(A) 2

(B) 4

(C) 5

(D) 7

(E) 14

Explanation

Let n represent the number of novels the club discussed last year. Since the club discussed a total of 12 books, the number of nonfiction books is represented by $12 - n$. This, together with the information that the club met 3 times to discuss each novel and 5 times to discuss each nonfiction book, tells you that the number of times the club met last year can be expressed as $3n + 5(12 - n)$. Since you know that the club met 52 times last year, it follows that $3n + 5(12 - n) = 52$. This equation can be solved for n as follows.

$$3n + 5(12 - n) = 52$$
$$3n + 60 - 5n = 52$$
$$8 = 2n$$
$$4 = n$$

Thus the club discussed 4 novels. The correct answer is **Choice B**.

This explanation uses the following strategies.
Strategy 1: Translate from Words to an Arithmetic or Algebraic Representation
Strategy 5: Simplify an Arithmetic or Algebraic Representation
Strategy 8: Search for a Mathematical Relationship

---

13. If $-1 < x < y < 0$, which of the following shows the expressions xy, x^2y, and xy^2 listed in order from least to greatest?

(A) $xy,\ x^2y,\ xy^2$

(B) $xy,\ xy^2,\ x^2y$

(C) $xy^2,\ xy,\ x^2y$

(D) $xy^2,\ x^2y,\ xy$

(E) $x^2y,\ xy^2,\ xy$

Explanation

You are given that $-1 < x < y < 0$. Since x and y are both negative numbers, it follows that xy is positive and both x^2y and xy^2 are negative. So xy is greater than both x^2y and xy^2. Now you need to determine which is greater, x^2y or xy^2. You can do this by multiplying the inequality $x < y$ by the positive number xy to get $x^2y < xy^2$. Thus $x^2y < xy^2 < xy$, and the correct answer is **Choice E**.

This explanation uses the following strategies.
Strategy 1: Translate from Words to an Arithmetic or Algebraic Representation
Strategy 8: Search for a Mathematical Relationship

---

14. The 5 letters in the list G, H, I, J, K are to be rearranged so that G is the 3rd letter in the list and H is <u>not</u> next to G. How many such rearrangements are there?

    (A) 60

    (B) 36

    (C) 24

    (D) 12

    (E) 6

Explanation

When the 5 letters are rearranged, G is to be listed in the 3rd position and H cannot be next to G, so there are only two possible positions for H: 1st and 5th.

Case 1: In the rearranged list, G is in the 3rd position, H is in the 1st position, and each of the remaining 3 letters can be in any of the remaining 3 positions. The number of ways these remaining 3 letters can be arranged is 3!, or 6. Thus the total number of rearrangements in case 1 is 6.

Case 2: In the rearranged list, G is in the 3rd position, H is in the 5th position, and each of the remaining 3 letters can be in any of the remaining 3 positions. Thus, as in case 1, the total number of rearrangements in case 2 is 6.

Thus there are $6 + 6$, or 12, possible rearrangements, and the correct answer is **Choice D**.

This explanation uses the following strategies.
Strategy 1: Translate from Words to an Arithmetic or Algebraic Representation
Strategy 11: Divide into Cases

15. If j and k are even integers and $j < k$, which of the following equals the number of even integers that are greater than j and less than k ?

   (A) $\dfrac{k-j-2}{2}$

   (B) $\dfrac{k-j-1}{2}$

   (C) $\dfrac{k-j}{2}$

   (D) $k-j$

   (E) $k-j-1$

Explanation

Since j and k are even integers, it follows that $k = j + 2n$ for some integer n. Consider the sequence of even integers from j to k.

$$j,\ j+(2)(1),\ j+(2)(2),\ j+(2)(3),\ \ldots,\ j+(2)(n-1),\ j+2n$$

Note that there are $n-1$ integers in the sequence between j and k, and these are the even integers greater than j and less than k. Therefore the answer is $n-1$, but the answer must be given in terms of j and k. Since $k = j + 2n$, you have $n = \dfrac{k-j}{2}$ and so

$$n-1 = \dfrac{k-j}{2} - 1 = \dfrac{k-j-2}{2}.$$

Thus the correct answer is **Choice A**.

This explanation uses the following strategies.

Strategy 5: Simplify an Arithmetic or Algebraic Representation
Strategy 8: Search for a Mathematical Relationship

16. Which of the following is closest to $\sqrt{2.3 \times 10^9}$?

    (A) 50,000

    (B) 150,000

    (C) 500,000

    (D) 1,500,000

    (E) 5,000,000

Explanation

The expression $\sqrt{2.3 \times 10^9}$ can be simplified as follows.

$$\sqrt{2.3 \times 10^9} = \sqrt{2.3 \times 10 \times 10^8}$$
$$= \sqrt{23 \times 10^8}$$
$$= 10^4 \sqrt{23}$$

Since $\sqrt{23}$ is between 4 and 5, it follows that $10^4 \sqrt{23}$ is between 40,000 and 50,000. Therefore, of the five answer choices listed, 50,000 is closest to $\sqrt{2.3 \times 10^9}$. The correct answer is **Choice A**.

This explanation uses the following strategies.
Strategy 5: Simplify an Arithmetic or Algebraic Representation
Strategy 9: Estimate

---

17. The interior dimensions of a rectangular tank are as follows: length 110 centimeters, width 90 centimeters, and height 270 centimeters. The tank rests on level ground. Based on the assumption that the volume of water increases by 10 percent when it freezes, which of the following is closest to the maximum height, in centimeters, to which the tank can be filled with water so that when the water freezes, the ice would not rise above the top of the tank?

    (A) 230

    (B) 235

    (C) 240

    (D) 245

    (E) 250

Explanation

Let x be the maximum height, in centimeters, to which the tank can be filled with water, so that when the water freezes, the ice will not rise above the top of the tank. Based on the assumption that the volume of water increases by 10 percent when it freezes and the fact that the length and width of the tank will not change, the maximum height of the ice is $1.1x$ centimeters. Since the height of the tank is 270 centimeters, it follows that $1.1x = 270$, or, to the nearest whole number, $x = 245$. The correct answer is **Choice D**.

This explanation uses the following strategy.
Strategy 1: Translate from Words to an Arithmetic or Algebraic Representation

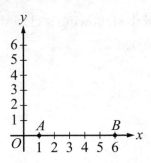

18. Points A and B are shown in the xy-plane above. Point C (not shown) is above the x-axis so that the area of triangle ABC is 10. Which of the following could be the coordinates of C?

Indicate <u>all</u> such coordinates.

A (0, 4)
B (1, 3)
C (2, 5)
D (3, 4)
E (4, 5)

Explanation

From the figure, you can see that points A and B are on the x-axis. Since the x-coordinate of A is 1 and the x-coordinate of B is 6, the length of side AB is 5. Point C is not shown, but you know that C is above the x-axis and that the area of triangle ABC is 10. Using the formula for the area of a triangle, you can see that the height h from point C to the corresponding base AB satisfies the equation $10 = \dfrac{5h}{2}$.

Therefore $h = 4$.

There are many possibilities for triangle ABC subject to these conditions. The following figures show three examples.

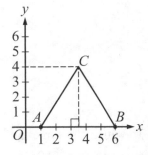
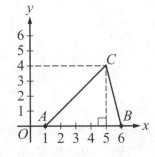
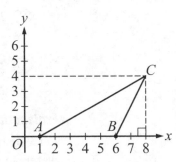

In the three examples, the dashed vertical line segments represent the height from point C to the base AB, and the coordinates of C are (3.5, 4), (5, 4), and (8, 4), respectively. Note that in all three cases, the y-coordinate of C is 4. In fact, for any triangle

ABC that satisfies the conditions in the question, point *C* is a point with a *y*-coordinate of 4. Of the answer choices, only (0, 4) and (3, 4) have a *y*-coordinate of 4. The correct answer consists of **Choices A and D**.

This explanation uses the following strategies.
Strategy 4: Translate from a Figure to an Arithmetic or Algebraic Representation
Strategy 6: Add to a Geometric Figure
Strategy 8: Search for a Mathematical Relationship

---

19. In a factory, machine *A* operates on a cycle of 20 hours of work followed by 4 hours of rest, and machine *B* operates on a cycle of 40 hours of work followed by 8 hours of rest. Last week, the two machines began their respective cycles at 12 noon on Monday and continued until 12 noon on the following Saturday. On which days during that time period was there a time when both machines were at rest?

    Indicate <u>all</u> such days.

    A Monday
    B Tuesday
    C Wednesday
    D Thursday
    E Friday
    F Saturday

Explanation

Both machines began their respective cycles at 12 noon on Monday and continued until 12 noon on the following Saturday. Note that 1 day has 24 hours and 2 days have 48 hours.

Machine *A* operates on a cycle of 20 hours of work followed by 4 hours of rest, so it was at rest from 8 o'clock in the morning until 12 noon every day from Tuesday to Saturday.

Machine *B* operates on a cycle of 40 hours of work followed by 8 hours of rest, so it was at rest from 4 o'clock in the morning until 12 noon on Wednesday and Friday.

Thus both machines were at rest from 8 o'clock in the morning until 12 noon on Wednesday and Friday. The correct answer consists of **Choices C and E**.

This explanation uses the following strategies.
Strategy 1: Translate from Words to an Arithmetic or Algebraic Representation
Strategy 7: Find a Pattern

AVERAGE RATING OF PRODUCT X
GIVEN BY THREE GROUPS OF PEOPLE

Group	Number of People in Group	Average Rating
A	45	3.8
B	25	4.6
C	30	4.2

20. Each of the people in three groups gave a rating of Product X on a scale from 1 through 5. For each of the groups, the table above shows the number of people in the group and the average (arithmetic mean) of their ratings. What is the average of the ratings of the product given by the 100 people in the three groups combined?

Give your answer to the <u>nearest 0.1</u>.

Explanation

For each of the three groups, the sum of the ratings given by the people in the group is equal to the number of people in the group times the average of their ratings. Therefore the sum of the ratings given by the 100 people in the three groups combined is $45(3.8) + 25(4.6) + 30(4.2)$, or 412, and the average of the 100 ratings is $\dfrac{412}{100}$, or 4.12. Therefore, to the nearest 0.1, the correct answer is **4.1**.

This explanation uses the following strategies.
Strategy 1: Translate from Words to an Arithmetic or Algebraic Representation
Strategy 4: Translate from a Figure to an Arithmetic or Algebraic Representation

21. The first term in a certain sequence is 1, the 2nd term in the sequence is 2, and, for all integers $n \geq 3$, the nth term in the sequence is the average (arithmetic mean) of the first $n - 1$ terms in the sequence. What is the value of the 6th term in the sequence?

Give your answer as a fraction.

Explanation

For all integers $n \geq 3$, the nth term in the sequence is the average of the first $n - 1$ terms in the sequence.

The 3rd term, which is the average of the first 2 terms, is $\dfrac{1+2}{2}$, or 1.5.

The 4th term, which is the average of the first 3 terms, is $\dfrac{1+2+1.5}{3}$, or 1.5.

Similarly, the 5th term is $\dfrac{1+2+1.5+1.5}{4} = \dfrac{6}{4}$, or 1.5, and the 6th term

is $\dfrac{1+2+1.5+1.5+1.5}{5} = \dfrac{7.5}{5}$, or 1.5. Since you must give your answer as a fraction, the

correct answer is $\dfrac{3}{2}$.

This explanation uses the following strategies.
Strategy 1: Translate from Words to an Arithmetic or Algebraic Representation
Strategy 7: Find a Pattern

SIGHTINGS OF SELECTED BIRD SPECIES
IN PARK *H* IN 1999, BY SEASON

Species	Number of Sightings			
	Winter	Spring	Summer	Fall
Cardinal	30	18	11	20
Goldfinch	6	12	6	9
Junco	12	0	0	6
Nuthatch	8	2	0	4
Robin	6	12	28	18
Sparrow	20	19	23	22
Wren	0	18	30	12

22. In the winter, $\frac{2}{3}$ of the cardinal sightings, $\frac{1}{2}$ of the junco sightings, and $\frac{1}{4}$ of the sparrow sightings were in January. What fraction of the total number of sightings of these three bird species in the winter were in January?

Ⓐ $\frac{1}{4}$

Ⓑ $\frac{1}{3}$

Ⓒ $\frac{1}{2}$

Ⓓ $\frac{2}{3}$

Ⓔ $\frac{3}{4}$

Explanation

The total number of sightings of cardinals, juncos, and sparrows in the winter was

$30 + 12 + 20$, or 62. In the question, you are given that $\frac{2}{3}$ of the 30 cardinal sightings,

$\frac{1}{2}$ of the 12 junco sightings, and $\frac{1}{4}$ of the 20 sparrow sightings were in January.

Therefore the number of sightings of these three bird species in January was

$\frac{2}{3}(30)+\frac{1}{2}(12)+\frac{1}{4}(20)$, or 31, which accounted for $\frac{31}{62}$, or $\frac{1}{2}$, of the total number of

sightings of these three bird species in the winter. Thus the correct answer is **Choice C.**

This explanation uses the following strategies.
Strategy 1: Translate from Words to an Arithmetic or Algebraic Representation
Strategy 4: Translate from a Figure to an Arithmetic or Algebraic Representation

23. For which of the following bird species is the standard deviation of the numbers of sightings shown for the four seasons least?

   (A) Cardinal

   (B) Junco

   (C) Robin

   (D) Sparrow

   (E) Wren

Explanation

Recall that the standard deviation of the numbers in a list is a measure of the spread of the numbers about the mean of the numbers. The standard deviation is directly related to the differences $|x - m|$ between the mean m and each number x in the list. The smaller the differences, the smaller the standard deviation. Thus to answer the question, look at the values of $|x - m|$ for each of the five bird species in the answer choices and determine which species has the smallest values.

   Choice A, Cardinal. For cardinals, the numbers of sightings are 30, 18, 11, and 20. The mean is approximately 20. Therefore the differences between the mean and the four numbers in the list are approximately 10, 2, 9, and 0.

   Choice B, Junco. For juncos, the numbers of sightings are 12, 0, 0, and 6. The mean is approximately 5. Therefore the differences between the mean and the four numbers in the list are approximately 7, 5, 5, and 1.

   Choice C, Robin. For robins, the numbers of sightings are 6, 12, 28, and 18. The mean is 16, and the differences between the mean and the four numbers in the list are 10, 4, 12, and 2.

   Choice D, Sparrow. For sparrows, the numbers of sightings are 20, 19, 23, and 22. The mean is 21, and the differences between the mean and the four numbers in the list are 1, 2, 2, and 1.

   Choice E, Wren. For wrens, the numbers of sightings are 0, 18, 30, and 12. The mean is 15, and the differences between the mean and the four numbers in the list are 15, 3, 15, and 3.

   Consider how consistently small the differences are for the numbers of sightings of sparrows as compared to the differences for the other four species. From this you can judge that the numbers of sightings of sparrows has the least standard deviation. Thus the correct answer is **Choice D**.

This explanation uses the following strategies.

Strategy 4: Translate from a Figure to an Arithmetic or Algebraic Representation
Strategy 9: Estimate

24. Which of the following is closest to the average (arithmetic mean) number of cardinal sightings for the 4 seasons?

    (A) 12

    (B) 14

    (C) 16

    (D) 18

    (E) 20

Explanation

The average (arithmetic mean) number of cardinal sightings for the 4 seasons

is $\dfrac{30+18+11+20}{4} = \dfrac{79}{4}$, or 19.75. Of the answer choices given, 20 is closest to 19.75.

Thus the correct answer is **Choice E.**

This explanation uses the following strategies.
Strategy 4: Translate from a Figure to an Arithmetic or Algebraic Representation
Strategy 9: Estimate

---

25. By what percent did the number of wren sightings increase from spring to summer?

    Give your answer to the nearest whole percent.

    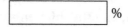 %

Explanation

From spring to summer, the number of wren sightings increased from 18 to 30.

Therefore the percent increase was $\left(\dfrac{30-18}{18}\right)(100\%)$, or $66.\overline{6}\%$. To the nearest whole

percent, the percent increase was 67%. Thus the correct answer is **67**.

This explanation uses the following strategy.
Strategy 4: Translate from a Figure to an Arithmetic or Algebraic Representation

Appendix A

GRE® Math Review

Your goals for this material

⇨ Review the math topics likely to appear on the *GRE®* Quantitative Reasoning measure
⇨ Study examples with worked-out solutions
⇨ Test your skills with practice exercises

This Math Review will familiarize you with the mathematical skills and concepts that are important to understand in order to solve problems and to reason quantitatively on the Quantitative Reasoning measure of the GRE revised General Test. The following material includes many definitions, properties, and examples, as well as a set of exercises (with answers) at the end of each review section. Note, however, that this review is not intended to be all-inclusive—there may be some concepts on the test that are not explicitly presented in this review. Also, if any topics in this review seem especially unfamiliar or are covered too briefly, we encourage you to consult appropriate mathematics texts for a more detailed treatment.

The Math Review covers the following topics:

1. Arithmetic
1.1   Integers
1.2   Fractions
1.3   Exponents and Roots
1.4   Decimals
1.5   Real Numbers
1.6   Ratio
1.7   Percent

2. Algebra
2.1   Operations with Algebraic Expressions
2.2   Rules of Exponents
2.3   Solving Linear Equations
2.4   Solving Quadratic Equations
2.5   Solving Linear Inequalities
2.6   Functions
2.7   Applications
2.8   Coordinate Geometry
2.9   Graphs of Functions

3. Geometry
3.1   Lines and Angles
3.2   Polygons
3.3   Triangles
3.4   Quadrilaterals
3.5   Circles
3.6   Three-dimensional Figures

4. Data Analysis
4.1   Graphical Methods for Describing Data
4.2   Numerical Methods for Describing Data
4.3   Counting Methods
4.4   Probability
4.5   Distributions of Data, Random Variables, and Probability Distributions
4.6   Data Interpretation Examples

1. ARITHMETIC

The review of arithmetic begins with integers, fractions, and decimals and progresses to the set of real numbers. The basic arithmetic operations of addition, subtraction, multiplication, and division are discussed, along with exponents and roots. The section ends with the concepts of ratio and percent.

1.1 Integers

The **integers** are the numbers 1, 2, 3, and so on, together with their negatives, $-1, -2, -3, \ldots$, and 0. Thus, the set of integers is $\{\ldots, -3, -2, -1, 0, 1, 2, 3, \ldots\}$.

The positive integers are greater than 0, the negative integers are less than 0, and 0 is neither positive nor negative. When integers are added, subtracted, or multiplied, the result is always an integer; division of integers is addressed below. The many elementary number facts for these operations, such as $7 + 8 = 15$, $78 - 87 = -9$, $7 - (-18) = 25$, and $(7)(8) = 56$, should be familiar to you; they are not reviewed here. Here are some general facts regarding multiplication of integers.

- The product of two positive integers is a positive integer.
- The product of two negative integers is a positive integer.
- The product of a positive integer and a negative integer is a negative integer.

When integers are multiplied, each of the multiplied integers is called a **factor** or **divisor** of the resulting product. For example, $(2)(3)(10) = 60$, so 2, 3, and 10 are factors of 60. The integers 4, 15, 5, and 12 are also factors of 60, since $(4)(15) = 60$ and $(5)(12) = 60$. The positive factors of 60 are 1, 2, 3, 4, 5, 6, 10, 12, 15, 20, 30, and 60. The negatives of these integers are also factors of 60, since, for example, $(-2)(-30) = 60$. There are no other factors of 60. We say that 60 is a **multiple** of each of its factors and that 60 is **divisible** by each of its divisors. Here are some more examples of factors and multiples.

- The positive factors of 100 are 1, 2, 4, 5, 10, 20, 25, 50, and 100.
- 25 is a multiple of only six integers: 1, 5, 25, and their negatives.
- The list of positive multiples of 25 has no end: 25, 50, 75, 100, 125, 150, etc.; likewise, every nonzero integer has infinitely many multiples.
- 1 is a factor of every integer; 1 is not a multiple of any integer except 1 and -1.
- 0 is a multiple of every integer; 0 is not a factor of any integer except 0.

The **least common multiple** of two nonzero integers a and b is the least positive integer that is a multiple of both a and b. For example, the least common multiple of 30 and 75 is 150. This is because the positive multiples of 30 are 30, 60, 90, 120, 150, 180, 210, 240, 270, 300, etc., and the positive multiples of 75 are 75, 150, 225, 300, 375, 450, etc. Thus, the *common* positive multiples of 30 and 75 are 150, 300, 450, etc., and the least of these is 150.

The **greatest common divisor** (or **greatest common factor**) of two nonzero integers a and b is the greatest positive integer that is a divisor of both a and b. For example, the greatest common divisor of 30 and 75 is 15. This is because the positive divisors of 30 are 1, 2, 3, 5, 6, 10, 15, and 30, and the positive divisors of 75 are 1, 3, 5, 15, 25, and 75. Thus, the *common* positive divisors of 30 and 75 are 1, 3, 5, and 15, and the greatest of these is 15.

When an integer a is divided by an integer b, where b is a divisor of a, the result is always a divisor of a. For example, when 60 is divided by 6 (one of its divisors), the result is 10, which is another divisor of 60. If b is *not* a divisor of a, then the result can be viewed in three different ways. The result can be viewed as a fraction or as a decimal, both of which are discussed later, or the result can be viewed as a **quotient** with a **remainder**, where both are integers. Each view is useful, depending on the context. Fractions and decimals are useful when the result must be viewed as a single number, while **quotients** with **remainders** are useful for describing the result in terms of integers only.

Regarding quotients with remainders, consider two positive integers a and b for which b is *not* a divisor of a; for example, the integers 19 and 7. When 19 is divided by 7, the result is greater than 2, since $(2)(7) < 19$, but less than 3, since $19 < (3)(7)$. Because 19 is 5 more than $(2)(7)$, we say that the result of 19 divided by 7 is the quotient 2 with remainder 5, or simply "2 remainder 5." In general, when a positive integer a is divided by a positive integer b, you first find the greatest multiple of b that is less than or equal to a. That multiple of b can be expressed as the product qb, where q is the quotient. Then the remainder is equal to a minus that multiple of b, or $r = a - qb$, where r is the remainder. The remainder is always greater than or equal to 0 and less than b.

Here are examples that illustrate a few different cases of division resulting in a quotient and remainder.

- 100 divided by 45 is 2 remainder 10, since the greatest multiple of 45 that's less than or equal to 100 is $(2)(45)$, or 90, which is 10 less than 100.
- 24 divided by 4 is 6 remainder 0, since the greatest multiple of 4 that's less than or equal to 24 is 24 itself, which is 0 less than 24. In general, the remainder is 0 if and only if a is divisible by b.
- 6 divided by 24 is 0 remainder 6, since the greatest multiple of 24 that's less than or equal to 6 is $(0)(24)$, or 0, which is 6 less than 6.

Here are some other examples.

- 100 divided by 3 is 33 remainder 1, since $100 = (33)(3) + 1$.
- 100 divided by 25 is 4 remainder 0, since $100 = (4)(25) + 0$.
- 80 divided by 100 is 0 remainder 80, since $80 = (0)(100) + 80$.
- When you divide 100 by 2, the remainder is 0.
- When you divide 99 by 2, the remainder is 1.

If an integer is divisible by 2, it is called an **even integer**; otherwise it is an **odd integer**. Note that when a positive odd integer is divided by 2, the remainder is always 1. The set of even integers is $\{\ldots, -6, -4, -2, 0, 2, 4, 6, \ldots\}$, and the set of odd integers is $\{\ldots, -5, -3, -1, 1, 3, 5, \ldots\}$. There are several useful facts regarding the sum and product of even and odd integers.

- The sum of two even integers is an even integer.
- The sum of two odd integers is an even integer.
- The sum of an even integer and an odd integer is an odd integer.
- The product of two even integers is an even integer.
- The product of two odd integers is an odd integer.
- The product of an even integer and an odd integer is an even integer.

A **prime number** is an integer greater than 1 that has only two positive divisors: 1 and itself. The first ten prime numbers are 2, 3, 5, 7, 11, 13, 17, 19, 23, and 29. The integer 14 is not a prime number, since it has four positive divisors: 1, 2, 7, and 14. The integer 1 is not a prime number, and the integer 2 is the only prime number that is even.

Every integer greater than 1 either is a prime number or can be uniquely expressed as a product of factors that are prime numbers, or **prime divisors**. Such an expression is called a **prime factorization**. Here are several examples of prime factorizations.

$$12 = (2)(2)(3) = (2^2)(3)$$
$$14 = (2)(7)$$
$$81 = (3)(3)(3)(3) = 3^4$$
$$338 = (2)(13)(13) = (2)(13^2)$$
$$800 = (2)(2)(2)(2)(2)(5)(5) = (2^5)(5^2)$$
$$1,155 = (3)(5)(7)(11)$$

An integer greater than 1 that is not a prime number is called a **composite number**. The first ten composite numbers are 4, 6, 8, 9, 10, 12, 14, 15, 16, and 18.

1.2 Fractions

A **fraction** is a number of the form $\frac{a}{b}$, where a and b are integers and $b \neq 0$. The integer a is called the **numerator** of the fraction, and b is called the **denominator**. For example, $\frac{-7}{5}$ is a fraction in which -7 is the numerator and 5 is the denominator. Such numbers are also called **rational numbers**.

If both the numerator a and denominator b are multiplied by the same nonzero integer, the resulting fraction will be equivalent to $\frac{a}{b}$. For example,

$$\frac{-7}{5} = \frac{(-7)(4)}{(5)(4)} = \frac{-28}{20}$$

$$\frac{-7}{5} = \frac{(-7)(-1)}{(5)(-1)} = \frac{7}{-5}$$

A fraction with a negative sign in either the numerator or denominator can be written with the negative sign in front of the fraction; for example, $\frac{-7}{5} = \frac{7}{-5} = -\frac{7}{5}$.

If both the numerator and denominator have a common factor, then the numerator and denominator can be factored and reduced to an equivalent fraction. For example,

$$\frac{40}{72} = \frac{(8)(5)}{(8)(9)} = \frac{5}{9}$$

To add two fractions with the same denominator, you add the numerators and keep the same denominator. For example,

$$-\frac{8}{11} + \frac{5}{11} = \frac{-8+5}{11} = \frac{-3}{11} = -\frac{3}{11}$$

To add two fractions with different denominators, first find a **common denominator**, which is a common multiple of the two denominators. Then convert both fractions to equivalent fractions with the same denominator. Finally, add the numerators and keep the common denominator. For example, to add the fractions $\frac{1}{3}$ and $-\frac{2}{5}$, use the common denominator 15:

$$\frac{1}{3}+\frac{-2}{5}=\left(\frac{1}{3}\right)\left(\frac{5}{5}\right)+\left(\frac{-2}{5}\right)\left(\frac{3}{3}\right)=\frac{5}{15}+\frac{-6}{15}=\frac{5+(-6)}{15}=-\frac{1}{15}$$

The same method applies to subtraction of fractions.

To multiply two fractions, multiply the two numerators and multiply the two denominators. For example,

$$\left(\frac{10}{7}\right)\left(\frac{-1}{3}\right)=\frac{(10)(-1)}{(7)(3)}=\frac{-10}{21}=-\frac{10}{21}$$

$$\left(\frac{8}{3}\right)\left(\frac{7}{3}\right)=\frac{56}{9}$$

To divide one fraction by another, first **invert** the second fraction—that is, find its **reciprocal**—then multiply the first fraction by the inverted fraction. For example,

$$\frac{17}{8}\div\frac{3}{4}=\left(\frac{17}{8}\right)\left(\frac{4}{3}\right)=\left(\frac{4}{8}\right)\left(\frac{17}{3}\right)=\left(\frac{1}{2}\right)\left(\frac{17}{3}\right)=\frac{17}{6}$$

$$\frac{\frac{3}{10}}{\frac{7}{13}}=\left(\frac{3}{10}\right)\left(\frac{13}{7}\right)=\frac{39}{70}$$

An expression such as $4\frac{3}{8}$ is called a **mixed number**. It consists of an integer part and a fraction part; the mixed number $4\frac{3}{8}$ means $4+\frac{3}{8}$. To convert a mixed number to an ordinary fraction, convert the integer part to an equivalent fraction and add it to the fraction part. For example,

$$4\frac{3}{8}=4+\frac{3}{8}=\left(\frac{4}{1}\right)\left(\frac{8}{8}\right)+\frac{3}{8}=\frac{32}{8}+\frac{3}{8}=\frac{35}{8}$$

Note that numbers of the form $\frac{a}{b}$, where either a or b is not an integer and $b\neq 0$, are fractional expressions that can be manipulated just like fractions. For example, the numbers $\frac{\pi}{2}$ and $\frac{\pi}{3}$ can be added together as follows.

$$\frac{\pi}{2}+\frac{\pi}{3}=\left(\frac{\pi}{2}\right)\left(\frac{3}{3}\right)+\left(\frac{\pi}{3}\right)\left(\frac{2}{2}\right)=\frac{3\pi}{6}+\frac{2\pi}{6}=\frac{5\pi}{6}$$

And the number $\dfrac{\frac{1}{\sqrt{2}}}{\frac{3}{\sqrt{5}}}$ can be simplified as follows.

$$\frac{\frac{1}{\sqrt{2}}}{\frac{3}{\sqrt{5}}} = \left(\frac{1}{\sqrt{2}}\right)\left(\frac{\sqrt{5}}{3}\right) = \frac{\sqrt{5}}{3\sqrt{2}}$$

1.3 Exponents and Roots

Exponents are used to denote the repeated multiplication of a number by itself; for example, $3^4 = (3)(3)(3)(3) = 81$ and $5^3 = (5)(5)(5) = 125$. In the expression 3^4, 3 is called the **base**, 4 is called the **exponent**, and we read the expression as "3 to the fourth power." So 5 to the third power is 125. When the exponent is 2, we call the process **squaring**. Thus, 6 squared is 36, $6^2 = (6)(6) = 36$, and 7 squared is 49, $7^2 = (7)(7) = 49$.

When negative numbers are raised to powers, the result may be positive or negative. For example, $(-3)^2 = (-3)(-3) = 9$, while $(-3)^5 = (-3)(-3)(-3)(-3)(-3) = -243$. A negative number raised to an even power is always positive, and a negative number raised to an odd power is always negative. Note that without the parentheses, the expression -3^2 means "the negative of '3 squared'"; that is, the exponent is applied before the negative sign. So $(-3)^2 = 9$, but $-3^2 = -9$.

Exponents can also be negative or zero; such exponents are defined as follows.

- For all nonzero numbers a, $a^0 = 1$. The expression 0^0 is undefined.

- For all nonzero numbers a, $a^{-1} = \dfrac{1}{a}$, $a^{-2} = \dfrac{1}{a^2}$, $a^{-3} = \dfrac{1}{a^3}$, etc. Note that
$(a)(a^{-1}) = (a)\left(\dfrac{1}{a}\right) = 1$.

A **square root** of a nonnegative number n is a number r such that $r^2 = n$. For example, 4 is a square root of 16 because $4^2 = 16$. Another square root of 16 is -4, since $(-4)^2 = 16$. All positive numbers have two square roots, one positive and one negative. The only square root of 0 is 0. The symbol $\sqrt{n}$ is used to denote the *nonnegative* square root of the nonnegative number n. Therefore, $\sqrt{100} = 10$, $-\sqrt{100} = -10$, and $\sqrt{0} = 0$. Square roots of negative numbers are not defined in the real number system.

Here are some important rules regarding operations with square roots, where $a > 0$ and $b > 0$.

Rule	Examples	
$\left(\sqrt{a}\right)^2 = a$	$\left(\sqrt{3}\right)^2 = 3$	$\left(\sqrt{\pi}\right)^2 = \pi$
$\sqrt{a^2} = a$	$\sqrt{4} = 2$	$\sqrt{\pi^2} = \pi$
$\sqrt{a}\sqrt{b} = \sqrt{ab}$	$\sqrt{3}\sqrt{10} = \sqrt{30}$	$\sqrt{24} = \sqrt{4}\sqrt{6} = 2\sqrt{6}$
$\dfrac{\sqrt{a}}{\sqrt{b}} = \sqrt{\dfrac{a}{b}}$	$\dfrac{\sqrt{5}}{\sqrt{15}} = \sqrt{\dfrac{5}{15}} = \sqrt{\dfrac{1}{3}}$	$\dfrac{\sqrt{18}}{\sqrt{2}} = \sqrt{\dfrac{18}{2}} = \sqrt{9} = 3$

A square root is a root of order 2. Higher-order roots of a positive number n are defined similarly. For orders 3 and 4, the **cube root** $\sqrt[3]{n}$ and **fourth root** $\sqrt[4]{n}$ represent numbers such that when they are raised to the powers 3 and 4, respectively, the result is n. These roots obey rules similar to those above (but with the exponent 2 replaced by 3 or 4 in the first two rules). There are some notable differences between odd-order roots and even-order roots (in the real number system):

- For odd-order roots, there is *exactly one* root for *every* number n, even when n is negative.
- For even-order roots, there are *exactly two* roots for every *positive* number n and *no* roots for any *negative* number n.

For example, 8 has exactly one cube root, $\sqrt[3]{8} = 2$, but 8 has two fourth roots: $\sqrt[4]{8}$ and $-\sqrt[4]{8}$; and −8 has exactly one cube root, $\sqrt[3]{-8} = -2$, but −8 has no fourth root, since it is negative.

1.4 Decimals

The decimal number system is based on representing numbers using powers of 10. The place value of each digit corresponds to a power of 10. For example, the digits of the number $7{,}532.418$ have the following place values.

Thousands		Hundreds	Tens	Ones or Units		Tenths	Hundredths	Thousandths
7	,	5	3	2	.	4	1	8

That is,

$$7{,}532.418 = 7(1{,}000) + 5(100) + 3(10) + 2(1) + 4\left(\frac{1}{10}\right) + 1\left(\frac{1}{100}\right) + 8\left(\frac{1}{1{,}000}\right)$$

$$= 7(10^3) + 5(10^2) + 3(10^1) + 2(10^0) + 4(10^{-1}) + 1(10^{-2}) + 8(10^{-3})$$

If there are a finite number of digits to the right of the decimal point, converting a decimal to an equivalent fraction with integers in the numerator and denominator is a straightforward process. Since each place value is a power of 10, every decimal can be converted to an integer divided by a power of 10. For example,

$$2.3 = 2 + \frac{3}{10} = \frac{23}{10}$$

$$90.17 = 90 + \frac{17}{100} = \frac{9{,}000 + 17}{100} = \frac{9{,}017}{100}$$

$$0.612 = \frac{612}{1{,}000} = \frac{153}{250}$$

Conversely, every fraction with integers in the numerator and denominator can be converted to an equivalent decimal by dividing the numerator by the denominator using long division (which is not in this review). The decimal that results from the long division will either **terminate**, as in $\frac{1}{4} = 0.25$ and $\frac{52}{25} = 2.08$, or the decimal will **repeat** without end, as in $\frac{1}{9} = 0.111\ldots$, $\frac{1}{22} = 0.0454545\ldots$, and $\frac{25}{12} = 2.08333\ldots$. One way to indicate the repeating part of a decimal that repeats without end is to use a bar over the digits that repeat. Here are some examples of fractions converted to decimals.

$$\frac{3}{8} = 0.375$$

$$\frac{259}{40} = 6 + \frac{19}{40} = 6.475$$

$$-\frac{1}{3} = -0.\overline{3}$$

$$\frac{15}{14} = 1.0\overline{714285}$$

Every fraction with integers in the numerator and denominator is equivalent to a decimal that terminates or repeats. That is, every rational number can be expressed as a terminating or repeating decimal. The converse is also true; that is, every terminating or repeating decimal represents a rational number.

Not all decimals are terminating or repeating; for instance, the decimal that is equivalent to $\sqrt{2}$ is $1.41421356237\ldots$, and it can be shown that this decimal does not terminate or repeat. Another example is $0.010110111011110111110\ldots$, which has groups of consecutive 1's separated by a 0, where the number of 1's in each successive group increases by one. Since these two decimals do not terminate or repeat, they are not rational numbers. Such numbers are called **irrational numbers**.

1.5 Real Numbers

The set of **real numbers** consists of all rational numbers and all irrational numbers. The real numbers include all integers, fractions, and decimals. The set of real numbers can be represented by a number line called the **real number line**.

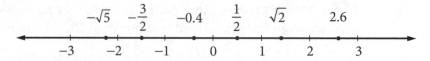

Every real number corresponds to a point on the number line, and every point on the number line corresponds to a real number. On the number line, all numbers to the left of 0 are negative and all numbers to the right of 0 are positive. Only the number 0 is neither negative nor positive.

A real number x is **less than** a real number y if x is to the left of y on the number line, which is written as $x < y$. A real number y is **greater than** x if y is to the right of x on the number line, which is written as $y > x$. For example,

$$-\sqrt{5} < -2$$

$$\frac{1}{2} > 0$$

$$1 < \sqrt{2} < 2$$

To say that a real number x is between 2 and 3 on the number line means that $x > 2$ and $x < 3$, which can also be written as the double inequality $2 < x < 3$. The set of all real numbers that are between 2 and 3 is called an **interval**, and the double inequality $2 < x < 3$ is often used to represent that interval. Note that the endpoints of the interval, 2 and 3, are not included in the interval. Sometimes one or both of the endpoints are to be included in an interval. The following inequalities represent four types of intervals, depending on whether the endpoints are included.

$$2 < x < 3$$

$$2 \leq x < 3$$

$$2 < x \leq 3$$

$$2 \leq x \leq 3$$

There are also four types of intervals with only one endpoint, each of which consists of all real numbers to the right or to the left of the endpoint, perhaps including the endpoint. The following inequalities represent these types of intervals.

$$x < 4$$

$$x \leq 4$$

$$x > 4$$

$$x \geq 4$$

The entire real number line is also considered to be an interval.

The distance between a number x and 0 on the number line is called the **absolute value** of x, written as $|x|$. Therefore, $|3| = 3$ and $|-3| = 3$ because each of the numbers 3 and -3 is a distance of 3 from 0. Note that if x is positive, then $|x| = x$; if x is negative, then $|x| = -x$; and lastly, $|0| = 0$. It follows that the absolute value of any nonzero number is positive. Here are some examples.

$$\left|\sqrt{5}\right| = \sqrt{5}$$

$$\left|-23\right| = -(-23) = 23$$

$$\left|-10.2\right| = 10.2$$

There are several general properties of real numbers that are used frequently. If a, b, and c are real numbers, then

- $a + b = b + a$ and $ab = ba$.
  For example, $8 + 2 = 2 + 8 = 10$ and $(-3)(17) = (17)(-3) = -51$.
- $(a + b) + c = a + (b + c)$ and $(ab)c = a(bc)$.
  For example, $(7 + 3) + 8 = 7 + (3 + 8) = 18$ and $\left(7\sqrt{2}\right)\sqrt{2} = 7\left(\sqrt{2}\sqrt{2}\right) = (7)(2) = 14$.

- $a(b + c) = ab + ac$
  For example, $5(3 + 16) = (5)(3) + (5)(16) = 95$.
- $a + 0 = a$, $(a)(0) = 0$, and $(a)(1) = a$.
- If $ab = 0$, then $a = 0$ or $b = 0$, or both.
  For example, if $-2b = 0$, then $b = 0$.
- Division by 0 is not defined; for example, $5 \div 0$, $\dfrac{-7}{0}$, and $\dfrac{0}{0}$ are undefined.
- If both a and b are positive, then both $a + b$ and ab are positive.
- If both a and b are negative, then $a + b$ is negative and ab is positive.
- If a is positive and b is negative, then ab is negative.
- $|a + b| \leq |a| + |b|$. This is known as the **triangle inequality**.
  For example, if $a = 5$ and $b = -2$, then $|5 + (-2)| = |5 - 2| = |3| = 3$ and $|5| + |-2| = 5 + 2 = 7$. Therefore, $|5 + (-2)| \leq |5| + |-2|$.
- $|a||b| = |ab|$. For example, $|5||-2| = |(5)(-2)| = |-10| = 10$.
- If $a > 1$, then $a^2 > a$. If $0 < b < 1$, then $b^2 < b$.

  For example, $5^2 = 25 > 5$, but $\left(\dfrac{1}{5}\right)^2 = \dfrac{1}{25} < \dfrac{1}{5}$.

1.6 Ratio

The **ratio** of one quantity to another is a way to express their relative sizes, often in the form of a fraction, where the first quantity is the numerator and the second quantity is the denominator. Thus, if s and t are positive quantities, then the ratio of s to t can be written as the fraction $\dfrac{s}{t}$. The notation "s to t" or "$s{:}t$" is also used to express this ratio. For example, if there are 2 apples and 3 oranges in a basket, we can say that the ratio of the number of apples to the number of oranges is $\dfrac{2}{3}$ or that it is 2 to 3 or that it is 2:3.

Like fractions, ratios can be reduced to lowest terms. For example, if there are 8 apples and 12 oranges in a basket, then the ratio of the numbers of apples to oranges is still 2 to 3. Similarly, the ratio 9 to 12 is equivalent to the ratio 3 to 4.

If three or more positive quantities are being considered, say r, s, and t, then their relative sizes can also be expressed as a ratio with the notation "r to s to t." For example, if there are 5 apples, 30 pears, and 20 oranges in a basket, then the ratio of the numbers of apples to pears to oranges is 5 to 30 to 20. This ratio can be reduced to 1 to 6 to 4 by dividing each number by the greatest common divisor of 5, 30, and 20, which is 5.

A **proportion** is an equation relating two ratios; for example, $\dfrac{9}{12} = \dfrac{3}{4}$. To solve a problem involving ratios, you can often write a proportion and solve it by **cross multiplication**.

Example 1.6.1: To find a number x so that the ratio of x to 49 is the same as the ratio of 3 to 21, you can write

$$\frac{x}{49} = \frac{3}{21}$$

Then cross multiply to get $21x = (3)(49)$, and solve for x to get $x = \dfrac{(3)(49)}{21} = 7$.

1.7 Percent

The term **percent** means *per hundred*, or *hundredths*. Percents are ratios that are often used to represent *parts of a whole*, where the whole is considered as having 100 parts.

- 1 percent means 1 part out of 100 parts, or $\frac{1}{100}$.

- 32 percent means 32 parts out of 100 parts, or $\frac{32}{100}$.

- 50 percent means 50 parts out of 100 parts, or $\frac{1}{2}$.

Note that the *part* is the numerator of the ratio and the *whole* is the denominator. Percents are often written with the % symbol; fractional and decimal equivalents are often used as well but without the % symbol, as follows.

$$1\% = \frac{1}{100} = 0.01$$

$$100\% = \frac{100}{100} = 1$$

$$32\% = \frac{32}{100} = 0.32$$

$$50\% = \frac{50}{100} = 0.5$$

$$0.3\% = \frac{0.3}{100} = 0.003$$

Be careful not to confuse 0.01 with 0.01%. The percent symbol matters. For example, $0.01 = 1\%$ but $0.01\% = \frac{0.01}{100} = 0.0001$.

- To compute a *percent*, given the *part* and the *whole*, divide the part by the whole. The result will be the decimal equivalent, so multiply the result by 100 to convert to percent.

   Example 1.7.1: If the whole is 20 and the part is 13, you can find the percent as follows.

   $$\frac{part}{whole} = \frac{13}{20} = 0.65 = 65\%$$

   Example 1.7.2: What percent of 150 is 12.9?

   Solution: Here the whole is 150 and the part is 12.9.

   $$\frac{part}{whole} = \frac{12.9}{150} = 0.086 = 8.6\%$$

- To find the *part* that is a certain *percent* of a *whole*, you can either multiply the *whole* by the decimal equivalent of the percent or set up a proportion to find the part.

Example 1.7.3: To find 30% of 350, multiply 350 by the decimal equivalent of 30%, or 0.3, as follows.

$$x = (350)(0.3) = 105$$

To use a proportion, you need to find the number of parts of 350 that yields the same ratio as 30 out of 100 parts. You want a number x that satisfies the proportion

$$\frac{part}{whole} = \frac{30}{100}$$

$$\frac{x}{350} = \frac{30}{100}$$

Solving for x yields $x = \frac{(30)(350)}{100} = 105$, so 30% of 350 is 105.

- Given the *percent* and the *part*, you can calculate the *whole*. To do this you can either use the decimal equivalent of the percent or you can set up a proportion and solve it.

Example 1.7.4: 15 is 60% of what number?

Solution: Use the decimal equivalent of 60%. Because 60% of some number z is 15, multiply z by the decimal equivalent of 60%, or 0.6.

$$0.6z = 15$$

Now solve for z by dividing both sides of the equation by 0.6 as follows.

$$z = \frac{15}{0.6} = 25$$

Using a proportion, look for a number z such that

$$\frac{part}{whole} = \frac{60}{100}$$

$$\frac{15}{z} = \frac{60}{100}$$

Hence, $60z = (15)(100)$, and therefore, $z = \frac{(15)(100)}{60} = \frac{1,500}{60} = 25$. That is, 15 is 60% of 25.

Although the discussion about percent so far assumes a context of a *part* and a *whole*, it is not necessary that the part be less than the whole. In general, the whole is called the **base** of the percent. When the numerator of a percent is greater than the base, the percent is greater than 100%. For example, 15 is 300% of 5, since

$$\frac{15}{5} = \frac{300}{100}$$

and 250% of 16 is $\left(\frac{250}{100}\right)(16) = (2.5)(16) = 40$. Note that the decimal equivalent of 250% is 2.5.

It is also not necessary for the part to be related to the whole at all, as in the question, "a teacher's salary is what percent of a banker's salary?"

When a quantity changes from an initial positive amount to another positive amount, for example, an employee's salary that is raised, you can compute the amount of change as a percent of the initial amount. This is called **percent change**. If a quantity increases from 600 to 750, then the **percent increase** is found by dividing the amount of increase, 150, by the base, 600, which is the initial number given:

$$\frac{amount\ of\ increase}{base} = \frac{750 - 600}{600} = \frac{150}{600} = \frac{25}{100} = 0.25 = 25\%$$

We say the percent increase is 25%. Sometimes this computation is written as

$$\left(\frac{750 - 600}{600}\right)(100\%) = \left(\frac{150}{600}\right)(100\%) = 25\%$$

If a quantity doubles in size, then the percent increase is 100%. For example, if a quantity changes from 150 to 300, then the percent increase is

$$\frac{change}{base} = \frac{300 - 150}{150} = \frac{150}{150} = 100\%$$

If a quantity decreases from 500 to 400, calculate the **percent decrease** as follows.

$$\frac{change}{base} = \frac{500 - 400}{500} = \frac{100}{500} = \frac{20}{100} = 0.20 = 20\%$$

The quantity decreased by 20%.

When computing a percent *increase*, the base is the *smaller* number. When computing a percent *decrease*, the base is the *larger* number. In either case, the base is the initial number, before the change.

> **Example 1.7.5:** An investment in a mutual fund increased by 12% in a single day. If the value of the investment before the increase was $1,300, what was the value after the increase?
>
> **Solution:** The percent increase is 12%. Therefore, the value of the increase is 12% of $1,300, or, using the decimal equivalent, the increase is $(0.12)(\$1,300) = \$156$. Thus, the value of the investment after the change is
>
> $$\$1,300 + \$156 = \$1,456$$
>
> Because the final result is the sum of the initial investment—100% of $1,300—and the increase—12% of $1,300—the final result is $100\% + 12\% = 112\%$ of $1,300.
>
> Thus, another way to get the final result is to multiply the value of the investment by the decimal equivalent of 112%, which is 1.12:
>
> $$(\$1,300)(1.12) = \$1,456$$

A quantity may have several successive percent changes. The base of each successive percent change is the result of the preceding percent change.

Example 1.7.6: The monthly enrollment at a preschool decreased by 8% during one month and increased by 6% during the next month. What was the cumulative percent change for the two months?

Solution: If E is the enrollment before the first month, then the enrollment as a result of the 8% decrease can be found by multiplying the base E by the decimal equivalent of $100\% - 8\% = 92\%$, which is 0.92:

$$0.92E$$

The enrollment as a result of the second percent change—the 6% increase—can be found by multiplying the *new* base $0.92E$ by the decimal equivalent of $100\% + 6\% = 106\%$, which is 1.06:

$$(1.06)(0.92)E = 0.9752E$$

The percent equivalent of 0.9752 is 97.52%, which is 2.48% less than 100%. Thus, the cumulative percent change in the enrollment for the two months is a 2.48% decrease.

ARITHMETIC EXERCISES

1. Evaluate the following.

   (a) $15 - (6 - 4)(-2)$
   (b) $(2 - 17) \div 5$
   (c) $(60 \div 12) - (-7 + 4)$
   (d) $(3)^4 - (-2)^3$

   (e) $(-5)(-3) - 15$
   (f) $(-2)^4(15 - 18)^4$
   (g) $(20 \div 5)^2(-2 + 6)^3$
   (h) $(-85)(0) - (-17)(3)$

2. Evaluate the following.

   (a) $\dfrac{1}{2} - \dfrac{1}{3} + \dfrac{1}{12}$

   (b) $\left(\dfrac{3}{4} + \dfrac{1}{7}\right)\left(\dfrac{-2}{5}\right)$

   (c) $\left(\dfrac{7}{8} - \dfrac{4}{5}\right)^2$

   (d) $\left(\dfrac{3}{-8}\right) \div \left(\dfrac{27}{32}\right)$

3. Which of the integers 312, 98, 112, and 144 are divisible by 8 ?

4. (a) What is the prime factorization of 372?
   (b) What are the positive divisors of 372?

5. (a) What are the prime divisors of 100?
   (b) What are the prime divisors of 144?

6. Which of the integers 2, 9, 19, 29, 30, 37, 45, 49, 51, 83, 90, and 91 are prime numbers?

7. What is the prime factorization of 585 ?

8. Which of the following statements are true?

(a) $-5 < 3.1$

(b) $\sqrt{16} = 4$

(c) $7 \div 0 = 0$

(d) $0 < \left| -\dfrac{1}{7} \right|$

(e) $0.3 < \dfrac{1}{3}$

(f) $(-1)^{87} = -1$

(g) $\sqrt{(-3)^2} < 0$

(h) $\dfrac{21}{28} = \dfrac{3}{4}$

(i) $-|-23| = 23$

(j) $\dfrac{1}{2} > \dfrac{1}{17}$

(k) $(59)^3(59)^2 = 59^6$

(l) $-\sqrt{25} < -4$

9. Find the following.

(a) 40% of 15

(b) 150% of 48

(c) 0.6% of 800

(d) 15 is 30% of which number?

(e) 11 is what percent of 55?

10. If a person's salary increased from \$200 per week to \$234 per week, what was the percent increase in the person's salary?

11. If an athlete's weight decreased from 160 pounds to 152 pounds, what was the percent decrease in the athlete's weight?

12. A particular stock is valued at \$40 per share. If the value increases by 20 percent and then decreases by 25 percent, what will be the value of the stock per share after the decrease?

13. If the ratio of the number of men to the number of women on a committee of 20 members is 3 to 2, how many members of the committee are women?

14. The integer a is even and the integer b is odd. For each of the following integers, indicate whether the integer is even or odd.

Integer	Even	Odd
$a + 2b$		
$2a + b$		
ab		
a^b		
$(a + b)^2$		
$a^2 - b^2$		

15. When the positive integer n is divided by 3, the remainder is 2 and when n is divided by 5, the remainder is 1. What is the least possible value of n?

ANSWERS TO ARITHMETIC EXERCISES

1. (a) 19   (e) 0
    (b) −3   (f) 1,296
    (c) 8   (g) 1,024
    (d) 89   (h) 51

2. (a) $\dfrac{1}{4}$ (c) $\dfrac{9}{1,600}$

    (b) $-\dfrac{5}{14}$ (d) $-\dfrac{4}{9}$

3. 312, 112, and 144

4. (a) $372 = (2^2)(3)(31)$
    (b) The positive divisors of 372 are 1, 2, 3, 4, 6, 12, 31, 62, 93, 124, 186, and 372.

5. (a) $100 = (2^2)(5^2)$, so the prime divisors are 2 and 5.
    (b) $144 = (2^4)(3^2)$, so the prime divisors are 2 and 3.

6. 2, 19, 29, 37, and 83

7. $585 = (3^2)(5)(13)$

8. (a) True   (g) False; $\sqrt{(-3)^2} = \sqrt{9} = 3 > 0$
    (b) True   (h) True
    (c) False; division by 0 is undefined   (i) False; $-|-23| = -23$
    (d) True   (j) True
    (e) True   (k) False; $(59)^3(59)^2 = 59^{3+2} = 59^5$
    (f) True   (l) True

9. (a) 6   (d) 50
    (b) 72   (e) 20%
    (c) 4.8

10. 17%

11. 5%

12. $36 per share

13. 8 women

14.

Integer	Even	Odd
$a + 2b$	✓	
$2a + b$		✓
ab	✓	
a^b	✓	
$(a + b)^2$		✓
$a^2 - b^2$		✓

15. 11

2. ALGEBRA

Basic algebra can be viewed as an extension of arithmetic. The main concept that distinguishes algebra from arithmetic is that of a **variable**, which is a letter that represents a quantity whose value is unknown. The letters x and y are often used as variables, although any letter can be used. Variables enable you to present a word problem in terms of unknown quantities by using algebraic expressions, equations, inequalities, and functions. This section reviews these algebraic tools and then progresses to several examples of applying them to solve real-life word problems. The section ends with coordinate geometry and graphs of functions as other important algebraic tools for solving problems.

2.1 Operations with Algebraic Expressions

An **algebraic expression** has one or more variables and can be written as a single **term** or as a sum of terms. Here are some examples of algebraic expressions.

$$2x \qquad y - \frac{1}{4} \qquad w^3z + 5z^2 - z^2 + 6 \qquad \frac{8}{n+p}$$

In the examples above, $2x$ is a single term, $y - \frac{1}{4}$ has two terms, $w^3z + 5z^2 - z^2 + 6$ has four terms, and $\frac{8}{n+p}$ has one term. In the expression $w^3z + 5z^2 - z^2 + 6$, the terms $5z^2$ and $-z^2$ are called **like terms** because they have the same variables and the corresponding variables have the same exponents. A term that has no variable is called a **constant** term. A number that is multiplied by variables is called the **coefficient** of a term. For example, in the expression $2x^2 + 7x - 5$, 2 is the coefficient of the term $2x^2$, 7 is the coefficient of the term $7x$, and -5 is a constant term.

The same rules that govern operations with numbers apply to operations with algebraic expressions. One additional rule, which helps in simplifying algebraic expressions, is that like terms can be combined by simply adding their coefficients, as the following examples show.

$$2x + 5x = 7x$$
$$w^3z + 5z^2 - z^2 + 6 = w^3z + 4z^2 + 6$$
$$3xy + 2x - xy - 3x = 2xy - x$$

A number or variable that is a factor of each term in an algebraic expression can be factored out, as the following examples show.

$$4x + 12 = 4(x + 3)$$
$$15y^2 - 9y = 3y(5y - 3)$$
$$\frac{7x^2 + 14x}{2x + 4} = \frac{7x(x+2)}{2(x+2)} = \frac{7x}{2} \text{ (where } x \neq -2, \text{ since division by 0 is not defined)}$$

To multiply two algebraic expressions, each term of the first expression is multiplied by each term of the second expression, and the results are added, as the following examples show.

$$(x + 2)(3x - 7) = x(3x) + x(-7) + 2(3x) + 2(-7)$$
$$= 3x^2 - 7x + 6x - 14$$
$$= 3x^2 - x - 14$$

A statement of equality between two algebraic expressions that is true for all possible values of the variables involved is called an **identity**. All of the preceding equality statements in this section are identities. Here are some standard identities that are useful.

$$(a + b)^2 = a^2 + 2ab + b^2$$
$$(a - b)^3 = a^3 - 3a^2b + 3ab^2 - b^3$$
$$a^2 - b^2 = (a + b)(a - b)$$

All of the identities above can be used to modify and simplify algebraic expressions. For example, the identity $a^2 - b^2 = (a + b)(a - b)$ can be used to simplify the following algebraic expression.

$$\frac{x^2 - 9}{4x - 12} = \frac{(x+3)(x-3)}{4(x-3)} = \frac{x+3}{4} \quad \text{(where } x \neq 3\text{)}$$

A statement of equality between two algebraic expressions that is true for only certain values of the variables involved is called an **equation.** The values are called the **solutions** of the equation.

The following are examples of some basic types of equations.

$$3x + 5 = -2 \quad \text{A \textbf{linear equation in one variable, } } x$$

$$x - 3y = 10 \quad \text{A \textbf{linear equation in two variables, } } x \text{ and } y$$

$$20y^2 + 6y - 17 = 0 \quad \text{A \textbf{quadratic equation in one variable, } } y$$

2.2 Rules of Exponents

In the algebraic expression x^a, where x is raised to the power a, x is called the **base** and a is called the **exponent**. For some equations involving bases and exponents, the following property is very useful: if $x^a = x^b$, then $a = b$. This is true for all positive numbers x, except $x = 1$, and for all integers a and b. For example, if $2^y = 64$, then since 64 is 2^6, you have $2^y = 2^6$, and you can conclude that $y = 6$.

Here are the basic rules of exponents, where the bases x and y are nonzero real numbers and the exponents a and b are integers.

1. $x^{-a} = \dfrac{1}{x^a}$

    Examples: $4^{-3} = \dfrac{1}{4^3} = \dfrac{1}{64}$, $x^{-10} = \dfrac{1}{x^{10}}$, and $\dfrac{1}{2^{-a}} = 2^a$

2. $(x^a)(x^b) = x^{a+b}$

    Examples: $(3^2)(3^4) = 3^{2+4} = 3^6 = 729$ and $(y^3)(y^{-1}) = y^2$

3. $\dfrac{x^a}{x^b} = x^{a-b} = \dfrac{1}{x^{b-a}}$

    Examples: $\dfrac{5^7}{5^4} = 5^{7-4} = 5^3 = 125$ and $\dfrac{t^3}{t^8} = t^{-5} = \dfrac{1}{t^5}$

4. $x^0 = 1$

    Examples: $7^0 = 1$ and $(-3)^0 = 1$. Note that 0^0 is not defined.

5. $(x^a)(y^a) = (xy)^a$

    Examples: $(2^3)(3^3) = 6^3 = 216$ and $(10z)^3 = 10^3 z^3 = 1{,}000z^3$

6. $\left(\dfrac{x}{y}\right)^a = \dfrac{x^a}{y^a}$

    Examples: $\left(\dfrac{3}{4}\right)^2 = \dfrac{3^2}{4^2} = \dfrac{9}{16}$ and $\left(\dfrac{r}{4t}\right)^3 = \dfrac{r^3}{64t^3}$

7. $(x^a)^b = x^{ab}$

    Examples: $(2^5)^2 = 2^{10} = 1{,}024$ and $(3y^6)^2 = (3^2)(y^6)^2 = 9y^{12}$

The rules above are identities that are used to simplify expressions. Sometimes algebraic expressions look like they can be simplified in similar ways, but in fact they cannot. Here are several pairs of expressions that are *commonly mistaken* to be identities.

- $x^a y^b \neq (xy)^{a+b}$
  Note that the bases are not the same.
- $(x^a)^b \neq x^a x^b$
  Instead, $(x^a)^b = x^{ab}$ and $x^a x^b = x^{a+b}$; for example, $(4^2)^3 = 4^6$ and $4^2 4^3 = 4^5$.
- $(x + y)^a \neq x^a + y^a$
  Recall that $(x + y)^2 = x^2 + 2xy + y^2$; that is, the correct expansion contains terms such as $2xy$.
- $(-x)^2 \neq -x^2$
  Instead, $(-x)^2 = x^2$. Note carefully where each minus sign appears.
- $\sqrt{x^2 + y^2} \neq x + y$
- $\dfrac{a}{x + y} \neq \dfrac{a}{x} + \dfrac{a}{y}$
  But it *is* true that $\dfrac{x+y}{a} = \dfrac{x}{a} + \dfrac{y}{a}$.

2.3 Solving Linear Equations

To **solve an equation** means to find the values of the variables that make the equation true, that is, the values that **satisfy the equation.** Two equations that have the same solutions are called **equivalent equations.** For example, $x + 1 = 2$ and $2x + 2 = 4$ are equivalent equations; both are true when $x = 1$ and are false otherwise. The general method for solving an equation is to find successively simpler equivalent equations so that the simplest equivalent equation makes the solutions obvious.

The following rules are important for producing equivalent equations.

- When the same constant is added to or subtracted from both sides of an equation, the equality is preserved and the new equation is equivalent to the original equation.
- When both sides of an equation are multiplied or divided by the same nonzero constant, the equality is preserved and the new equation is equivalent to the original equation.

A **linear equation** is an equation involving one or more variables in which each term in the equation is either a constant term or a variable multiplied by a coefficient. None of the variables are multiplied together or raised to a power greater than 1. For example, $2x + 1 = 7x$ and $10x - 9y - z = 3$ are linear equations, but $x + y^2 = 0$ and $xz = 3$ are not.

Linear Equations in One Variable

To solve a linear equation in one variable, simplify each side of the equation by combining like terms. Then use the rules for producing simpler equivalent equations.

Example 2.3.1:

$$11x - 4 - 8x = 2(x + 4) - 2x$$
$$3x - 4 = 2x + 8 - 2x \quad \text{(like terms combined)}$$
$$3x - 4 = 8 \quad \text{(simplified)}$$
$$3x - 4 + 4 = 8 + 4 \quad \text{(4 added to both sides)}$$
$$3x = 12$$
$$\frac{3x}{3} = \frac{12}{3} \quad \text{(both sides divided by 3)}$$
$$x = 4$$

You can always check your solution by substituting it into the original equation.

Note that it is possible for a linear equation to have no solutions. For example, the equation $2x + 3 = 2(7 + x)$ has no solution, since it is equivalent to the equation $3 = 14$, which is false. Also, it is possible that what looks to be a linear equation turns out to be an identity when you try to solve it. For example, $3x - 6 = -3(2 - x)$ is true for all values of x, so it is an identity.

Linear Equations in Two Variables

A linear equation in two variables, x and y, can be written in the form

$$ax + by = c$$

where a, b, and c are real numbers and a and b are not both zero. For example, $3x + 2y = 8$ is a linear equation in two variables.

A solution of such an equation is an **ordered pair** of numbers (x, y) that makes the equation true when the values of x and y are substituted into the equation. For example, both $(2, 1)$ and $\left(-\frac{2}{3}, 5\right)$ are solutions of the equation $3x + 2y = 8$, but $(1, 2)$ is not a solution. A linear equation in two variables has infinitely many solutions. If another linear equation in the same variables is given, it is usually possible to find a unique solution of both equations. Two equations with the same variables are called a **system of equations,** and the equations in the system are called **simultaneous equations.** To solve a system of two equations means to find an ordered pair of numbers that satisfies *both* equations in the system.

There are two basic methods for solving systems of linear equations, by **substitution** or by **elimination.** In the substitution method, one equation is manipulated to express one variable in terms of the other. Then the expression is substituted in the other equation. For example, to solve the system of equations

$$4x + 3y = 13$$
$$x + 2y = 2$$

you can express x in the second equation in terms of y as $x = 2 - 2y$. Then substitute $2 - 2y$ for x in the first equation to find the value of y.

$$4(2 - 2y) + 3y = 13$$
$$8 - 8y + 3y = 13$$
$$-8y + 3y = 5 \quad \text{(8 subtracted from both sides)}$$
$$-5y = 5 \quad \text{(like terms combined)}$$
$$y = -1 \quad \text{(both sides divided by } -5)$$

Then -1 can be substituted for y in either equation to find the value of x. We use the second equation:

$$x + 2y = 2$$
$$x + 2(-1) = 2$$
$$x - 2 = 2$$
$$x = 4 \quad \text{(2 added to both sides)}$$

In the elimination method, the object is to make the coefficients of one variable the same in both equations so that one variable can be eliminated either by adding the equations together or by subtracting one from the other. In the example above, multiplying both sides of the second equation by 4 yields $4(x + 2y) = 4(2)$, or $4x + 8y = 8$. Now you have two equations with the same coefficient of x.

$$4x + 3y = 13$$
$$4x + 8y = 8$$

If you subtract the second equation from the first, the result is $-5y = 5$. Thus, $y = -1$, and substituting -1 for y in either of the original equations yields $x = 4$.

By either method, the solution of the system is $x = 4$ and $y = -1$, or $(x, y) = (4, -1)$.

2.4 Solving Quadratic Equations

A **quadratic equation** in the variable x is an equation that can be written in the form

$$ax^2 + bx + c = 0$$

where a, b, and c are real numbers and $a \neq 0$. When such an equation has solutions, they can be found using the **quadratic formula:**

$$x = \frac{-b \pm \sqrt{b^2 - 4ac}}{2a}$$

where the notation $\pm$ is shorthand for indicating two solutions—one that uses the plus sign and the other that uses the minus sign.

Example 2.4.1: In the quadratic equation $2x^2 - x - 6 = 0$, we have $a = 2$, $b = -1$, and $c = -6$. Therefore, the quadratic formula yields

$$x = \frac{-(-1) \pm \sqrt{(-1)^2 - 4(2)(-6)}}{2(2)}$$

$$= \frac{1 \pm \sqrt{49}}{4}$$

$$= \frac{1 \pm 7}{4}$$

Hence the two solutions are $x = \dfrac{1+7}{4} = 2$ and $x = \dfrac{1-7}{4} = -\dfrac{3}{2}$.

Quadratic equations have at most two real solutions, as in the example above. However, some quadratic equations have only one real solution. For example, the quadratic equation $x^2 + 4x + 4 = 0$ has only one solution, which is $x = -2$. In this case, the expression under the square root symbol in the quadratic formula is equal to 0, and so adding or subtracting 0 yields the same result. Other quadratic equations have no real solutions; for example, $x^2 + x + 5 = 0$. In this case, the expression under the square root symbol is negative, so the entire expression is not a real number.

Some quadratic equations can be solved more quickly by factoring. For example, the quadratic equation $2x^2 - x - 6 = 0$ in example 2.4.1 can be factored as $(2x + 3)(x - 2) = 0$. When a product is equal to 0, at least one of the factors must be equal to 0, which leads to two cases: either $2x + 3 = 0$ or $x - 2 = 0$. Therefore,

$$2x + 3 = 0 \qquad\qquad x - 2 = 0$$
$$2x = -3 \qquad \text{OR} \qquad x = 2$$
$$x = -\frac{3}{2}$$

and the solutions are $-\dfrac{3}{2}$ and 2.

Example 2.4.2: Here is another example of a quadratic equation that can be easily factored.

$$5x^2 + 3x - 2 = 0$$
$$(5x - 2)(x + 1) = 0$$

Therefore,

$$5x - 2 = 0 \qquad\qquad x + 1 = 0$$
$$\qquad\qquad \text{OR} \qquad x = -1$$
$$x = \frac{2}{5}$$

2.5 Solving Linear Inequalities

A mathematical statement that uses one of the following inequality signs is called an **inequality.**

$\quad<\quad$ less than
$\quad>\quad$ greater than
$\quad\leq\quad$ less than or equal to
$\quad\geq\quad$ greater than or equal to

Inequalities can involve variables and are similar to equations, except that the two sides are related by one of the inequality signs instead of the equality sign used in equations. For example, the inequality $4x - 1 \leq 7$ is a linear inequality in one variable, which states that "$4x - 1$ is less than or equal to 7." To **solve an inequality** means to find the set of all values of the variable that make the inequality true. This set of values is also known as the **solution set** of an inequality. Two inequalities that have the same solution set are called **equivalent inequalities.**

The procedure used to solve a linear inequality is similar to that used to solve a linear equation, which is to simplify the inequality by isolating the variable on one side of the inequality, using the following two rules.

- When the same constant is added to or subtracted from both sides of an inequality, the direction of the inequality is preserved and the new inequality is equivalent to the original.
- When both sides of the inequality are multiplied or divided by the same nonzero constant, the direction of the inequality is *preserved if the constant is positive* but the direction is *reversed if the constant is negative*. In either case, the new inequality is equivalent to the original.

Example 2.5.1: The inequality $-3x + 5 \leq 17$ can be solved as follows.

$$-3x + 5 \leq 17$$
$$-3x \leq 12 \qquad \text{(5 subtracted from both sides)}$$
$$\frac{-3x}{-3} \geq \frac{12}{-3} \qquad \text{(both sides divided by } -3\text{, which reverses the direction of the inequality)}$$
$$x \geq -4$$

Therefore, the solution set of $-3x + 5 \leq 17$ consists of all real numbers greater than or equal to -4.

Example 2.5.2:

$$\frac{4x+9}{11} < 5$$
$$4x + 9 < 55 \qquad \text{(both sides multiplied by 11)}$$
$$4x < 46 \qquad \text{(9 subtracted from both sides)}$$
$$x < \frac{46}{4} \qquad \text{(both sides divided by 4)}$$
$$x < 11.5$$

Therefore, the solution set of $\dfrac{4x+9}{11} < 5$ consists of all real numbers less than 11.5.

2.6 Functions

An algebraic expression in one variable can be used to define a **function** of that variable. Functions are usually denoted by letters such as f, g, and h. For example, the algebraic expression $3x + 5$ can be used to define a function f by

$$f(x) = 3x + 5$$

where $f(x)$ is called the value of f at x and is obtained by substituting the value of x in the expression above. For example, if $x = 1$ is substituted in the expression above, the result is $f(1) = 8$.

It might be helpful to think of a function f as a machine that takes an input, which is a value of the variable x, and produces the corresponding output, $f(x)$. For any function, each input x gives exactly one output $f(x)$. However, more than one value of x can give the same output $f(x)$. For example, if g is the function defined by $g(x) = x^2 - 2x + 3$, then $g(0) = 3$ and $g(2) = 3$.

The **domain** of a function is the set of all permissible inputs, that is, all permissible values of the variable x. For the functions f and g defined above, the domain is the set of all real numbers. Sometimes the domain of the function is given explicitly and is restricted to a specific set of values of x. For example, we can define the function h by $h(x) = x^2 - 4$ for $-2 \leq x \leq 2$. Without an explicit restriction, the domain is assumed to be the set of all values of x for which $f(x)$ is a real number.

Example 2.6.1: Let f be the function defined by $f(x) = \dfrac{2x}{x-6}$. In this case, f is not defined at $x = 6$ because $\dfrac{12}{0}$ is not defined. Hence, the domain of f consists of all real numbers except for 6.

Example 2.6.2: Let g be the function defined by $g(x) = x^3 + \sqrt{x+2} - 10$. In this case, $g(x)$ is not a real number if $x < -2$. Hence, the domain of g consists of all real numbers x such that $x \geq -2$.

Example 2.6.3: Let h be the function defined by $h(x) = |x|$, the **absolute value** of x, which is the distance between x and 0 on the number line (see section 1.5). The domain of h is the set of all real numbers. Also, $h(x) = h(-x)$ for all real numbers x, which reflects the property that on the number line the distance between x and 0 is the same as the distance between $-x$ and 0.

2.7 Applications

Translating verbal descriptions into algebraic expressions is an essential initial step in solving word problems. Some examples are given below.

- If the square of the number x is multiplied by 3, and then 10 is added to that product, the result can be represented by $3x^2 + 10$.
- If John's present salary s is increased by 14 percent, then his new salary is $1.14s$.
- If y gallons of syrup are to be distributed among 5 people so that one particular person gets 1 gallon and the rest of the syrup is divided equally among the remaining 4, then each of those 4 people will get $\dfrac{y-1}{4}$ gallons of syrup.

Here are several examples of using algebraic techniques to solve word problems.

Example 2.7.1: Ellen has received the following scores on 3 exams: 82, 74, and 90. What score will Ellen need to receive on the next exam so that the average (arithmetic mean) score for the 4 exams will be 85?

Solution: Let x represent the score on Ellen's next exam. This initial step of assigning a variable to the quantity that is sought is an important beginning to solving the problem. Then in terms of x, the average of the 4 exams is

$$\frac{82+74+90+x}{4}$$

which is supposed to equal 85. Now simplify the expression and set it equal to 85:

$$\frac{82+74+90+x}{4} = \frac{246+x}{4} = 85$$

Solving the resulting linear equation for x, you get

$$246 + x = 340$$
$$x = 94$$

Therefore, Ellen will need to attain a score of 94 on the next exam.

Example 2.7.2: A mixture of 12 ounces of vinegar and oil is 40 percent vinegar, where all of the measurements are by weight. How many ounces of oil must be added to the mixture to produce a new mixture that is only 25 percent vinegar?

Solution: Let x represent the number of ounces of oil to be added. Then the total number of ounces of the new mixture will be $12 + x$, and the total number of ounces of vinegar in the new mixture will be $(0.40)(12)$. Since the new mixture must be 25 percent vinegar,

$$\frac{(0.40)(12)}{12+x} = 0.25$$

Therefore,

$$(0.40)(12) = (12 + x)(0.25)$$
$$4.8 = 3 + 0.25x$$
$$1.8 = 0.25x$$
$$7.2 = x$$

Thus, 7.2 ounces of oil must be added to produce a new mixture that is 25 percent vinegar.

Example 2.7.3: In a driving competition, Jeff and Dennis drove the same course at average speeds of 51 miles per hour and 54 miles per hour, respectively. If it took Jeff 40 minutes to drive the course, how long did it take Dennis?

Solution: Let x be the time, in minutes, that it took Dennis to drive the course. The distance d, in miles, is equal to the product of the rate r, in miles per hour, and the time t, in hours; that is,

$$d = rt$$

Note that since the rates are given in miles per *hour*, it is necessary to express the times in hours; for example, 40 minutes equals $\dfrac{40}{60}$ of an hour. Thus, the distance traveled by Jeff is the product of his speed and his time, $(51)\left(\dfrac{40}{60}\right)$ miles, and the distance traveled by Dennis is similarly represented by $(54)\left(\dfrac{x}{60}\right)$ miles. Since the distances are equal,

$$(51)\left(\frac{40}{60}\right) = (54)\left(\frac{x}{60}\right)$$

$$(51)(40) = 54x$$

$$x = \frac{(51)(40)}{54} \approx 37.8$$

Thus, it took Dennis approximately 37.8 minutes to drive the course.

Example 2.7.4: Working alone at its constant rate, machine A takes 3 hours to produce a batch of identical computer parts. Working alone at its constant rate, machine B takes 2 hours to produce an identical batch of parts. How long will it take the two machines, working simultaneously at their respective constant rates, to produce an identical batch of parts?

Solution: Since machine A takes 3 hours to produce a batch, machine A can produce $\dfrac{1}{3}$ of the batch in 1 hour. Similarly, machine B can produce $\dfrac{1}{2}$ of the batch in 1 hour. If we let x represent the number of hours it takes both machines, working simultaneously, to produce the batch, then the two machines will produce $\dfrac{1}{x}$ of the job in 1 hour. When the two machines work together, adding their individual production rates, $\dfrac{1}{3}$ and $\dfrac{1}{2}$, gives their combined production rate $\dfrac{1}{x}$. Therefore,

$$\frac{1}{3} + \frac{1}{2} = \frac{1}{x}$$

$$\frac{2}{6} + \frac{3}{6} = \frac{1}{x}$$

$$\frac{5}{6} = \frac{1}{x}$$

$$\frac{6}{5} = x$$

Thus, working together, the machines will take $\dfrac{6}{5}$ hours, or 1 hour 12 minutes, to produce a batch of parts.

Example 2.7.5: At a fruit stand, apples can be purchased for $0.15 each and pears for $0.20 each. At these rates, a bag of apples and pears was purchased for $3.80. If the bag contained 21 pieces of fruit, how many of the pieces were pears?

Solution: If a represents the number of apples purchased and p represents the number of pears purchased, the information can be translated into the following system of equations.

$$0.15a + 0.20p = 3.80 \quad \text{(total cost)}$$
$$a + p = 21 \quad \text{(total number of fruit)}$$

From the second equation, $a = 21 - p$. Substituting $21 - p$ into the first equation for a gives

$$0.15(21 - p) + 0.20p = 3.80$$
$$(0.15)(21) - 0.15p + 0.20p = 3.80$$
$$3.15 - 0.15p + 0.20p = 3.80$$
$$0.05p = 0.65$$
$$p = 13$$

Thus, of the 21 pieces of fruit, 13 were pears.

Example 2.7.6: To produce a particular radio model, it costs a manufacturer $30 per radio, and it is assumed that if 500 radios are produced, all of them will be sold. What must be the selling price per radio to ensure that the profit (revenue from the sales minus the total production cost) on the 500 radios is greater than $8,200?

Solution: If y represents the selling price per radio, then the profit is $500(y - 30)$. Therefore, we set

$$500(y - 30) > 8,200$$

Solving the inequality, we get

$$500y - 15,000 > 8,200$$
$$500y > 23,200$$
$$y > 46.4$$

Thus, the selling price must be greater than $46.40 to ensure that the profit is greater than $8,200.

Some applications involve computing **interest** earned on an investment during a specified time period. The interest can be computed as simple interest or compound interest.

Simple interest is based only on the initial deposit, which serves as the amount on which interest is computed, called the **principal**, for the entire time period. If the amount P is invested at a *simple annual interest rate of r percent,* then the value V of the investment at the end of t years is given by the formula

$$V = P\left(1 + \frac{rt}{100}\right)$$

where P and V are in dollars.

In the case of **compound interest**, interest is added to the principal at regular time intervals, such as annually, quarterly, and monthly. Each time interest is added to the principal, the interest is said to be compounded. After each compounding, interest is earned on the new principal, which is the sum of the preceding principal and the interest just added. If the amount P is invested at an *annual interest rate of r percent, compounded annually,* then the value V of the investment at the end of t years is given by the formula

$$V = P\left(1 + \frac{r}{100}\right)^t$$

If the amount P is invested at an *annual interest rate of r percent, compounded n times per year,* then the value V of the investment at the end of t years is given by the formula

$$V = P\left(1 + \frac{r}{100n}\right)^{nt}$$

Example 2.7.7: If $10,000 is invested at a simple annual interest rate of 6 percent, what is the value of the investment after half a year?

Solution: According to the formula for simple interest, the value of the investment after $\frac{1}{2}$ year is

$$\$10,000\left(1 + 0.06\left(\frac{1}{2}\right)\right) = \$10,000(1.03) = \$10,300$$

Example 2.7.8: If an amount P is to be invested at an annual interest rate of 3.5 percent, compounded annually, what should be the value of P so that the value of the investment is $1,000 at the end of 3 years?

Solution: According to the formula for 3.5 percent annual interest, compounded annually, the value of the investment after 3 years is

$$P(1 + 0.035)^3$$

and we set it to be equal to $1,000

$$P(1 + 0.035)^3 = \$1,000$$

To find the value of P, we divide both sides of the equation by $(1 + 0.035)^3$.

$$P = \frac{\$1,000}{(1 + 0.035)^3} \approx \$901.94$$

Thus, an amount of approximately $901.94 should be invested.

Example 2.7.9: A college student expects to earn at least $1,000 in interest on an initial investment of $20,000. If the money is invested for one year at interest compounded quarterly, what is the least annual interest rate that would achieve the goal?

Solution: According to the formula for r percent annual interest, compounded quarterly, the value of the investment after 1 year is

$$\$20,000\left(1 + \frac{r}{400}\right)^4$$

By setting this value greater than or equal to \$21,000 and solving for r, we get

$$\$20{,}000\left(1+\frac{r}{400}\right)^4 \geq \$21{,}000$$

$$\left(1+\frac{r}{400}\right)^4 \geq 1.05$$

We can use the fact that taking the positive fourth root of each side of an inequality preserves the direction of the inequality. This is also true for the positive square root or any other positive root.

$$1+\frac{r}{400} \geq \sqrt[4]{1.05}$$

$$r \geq 400\left(\sqrt[4]{1.05}-1\right)$$

To compute the fourth root, we can use the fact that $\sqrt[4]{x}=\sqrt{\sqrt{x}}$ for $x \geq 0$; that is, we can compute a fourth root by taking a square root twice:

$$r \geq 400\left(\sqrt[4]{1.05}-1\right)=400\left(\sqrt{\sqrt{1.05}}-1\right)\approx 4.91$$

So the least annual interest rate is approximately 4.91 percent.

2.8 Coordinate Geometry

Two real number lines that are perpendicular to each other and that intersect at their respective zero points define a **rectangular coordinate system,** often called the *xy-coordinate system* or *xy*-**plane.** The horizontal number line is called the **x-axis** and the vertical number line is called the **y-axis.** The point where the two axes intersect is called the **origin,** denoted by O. The positive half of the x-axis is to the right of the origin, and the positive half of the y-axis is above the origin. The two axes divide the plane into four regions called **quadrants I, II, III,** and **IV,** as shown in the figure below.

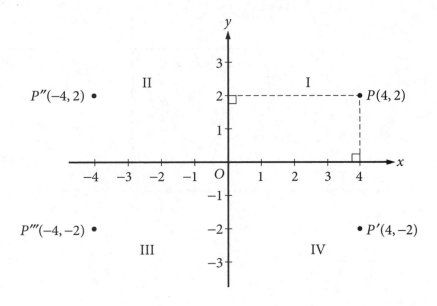

Each point P in the xy-plane can be identified with an ordered pair (x, y) of real numbers and is denoted by $P(x, y)$. The first number is called the **x-coordinate,** and the second number is called the **y-coordinate.** A point with coordinates (x, y) is located $|x|$ units to the right of the y-axis if x is positive or to the left of the y-axis if x is negative. Also, the point is located $|y|$ units above the x-axis if y is positive or below the x-axis if y is negative. If $x = 0$, the point lies on the y-axis, and if $y = 0$, the point lies on the x-axis. The origin has coordinates $(0, 0)$. Unless otherwise noted, the units used on the x-axis and the y-axis are the same.

In the figure above, the point $P(4, 2)$ is 4 units to the right of the y-axis and 2 units above the x-axis, and the point $P'''(-4, -2)$ is 4 units to the left of the y-axis and 2 units below the x-axis.

Note that the three points $P'(4, -2)$, $P''(-4, 2)$, and $P'''(-4, -2)$ have the same coordinates as P except for the sign. These points are geometrically related to P as follows.

- P' is the **reflection of P about the x-axis,** or P' and P are **symmetric about the x-axis.**
- P'' is the **reflection of P about the y-axis,** or P'' and P are **symmetric about the y-axis.**
- P''' is the **reflection of P about the origin,** or P''' and P are **symmetric about the origin.**

The distance between two points in the xy-plane can be found by using the Pythagorean theorem. For example, the distance between the two points $Q(-2, -3)$ and $R(4, 1.5)$ in the figure that follows is the length of line segment QR. To find this distance, construct a right triangle (indicated by the dashed lines) and then note that the two shorter sides of the triangle have lengths $QS = 4 - (-2) = 6$ and $RS = 1.5 - (-3) = 4.5$.

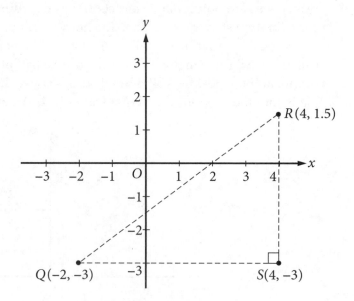

Since line segment QR is the hypotenuse of the triangle, you can apply the Pythagorean theorem:

$$QR = \sqrt{6^2 + 4.5^2} = \sqrt{56.25} = 7.5$$

(For a discussion of right triangles and the Pythagorean theorem, see section 3.3.)

Equations in two variables can be represented as graphs in the coordinate plane. In the xy-plane, the **graph of an equation** in the variables x and y is the set of all points whose ordered pairs (x, y) satisfy the equation.

The graph of a linear equation of the form $y = mx + b$ is a straight line in the xy-plane, where m is called the **slope** of the line and b is called the **y-intercept.**

The **x-intercepts** of a graph are the x-coordinates of the points at which the graph intersects the x-axis. Similarly, the **y-intercepts** of a graph are the y-coordinates of the points at which the graph intersects the y-axis. Sometimes the terms **x-intercept** and **y-intercept** refer to the actual intersection points.

The slope of a line passing through two points $Q(x_1, y_1)$ and $R(x_2, y_2)$, where $x_1 \neq x_2$, is defined as

$$\frac{y_2 - y_1}{x_2 - x_1}$$

This ratio is often called "rise over run," where *rise* is the change in y when moving from Q to R and *run* is the change in x when moving from Q to R. A horizontal line has a slope of 0, since the rise is 0 for any two points on the line. So the equation of every horizontal line has the form $y = b$, where b is the y-intercept. The slope of a vertical line is not defined, since the run is 0. The equation of every vertical line has the form $x = a$, where a is the x-intercept.

Two lines are **parallel** if their slopes are equal. Two lines are **perpendicular** if their slopes are negative reciprocals of each other. For example, the line with equation $y = 2x + 5$ is perpendicular to the line with equation $y = -\frac{1}{2}x + 9$.

Example 2.8.1: In the preceding figure, the slope of the line passing through the points $Q(-2, -3)$ and $R(4, 1.5)$ is

$$\frac{1.5 - (-3)}{4 - (-2)} = \frac{4.5}{6} = 0.75$$

Line QR appears to intersect the y-axis close to the point $(0, -1.5)$, so the y-intercept of the line must be close to -1.5. To get the exact value of the y-intercept, substitute the coordinates of any point on the line, say $Q(-2, -3)$, into the equation $y = 0.75x + b$, and solve it for b as follows.

$$y = 0.75x + b$$
$$-3 = (0.75)(-2) + b$$
$$b = -3 + (0.75)(2)$$
$$b = -1.5$$

Therefore, the equation of line QR is $y = 0.75x - 1.5$.

You can see from the graph that the *x*-intercept of line *QR* is 2, since *QR* passes through the point (2, 0). More generally, you can find the *x*-intercept by setting $y = 0$ in an equation of the line and solving it for *x* as follows.

$$0 = 0.75x - 1.5$$
$$1.5 = 0.75x$$
$$x = \frac{1.5}{0.75} = 2$$

Graphs of linear equations can be used to illustrate solutions of systems of linear equations and inequalities.

Example 2.8.2: Consider the system of linear equations in two variables in section 2.3:

$$4x + 3y = 13$$
$$x + 2y = 2$$

Solving each equation for *y* in terms of *x* yields

$$y = -\frac{4}{3}x + \frac{13}{3}$$

$$y = -\frac{1}{2}x + 1$$

The graphs of the two equations are below, and the solution of the system of equations is the point at which the two graphs intersect, which is (4, −1).

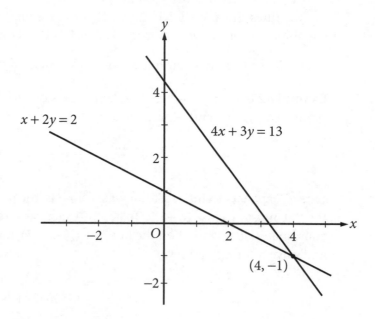

Example 2.8.3: Consider the following system of linear inequalities.

$$x - 3y \geq -6$$
$$2x + y \geq -1$$

Solving each inequality for y in terms of x yields

$$y \leq \frac{1}{3}x + 2$$

$$y \geq -2x - 1$$

Each point (x, y) that satisfies the first inequality $y \leq \frac{1}{3}x + 2$ is either on the line $y = \frac{1}{3}x + 2$ or *below* the line because the y-coordinate is either equal to or *less than* $\frac{1}{3}x + 2$. Therefore, the graph of $y \leq \frac{1}{3}x + 2$ consists of the line $y = \frac{1}{3}x + 2$ and the entire region below it. Similarly, the graph of $y \geq -2x - 1$ consists of the line $y = -2x - 1$ and the entire region *above* it. Thus, the solution set of the system of inequalities consists of all of the points that lie in the shaded region shown in the figure below, which is the intersection of the two regions described.

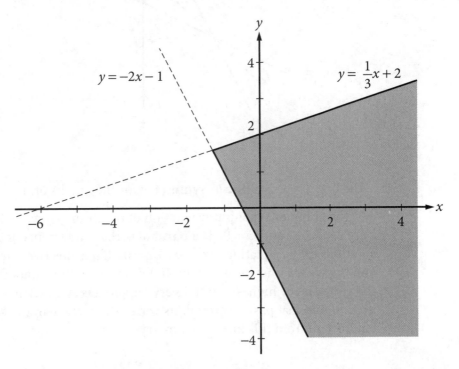

Symmetry with respect to the x-axis, the y-axis, and the origin is mentioned above. Another important symmetry is symmetry with respect to the line with equation $y = x$. The line $y = x$ passes through the origin, has a slope of 1, and makes a 45-degree angle with each axis. For any point with coordinates (a, b), the point with interchanged coordinates (b, a) is the reflection of (a, b) about the line $y = x$; that is, (a, b) and (b, a) are symmetric about the line $y = x$. It follows that interchanging x and y in the equation of any graph yields another graph that is the reflection of the original graph about the line $y = x$.

Example 2.8.4: Consider the line whose equation is $y = 2x + 5$. Interchanging x and y in the equation yields $x = 2y + 5$. Solving this equation for y yields $y = \frac{1}{2}x - \frac{5}{2}$. The line $y = 2x + 5$ and its reflection $y = \frac{1}{2}x - \frac{5}{2}$ are graphed below.

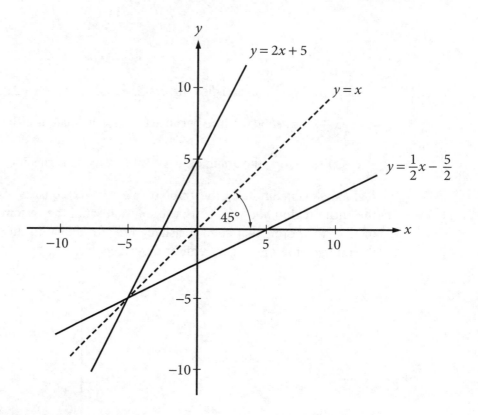

The line $y = x$ is a **line of symmetry** for the graphs of $y = 2x + 5$ and $y = \frac{1}{2}x - \frac{5}{2}$.

The graph of a quadratic equation of the form $y = ax^2 + bx + c$, where a, b, and c are constants and $a \neq 0$, is a **parabola**. The x-intercepts of the parabola are the solutions of the equation $ax^2 + bx + c = 0$. If a is positive, the parabola opens upward and the **vertex** is its lowest point. If a is negative, the parabola opens downward and the vertex is the highest point. Every parabola is symmetric with itself about the vertical line that passes through its vertex. In particular, the two x-intercepts are equidistant from this line of symmetry.

Example 2.8.5: The equation $y = x^2 - 2x - 3$ has the following graph.

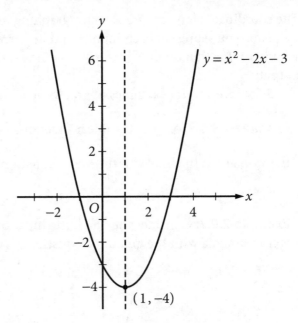

The graph indicates that the x-intercepts of the parabola are -1 and 3. The values of the x-intercepts can be confirmed by solving the quadratic equation $x^2 - 2x - 3 = 0$ to get $x = -1$ and $x = 3$. The point $(1, -4)$ is the vertex of the parabola, and the line $x = 1$ is its line of symmetry. The y-intercept is the y-coordinate of the point on the parabola at which $x = 0$, which is $y = 0^2 - 2(0) - 3 = -3$.

The graph of an equation of the form $(x - a)^2 + (y - b)^2 = r^2$ is a **circle** with its center at the point (a, b) and with radius r.

Example 2.8.6: The graph of $x^2 + y^2 = 100$ is a circle with its center at the origin and with radius 10, as shown in the figure below. The smaller circle has center $(6, -5)$ and radius 3, so its equation is $(x - 6)^2 + (y + 5)^2 = 9$.

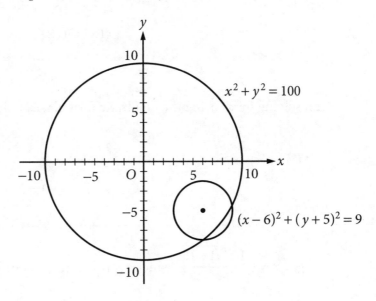

2.9 Graphs of Functions

The coordinate plane can be used for graphing functions. To graph a function in the xy-plane, you represent each input x and its corresponding output $f(x)$ as a point (x, y), where $y = f(x)$. In other words, you use the x-axis for the input and the y-axis for the output.

Below are several examples of graphs of elementary functions.

Example 2.9.1: Consider the linear function defined by $f(x) = -\frac{1}{2}x + 1$. Its graph in the xy-plane is the line with the linear equation $y = -\frac{1}{2}x + 1$, as shown in the figure below.

Example 2.9.2: Consider the quadratic function defined by $g(x) = x^2$. The graph of g is the parabola with the quadratic equation $y = x^2$, as shown in the figure below.

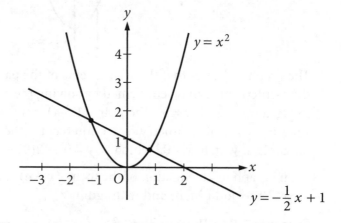

Note that the graphs of f and g from the two examples above intersect at two points. These are the points at which $g(x) = f(x)$. We can find these points algebraically by setting

$$g(x) = f(x)$$

$$x^2 = -\frac{1}{2}x + 1$$

and solving for x, using the quadratic formula, as follows.

$$x^2 = -\frac{1}{2}x + 1$$

$$x^2 + \frac{1}{2}x - 1 = 0$$

$$2x^2 + x - 2 = 0$$

We get $x = \dfrac{-1 \pm \sqrt{1 + 16}}{4}$, which represent the x-coordinates of the two solutions

$$x = \frac{-1 + \sqrt{17}}{4} \approx 0.78 \quad \text{and} \quad x = \frac{-1 - \sqrt{17}}{4} \approx -1.28$$

With these input values, the corresponding y-coordinates can be found using either f or g:

$$g\left(\frac{-1+\sqrt{17}}{4}\right)=\left(\frac{-1+\sqrt{17}}{4}\right)^2\approx 0.61 \quad \text{and} \quad g\left(\frac{-1-\sqrt{17}}{4}\right)=\left(\frac{-1-\sqrt{17}}{4}\right)^2\approx 1.64$$

Thus, the two intersection points can be approximated by $(0.78, 0.61)$ and $(-1.28, 1.64)$.

Example 2.9.3: Consider the absolute value function defined by $h(x)=|x|$. By using the definition of absolute value (see section 1.5), h can be expressed as a **piecewise-defined** function:

$$h(x)=\begin{cases} x, & x\geq 0 \\ -x, & x<0 \end{cases}$$

The graph of this function is V-shaped and consists of two linear pieces, $y=x$ and $y=-x$, joined at the origin, as shown in the figure below.

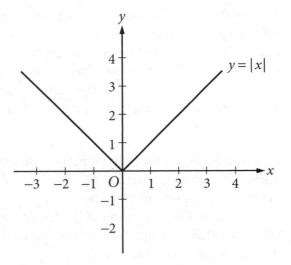

Example 2.9.4: Consider the positive square-root function defined by $j(x)=\sqrt{x}$ for $x\geq 0$, whose graph is half of a parabola lying on its side. Also consider the negative square-root function defined by $k(x)=-\sqrt{x}$ for $x\geq 0$, whose graph is the other half

of the parabola lying on its side—the dashed curve below the x-axis. Both graphs are shown in the figure below, along with the parabola $y = x^2$ (with its left half dashed).

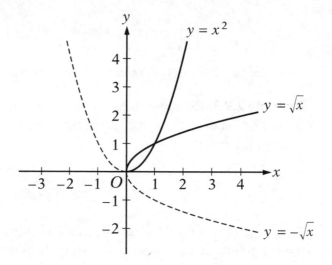

The graphs of $y = \sqrt{x}$ and $y = -\sqrt{x}$ are halves of a parabola because they are reflections of the right and left halves, respectively, of the parabola $y = x^2$ about the line $y = x$. This follows from squaring both sides of the two square root equations to get $y^2 = x$ and then interchanging x and y to get $y = x^2$.

Also note that $y = -\sqrt{x}$ is the reflection of $y = \sqrt{x}$ about the x-axis. In general, for any function h, the graph of $y = -h(x)$ is the **reflection** of the graph of $y = h(x)$ about the x-axis.

Example 2.9.5: Consider the functions defined by $f(x) = |x| + 2$ and $g(x) = (x + 1)^2$. These functions are related to the absolute value function $|x|$ and the quadratic function x^2, respectively, in simple ways.

The graph of f is the graph of $|x|$ shifted upward by 2 units, as shown in the figure below. Similarly, the graph of the function $|x| - 5$ is the graph of $|x|$ shifted downward by 5 units (not shown).

The graph of g is the graph of x^2 shifted to the left by 1 unit, as shown in the figure below. Similarly, the graph of the function $(x - 4)^2$ is the graph of x^2 shifted to the right by 4 units (not shown). To double-check the direction of the shift, you can plot some corresponding values of the original function and the shifted function.

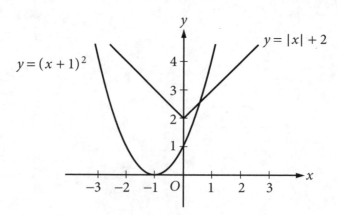

In general, for any function $h(x)$ and any positive number c, the following are true.

- The graph of $h(x) + c$ is the graph of $h(x)$ **shifted upward** by c units.
- The graph of $h(x) - c$ is the graph of $h(x)$ **shifted downward** by c units.
- The graph of $h(x + c)$ is the graph of $h(x)$ **shifted to the left** by c units.
- The graph of $h(x - c)$ is the graph of $h(x)$ **shifted to the right** by c units.

Example 2.9.6: Consider the function s defined by $f(x) = 2|x-1|$ and $g(x) = -\dfrac{x^2}{4}$.

These functions are related to the absolute value function $|x|$ and the quadratic function x^2, respectively, in more complicated ways than in the preceding example.

The graph of f is the graph of $|x|$ shifted to the right by 1 unit and then stretched vertically away from the x-axis by a factor of 2, as shown in the figure below. Similarly, the graph of the function $\dfrac{1}{2}|x - 1|$ is the graph of $|x|$ shifted to the right by 1 unit and then shrunk vertically toward the x-axis by a factor of $\dfrac{1}{2}$ (not shown).

The graph of g is the graph of x^2 shrunk vertically by a factor of $\dfrac{1}{4}$ and then reflected in the x-axis, as shown in the figure below.

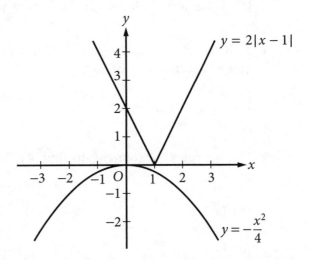

In general, for any function $h(x)$ and any positive number c, the following are true.

- The graph of $ch(x)$ is the graph of $h(x)$ **stretched vertically** by a factor of c if $c > 1$.
- The graph of $ch(x)$ is the graph of $h(x)$ **shrunk vertically** by a factor of c if $0 < c < 1$.

ALGEBRA EXERCISES

1. Find an algebraic expression to represent each of the following.
   (a) The square of y is subtracted from 5, and the result is multiplied by 37.
   (b) Three times x is squared, and the result is divided by 7.
   (c) The product of $(x+4)$ and y is added to 18.

2. Simplify each of the following algebraic expressions.
   (a) $3x^2 - 6 + x + 11 - x^2 + 5x$
   (b) $3(5x-1) - x + 4$
   (c) $\dfrac{x^2 - 16}{x-4}$, where $x \neq 4$
   (d) $(2x+5)(3x-1)$

3. (a) What is the value of $f(x) = 3x^2 - 7x + 23$ when $x = -2$?
   (b) What is the value of $h(x) = x^3 - 2x^2 + x - 2$ when $x = 2$?
   (c) What is the value of $k(x) = \dfrac{5}{3}x - 7$ when $x = 0$?

4. If the function g is defined for all nonzero numbers y by $g(y) = \dfrac{y}{|y|}$, find the value of each of the following.
   (a) $g(2)$
   (b) $g(-2)$
   (c) $g(2) - g(-2)$

5. Use the rules of exponents to simplify the following.
   (a) $(n^5)(n^{-3})$
   (b) $(s^7)(t^7)$
   (c) $\dfrac{r^{12}}{r^4}$
   (d) $\left(\dfrac{2a}{b}\right)^5$
   (e) $(w^5)^{-3}$
   (f) $(5^0)(d^3)$
   (g) $\dfrac{(x^{10})(y^{-1})}{(x^{-5})(y^5)}$
   (h) $\left(\dfrac{3x}{y}\right)^2 \div \left(\dfrac{1}{y}\right)^5$

6. Solve each of the following equations for x.
   (a) $5x - 7 = 28$
   (b) $12 - 5x = x + 30$
   (c) $5(x+2) = 1 - 3x$
   (d) $(x+6)(2x-1) = 0$
   (e) $x^2 + 5x - 14 = 0$
   (f) $x^2 - x - 1 = 0$

7. Solve each of the following systems of equations for x and y.
   (a) $x + y = 24$
   $x - y = 18$
   (b) $3x - y = -5$
   $x + 2y = 3$
   (c) $15x - 18 - 2y = -3x + y$
   $10x + 7y + 20 = 4x + 2$

8. Solve each of the following inequalities for x.
   (a) $-3x > 7 + x$
   (b) $25x + 16 \geq 10 - x$
   (c) $16 + x > 8x - 12$

9. For a given two-digit positive integer, the tens digit is 5 more than the units digit. The sum of the digits is 11. Find the integer.

10. If the ratio of $2x$ to $5y$ is 3 to 4, what is the ratio of x to y?

11. Kathleen's weekly salary was increased by 8 percent to $237.60. What was her weekly salary before the increase?

12. A theater sells children's tickets for half the adult ticket price. If 5 adult tickets and 8 children's tickets cost a total of $27, what is the cost of an adult ticket?

13. Pat invested a total of $3,000. Part of the money was invested in a money market account that paid 10 percent simple annual interest, and the remainder of the money was invested in a fund that paid 8 percent simple annual interest. If the interest earned at the end of the first year from these investments was $256, how much did Pat invest at 10 percent and how much at 8 percent?

14. Two cars started from the same point and traveled on a straight course in opposite directions for exactly 2 hours, at which time they were 208 miles apart. If one car traveled, on average, 8 miles per hour faster than the other car, what was the average speed of each car for the 2-hour trip?

15. A group can charter a particular aircraft at a fixed total cost. If 36 people charter the aircraft rather than 40 people, then the cost per person is greater by $12.
    (a) What is the fixed total cost to charter the aircraft?
    (b) What is the cost per person if 40 people charter the aircraft?

16. An antiques dealer bought c antique chairs for a total of x dollars. The dealer sold each chair for y dollars.
    (a) Write an algebraic expression for the profit, P, earned from buying and selling the chairs.
    (b) Write an algebraic expression for the profit per chair.

17. In the coordinate system below, find the following.
    (a) Coordinates of point Q
    (b) Lengths of PQ, QR, and PR
    (c) Perimeter of $\triangle PQR$
    (d) Area of $\triangle PQR$
    (e) Slope, y-intercept, and equation of the line passing through points P and R

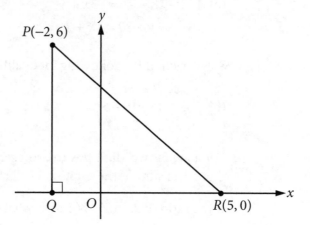

18. In the xy-plane, find the following.
    (a) Slope and y-intercept of the line with equation $2y + x = 6$
    (b) Equation of the line passing through the point $(3, 2)$ with y-intercept 1
    (c) The y-intercept of a line with slope 3 that passes through the point $(-2, 1)$
    (d) The x-intercepts of the graphs in (a), (b), and (c)

19. For the parabola $y = x^2 - 4x - 12$ in the xy-plane, find the following.
    (a) The x-intercepts
    (b) The y-intercept
    (c) Coordinates of the vertex

20. For the circle $(x - 1)^2 + (y + 1)^2 = 20$ in the xy-plane, find the following.
    (a) Coordinates of the center
    (b) Radius
    (c) Area

21. For each of the following functions, give the domain and a description of the graph $y = f(x)$ in the xy-plane, including its shape, and the x- and y-intercepts.
    (a) $f(x) = -4$
    (b) $f(x) = 100 - 900x$
    (c) $f(x) = 5 - (x + 20)^2$
    (d) $f(x) = \sqrt{x + 2}$
    (e) $f(x) = x + |x|$

ANSWERS TO ALGEBRA EXERCISES

1. (a) $37(5 - y^2)$, or $185 - 37y^2$

    (b) $\dfrac{(3x)^2}{7}$, or $\dfrac{9x^2}{7}$

    (c) $18 + (x + 4)(y)$, or $18 + xy + 4y$

2. (a) $2x^2 + 6x + 5$ (c) $x + 4$

    (b) $14x + 1$ (d) $6x^2 + 13x - 5$

3. (a) 49 (b) 0 (c) -7

4. (a) 1 (b) -1 (c) 2

5. (a) n^2 (e) $\dfrac{1}{w^{15}}$

    (b) $(st)^7$ (f) d^3

    (c) r^8 (g) $\dfrac{x^{15}}{y^6}$

    (d) $\dfrac{32a^5}{b^5}$ (h) $9x^2y^3$

6. (a) 7 (d) $-6, \dfrac{1}{2}$

    (b) -3 (e) $-7, 2$

    (c) $-\dfrac{9}{8}$ (f) $\dfrac{1 + \sqrt{5}}{2}, \dfrac{1 - \sqrt{5}}{2}$

7. (a) $\begin{aligned} x &= 21 \\ y &= 3 \end{aligned}$ (b) $\begin{aligned} x &= -1 \\ y &= 2 \end{aligned}$ (c) $\begin{aligned} x &= \dfrac{1}{2} \\ x &= -3 \end{aligned}$

8. (a) $x < -\dfrac{7}{4}$

    (b) $x \geq -\dfrac{3}{13}$

    (c) $x < 4$

9. 83

10. 15 to 8

11. $220

12. $3

13. $800 at 10% and $2,200 at 8%

14. 48 mph and 56 mph

15. (a) $4,320   (b) $108

16. (a) $P = cy - x$ (b) Profit per chair: $\dfrac{P}{c} = \dfrac{cy - x}{c} = y - \dfrac{x}{c}$

17. (a) $(-2, 0)$

(b) $PQ = 6$, $QR = 7$, $PR = \sqrt{85}$

(c) $13 + \sqrt{85}$

(d) 21

(e) Slope: $-\dfrac{6}{7}$; y-intercept: $-\dfrac{30}{7}$; equation of line: $y = -\dfrac{6}{7}x + \dfrac{30}{7}$, or

$7y + 6x = 30$

18. (a) Slope: $-\dfrac{1}{2}$; y-intercept: 3

(b) $y = \dfrac{x}{3} + 1$

(c) 7

(d) $6, -3, -\dfrac{7}{3}$

19. (a) $x = -2$ and $x = 6$

(b) $y = -12$

(c) $(2, -16)$

20. (a) $(1, -1)$

(b) $\sqrt{20}$

(c) 20π

21. (a) Domain: the set of all real numbers. The graph is a horizontal line with y-intercept -4 and no x-intercept.

(b) Domain: the set of all real numbers. The graph is a line with slope -900, y-intercept 100, and x-intercept $\dfrac{1}{9}$.

(c) Domain: the set of all real numbers. The graph is a parabola opening downward with vertex at $(-20, 5)$, line of symmetry $x = -20$, y-intercept -395, and x-intercepts $-20 \pm \sqrt{5}$.

(d) Domain: the set of numbers greater than or equal to -2. The graph is half a parabola opening to the right with vertex at $(-2, 0)$, x-intercept -2, and y-intercept $\sqrt{2}$.

(e) Domain: the set of all real numbers. The graph is two half-lines joined at the origin: one half-line is the negative x-axis and the other is a line starting at the origin with slope 2. Every nonpositive number is an x-intercept, and the y-intercept is 0. The function is equal to the following piecewise-defined function

$$f(x) = \begin{cases} 2x, & x \geq 0 \\ 0, & x < 0 \end{cases}$$

3. GEOMETRY

The review of geometry begins with lines and angles and progresses to other plane figures, such as polygons, triangles, quadrilaterals, and circles. The section ends with some basic three-dimensional figures. Coordinate geometry is covered in the Algebra section.

3.1 Lines and Angles

Plane geometry is devoted primarily to the properties and relations of plane figures, such as angles, triangles, other polygons, and circles. The terms "point," "line," and "plane" are familiar intuitive concepts. A **point** has no size and is the simplest geometric figure. All geometric figures consist of points. A **line** is understood to be a straight line that extends in both directions without ending. A **plane** can be thought of as a floor or a tabletop, except that a plane extends in all directions without ending and has no thickness.

Given any two points on a line, a **line segment** is the part of the line that contains the two points and all the points between them. The two points are called **endpoints**. Line segments that have equal lengths are called **congruent line segments**. The point that divides a line segment into two congruent line segments is called the **midpoint** of the line segment.

In the figure below, A, B, C, and D are points on line ℓ.

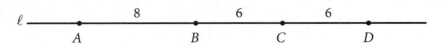

Line segment AB consists of points A and B and all the points on the line between A and B. Sometimes the notation AB denotes line segment AB, and sometimes it denotes the **length** of line segment AB. The meaning of the notation can be determined from the context. According to the figure above, the lengths of line segments AB, BC, and CD are 8, 6, and 6, respectively. Hence, line segments BC and CD are congruent. Since C is halfway between B and D, point C is the midpoint of line segment BD.

When two lines intersect at a point, they form four **angles**, as indicated below. Each angle has a **vertex** at point P, which is the point of intersection of the two lines.

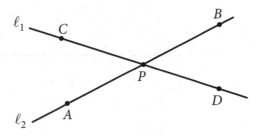

In the figure, angles APC and BPD are called **opposite angles**, also known as **vertical angles**. Angles APD and CPB are also opposite angles. Opposite angles have equal measures, and angles that have equal measures are called **congruent angles**. Hence, opposite angles are congruent. The sum of the measures of the four angles is 360°.

Sometimes the angle symbol $\angle$ is used instead of the word "angle." For example, angle APC can be written as $\angle APC$.

Two lines that intersect to form four congruent angles are called **perpendicular lines**. Each of the four angles has a measure of 90°. An angle with a measure of 90° is called a **right angle**. The figure below shows two lines, ℓ_1 and ℓ_2, that are perpendicular, denoted by $\ell_1 \perp \ell_2$.

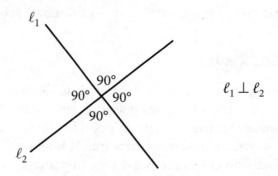

A common way to indicate that an angle is a right angle is to draw a small square at the vertex of the angle, as shown below, where *PON* is a right angle.

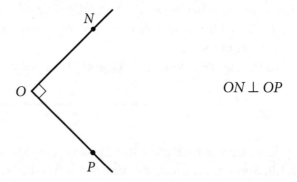

An angle with a measure less than 90° is called an **acute angle**, and an angle with a measure between 90° and 180° is called an **obtuse angle**.

Two lines in the same plane that do not intersect are called **parallel lines**. The figure below shows two lines, ℓ_1 and ℓ_2, that are parallel, denoted by $\ell_1 \| \ell_2$. The two lines are intersected by a third line, ℓ_3, forming eight angles. Note that four of the angles have the measure $x°$, and the remaining four angles have the measure $y°$, where $x + y = 180$.

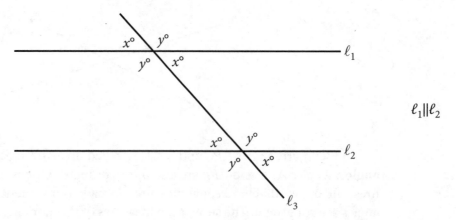

3.2 Polygons

A **polygon** is a closed figure formed by three or more line segments, called **sides**. Each side is joined to two other sides at its endpoints, and the endpoints are called **vertices**. In this discussion, the term "polygon" means "convex polygon," that is, a polygon in which the measure of each interior angle is less than 180°. The figures below are examples of such polygons.

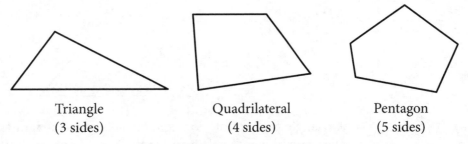

Triangle   Quadrilateral   Pentagon
(3 sides)   (4 sides)   (5 sides)

The simplest polygon is a **triangle**. Note that a **quadrilateral** can be divided into 2 triangles, and a **pentagon** can be divided into 3 triangles, as shown below.

If a polygon has n sides, it can be divided into $n - 2$ triangles. Since the sum of the measures of the interior angles of a triangle is 180°, it follows that the sum of the measures of the interior angles of an n-sided polygon is $(n - 2)(180°)$. For example, the sum for a quadrilateral $(n = 4)$ is $(4 - 2)(180°) = 360°$, and the sum for a **hexagon** $(n = 6)$ is $(6 - 2)(180°) = 720°$.

A polygon in which all sides are congruent and all interior angles are congruent is called a **regular polygon**. For example, in a **regular octagon** (8 sides), the sum of the measures of the interior angles is $(8 - 2)(180°) = 1,080°$. Therefore, the measure of each angle is $\dfrac{1,080°}{8} = 135°$.

The **perimeter** of a polygon is the sum of the lengths of its sides. The **area** of a polygon refers to the area of the region enclosed by the polygon.

In the next two sections, we will look at some basic properties of triangles and quadrilaterals.

3.3 Triangles

Every triangle has three sides and three interior angles. The measures of the interior angles add up to 180°. The length of each side must be less than the sum of the lengths of the other two sides. For example, the sides of a triangle could not have the lengths 4, 7, and 12 because 12 is greater than $4 + 7$.

The following are special triangles.

- A triangle with three congruent sides is called an **equilateral triangle**. The measures of the three interior angles of such a triangle are also equal, and each measure is 60°.

- A triangle with at least two congruent sides is called an **isosceles triangle**. If a triangle has two congruent sides, then the angles opposite the two sides are congruent. The converse is also true. For example, in $\triangle ABC$ below, since both $\angle A$ and $\angle C$ have measure 50°, it follows that $AB = BC$. Also, since $50 + 50 + x = 180$, the measure of $\angle B$ is 80°.

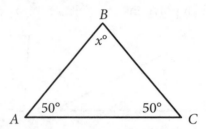

- A triangle with an interior right angle is called a **right triangle**. The side opposite the right angle is called the **hypotenuse**; the other two sides are called **legs**.

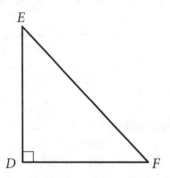

In right triangle *DEF* above, *EF* is the hypotenuse and *DE* and *DF* are legs. The **Pythagorean theorem** states that in a right triangle, the square of the length of the hypotenuse is equal to the sum of the squares of the lengths of the legs. Thus, for triangle *DEF* above,

$$(EF)^2 = (DE)^2 + (DF)^2$$

This relationship can be used to find the length of one side of a right triangle if the lengths of the other two sides are known. For example, if one leg of a right triangle has length 5 and the hypotenuse has length 8, then the length of the other side can be determined as follows.

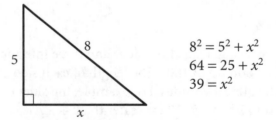

$$8^2 = 5^2 + x^2$$
$$64 = 25 + x^2$$
$$39 = x^2$$

Since $x^2 = 39$ and x must be positive, it follows that $x = \sqrt{39}$, or approximately 6.2.

The Pythagorean theorem can be used to determine the ratios of the lengths of the sides of two special right triangles. One special right triangle is an isosceles right triangle. Applying the Pythagorean theorem to such a triangle shows that the lengths of its sides are in the ratio 1 to 1 to $\sqrt{2}$, as indicated below.

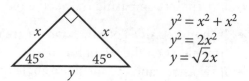

$$y^2 = x^2 + x^2$$
$$y^2 = 2x^2$$
$$y = \sqrt{2}x$$

The other special right triangle is a 30°-60°-90° right triangle, which is half of an equilateral triangle, as indicated below.

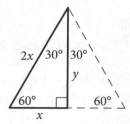

Note that the length of the shortest side, x, is one-half the length of the longest side, $2x$. By the Pythagorean theorem, the ratio of x to y is 1 to $\sqrt{3}$ because

$$x^2 + y^2 = (2x)^2$$
$$x^2 + y^2 = 4x^2$$
$$y^2 = 4x^2 - x^2$$
$$y^2 = 3x^2$$
$$y = \sqrt{3}x$$

Hence, the ratio of the lengths of the three sides of such a triangle is 1 to $\sqrt{3}$ to 2.

The **area** A of a triangle equals one-half the product of the length of a base and the height corresponding to the base. In the figure below, the base is denoted by b and the corresponding height is denoted by h.

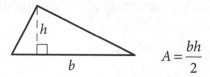

$$A = \frac{bh}{2}$$

Any side of a triangle can be used as a base; the height that corresponds to the base is the perpendicular line segment from the opposite vertex to the base (or to an extension of the base). The examples below show three different configurations of a base and the corresponding height.

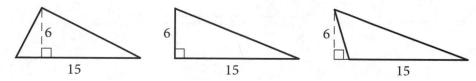

In all three triangles above, the area is $\dfrac{(15)(6)}{2}$, or 45.

Two triangles that have the same shape and size are called **congruent triangles**. More precisely, two triangles are congruent if their vertices can be matched up so that the corresponding angles and the corresponding sides are congruent.

The following three propositions can be used to determine whether two triangles are congruent by comparing only some of their sides and angles.

- If the three sides of one triangle are congruent to the three sides of another triangle, then the triangles are congruent.
- If two sides and the included angle of one triangle are congruent to two sides and the included angle of another triangle, then the triangles are congruent.
- If two angles and the included side of one triangle are congruent to two angles and the included side of another triangle, then the triangles are congruent.

Two triangles that have the same shape but not necessarily the same size are called **similar triangles**. More precisely, two triangles are similar if their vertices can be matched up so that the corresponding angles are congruent or, equivalently, the lengths of corresponding sides have the same ratio, called the scale factor of similarity. For example, all 30°-60°-90° right triangles, discussed above, are similar triangles, though they may differ in size.

When we say that triangles *ABC* and *DEF* are similar, it is assumed that angles *A* and *D* are congruent, angles *B* and *E* are congruent, and angles *C* and *F* are congruent, as shown in the figure below. In other words, the order of the letters indicates the correspondences.

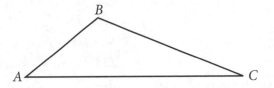

Since triangles *ABC* and *DEF* are similar, we have $\dfrac{AB}{DE} = \dfrac{BC}{EF} = \dfrac{AC}{DF}$. By cross

multiplication, we can obtain other proportions, such as $\dfrac{AB}{BC} = \dfrac{DE}{EF}$.

3.4 Quadrilaterals

Every quadrilateral has four sides and four interior angles. The measures of the interior angles add up to 360°. The following are special quadrilaterals.

- A quadrilateral with four right angles is called a **rectangle**. Opposite sides of a rectangle are parallel and congruent, and the two diagonals are also congruent.

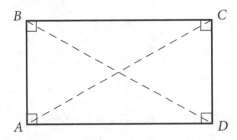

$AB \parallel CD$ and $AD \parallel BC$
$AB = CD$ and $AD = BC$
$AC = BD$

- A rectangle with four congruent sides is called a **square**.
- A quadrilateral in which both pairs of opposite sides are parallel is called a **parallelogram**. In a parallelogram, opposite sides are congruent and opposite angles are congruent.

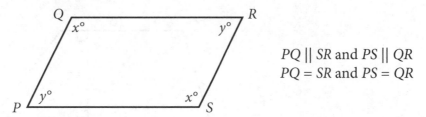

$PQ \parallel SR$ and $PS \parallel QR$
$PQ = SR$ and $PS = QR$

- A quadrilateral in which two opposite sides are parallel is called a **trapezoid**.

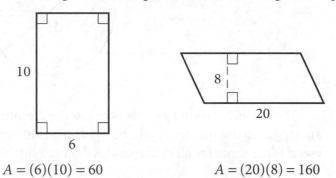

$KN \parallel LM$

For all parallelograms, including rectangles and squares, the **area** A equals the product of the length of a base b and the corresponding height h; that is,

$$A = bh$$

Any side can be used as a base. The height corresponding to the base is the perpendicular line segment from any point of a base to the opposite side (or to an extension of that side). Below are examples of finding the areas of a rectangle and a parallelogram.

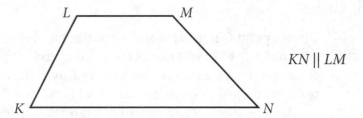

$A = (6)(10) = 60$ $\qquad\qquad$ $A = (20)(8) = 160$

The **area** A of a trapezoid equals half the product of the sum of the lengths of the two parallel sides b_1 and b_2 and the corresponding height h; that is,

$$A = \frac{1}{2}(b_1 + b_2)(h)$$

For example, for the trapezoid below with bases of length 10 and 18 and a height of 7.5, the area is

$$A = \frac{1}{2}(10+18)(7.5) = 105$$

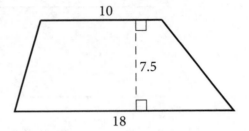

3.5 Circles

Given a point O in a plane and a positive number r, the set of points in the plane that are a distance of r units from O is called a **circle**. The point O is called the **center** of the circle and the distance r is called the **radius** of the circle. The **diameter** of the circle is twice the radius. Two circles with equal radii are called **congruent circles**.

Any line segment joining two points on the circle is called a **chord**. The terms "radius" and "diameter" can also refer to line segments: A **radius** is any line segment joining a point on the circle and the center of the circle, and a **diameter** is any chord that passes through the center of the circle. In the figure below, O is the center of the circle, r is the radius, PQ is a chord, and ST is a diameter.

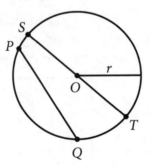

The distance around a circle is called the **circumference** of the circle, which is analogous to the perimeter of a polygon. The ratio of the circumference C to the diameter d is the same for all circles and is denoted by the Greek letter π; that is,

$$\frac{C}{d} = \pi$$

The value of π is approximately 3.14 and can also be approximated by the fraction $\frac{22}{7}$.

If r is the radius of a circle, then $\frac{C}{d} = \frac{C}{2r} = \pi$, and so the circumference is related to the radius by the equation

$$C = 2\pi r$$

For example, if a circle has a radius of 5.2, then its circumference is

$$(2)(\pi)(5.2)=(10.4)(\pi)\approx(10.4)(3.14)$$

which is approximately 32.7.

Given any two points on a circle, an **arc** is the part of the circle containing the two points and all the points between them. Two points on a circle are always the endpoints of two arcs. It is customary to identify an arc by three points to avoid ambiguity. In the figure below, arc *ABC* is the shorter arc between *A* and *C*, and arc *ADC* is the longer arc between *A* and *C*.

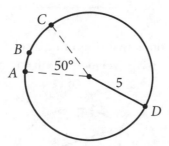

A **central angle** of a circle is an angle with its vertex at the center of the circle. The **measure of an arc** is the measure of its central angle, which is the angle formed by two radii that connect the center of the circle to the two endpoints of the arc. An entire circle is considered to be an arc with measure 360°. In the figure above, the measure of arc *ABC* is 50° and the measure of arc *ADC* is 310°.

To find the **length of an arc** of a circle, note that the ratio of the length of an arc to the circumference is equal to the ratio of the degree measure of the arc to 360°. The circumference of the circle above is 10π. Therefore,

$$\frac{\text{length of arc } ABC}{10\pi}=\frac{50}{360}$$

$$\text{length of arc } ABC=\left(\frac{50}{360}\right)(10\pi)=\frac{25\pi}{18}\approx\frac{(25)(3.14)}{18}\approx4.4$$

The **area** of a circle with radius *r* is equal to πr^2. For example, the area of the circle above with radius 5 is $\pi(5)^2=25\pi$.

A **sector** of a circle is a region bounded by an arc of the circle and two radii. In the circle above, the region bounded by arc *ABC* and the two dashed radii is a sector with central angle 50°. Just as in the case of the length of an arc, the ratio of the area of a sector of a circle to the area of the entire circle is equal to the ratio of the degree measure of its arc to 360°. Therefore, if *S* represents the area of the sector with central angle 50°, then

$$\frac{S}{25\pi}=\frac{50}{360}$$

$$S=\left(\frac{50}{360}\right)(25\pi)=\frac{125\pi}{36}\approx\frac{(125)(3.14)}{36}\approx10.9$$

A **tangent** to a circle is a line that intersects the circle at exactly one point, called the **point of tangency**, denoted by *P* in the figure that follows. If a line is tangent to a circle, then a radius drawn to the point of tangency is perpendicular to the tangent line.

The converse is also true; that is, if a line is perpendicular to a radius at its endpoint on the circle, then the line is a tangent to the circle at that endpoint.

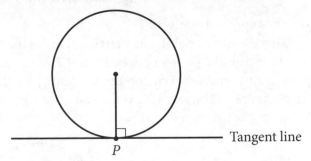

Tangent line

A polygon is **inscribed** in a circle if all its vertices lie on the circle, or equivalently, the circle is **circumscribed** about the polygon. Triangles *RST* and *XYZ* below are inscribed in the circles with centers *O* and *W*, respectively.

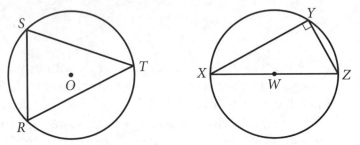

If one side of an inscribed triangle is a diameter of the circle, as in triangle *XYZ* above, then the triangle is a right triangle. Conversely, if an inscribed triangle is a right triangle, then one of its sides is a diameter of the circle.

A polygon is circumscribed about a circle if each side of the polygon is tangent to the circle, or equivalently, the circle is inscribed in the polygon. In the figure below, quadrilateral *ABCD* is circumscribed about the circle with center *O*.

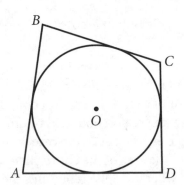

Two or more circles with the same center are called **concentric circles**, as shown in the figure below.

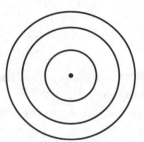

3.6 Three-dimensional Figures

Basic three-dimensional figures include rectangular solids, cubes, cylinders, spheres, pyramids, and cones. In this section, we look at some properties of rectangular solids and right circular cylinders.

A **rectangular solid** has six rectangular surfaces called **faces**, as shown in the figure below. Adjacent faces are perpendicular to each other. Each line segment that is the intersection of two faces is called an **edge**, and each point at which the edges intersect is called a **vertex**. There are 12 edges and 8 vertices. The dimensions of a rectangular solid are the length ℓ, the width w, and the height h.

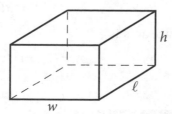

A rectangular solid with six square faces is called a **cube**, in which case $\ell = w = h$. The **volume** V of a rectangular solid is the product of its three dimensions, or

$$V = \ell w h$$

The **surface area** A of a rectangular solid is the sum of the areas of the six faces, or

$$A = 2(\ell w + \ell h + wh)$$

For example, if a rectangular solid has length 8.5, width 5, and height 10, then its volume is

$$V = (8.5)(5)(10) = 425$$

and its surface area is

$$A = 2((8.5)(5) + (8.5)(10) + (5)(10)) = 355$$

A **circular cylinder** consists of two bases that are congruent circles and a **lateral surface** made of all line segments that join points on the two circles and that are parallel to the line segment joining the centers of the two circles. The latter line segment is called the **axis** of the cylinder. A **right circular cylinder** is a circular cylinder whose axis is perpendicular to its bases.

The right circular cylinder shown in the figure below has circular bases with centers P and Q. Line segment PQ is the axis of the cylinder and is perpendicular to both bases. The length of PQ is called the height of the cylinder.

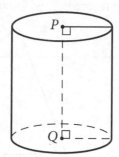

The **volume** V of a right circular cylinder that has height h and a base with radius r is the product of the height and the area of the base, or

$$V = \pi r^2 h$$

The **surface area** A of a right circular cylinder is the sum of the areas of the two bases and the lateral area, or

$$A = 2(\pi r^2) + 2\pi rh$$

For example, if a right circular cylinder has height 6.5 and a base with radius 3, then its volume is

$$V = \pi(3)^2(6.5) = 58.5\pi$$

and its surface area is

$$A = (2)(\pi)(3)^2 + (2)(\pi)(3)(6.5) = 57\pi$$

GEOMETRY EXERCISES

1. Lines ℓ and m below are parallel. Find the values of x and y.

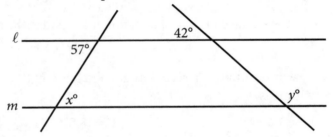

2. In the figure below, $AC = BC$. Find the values of x and y.

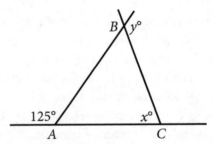

3. In the figure below, what is the relationship between x, y, and z?

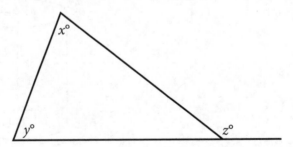

4.   What is the sum of the measures of the interior angles of a decagon (10-sided polygon)?

5.   If the decagon in exercise 4 is regular, what is the measure of each interior angle?

6.   The lengths of two sides of an isosceles triangle are 15 and 22, respectively. What are the possible values of the perimeter?

7.   Triangles *PQR* and *XYZ* are similar. If *PQ* = 6, *PR* = 4, and *XY* = 9, what is the length of side *XZ*?

8.   What are the lengths of sides *NO* and *OP* in triangle *NOP* below?

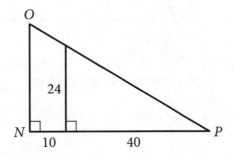

9.   In the figure below, *AB* = *BC* = *CD*. If the area of triangle *CDE* is 42, what is the area of triangle *ADG*?

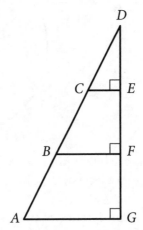

10. In rectangle *ABCD* below, *AB* = 5, *AF* = 7, and *FD* = 3. Find the following.
     (a) Area of *ABCD*
     (b) Area of triangle *AEF*
     (c) Length of *BD*
     (d) Perimeter of *ABCD*

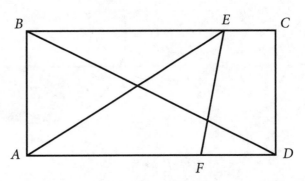

11. In parallelogram *ABCD* below, find the following.
    (a) Area of *ABCD*
    (b) Perimeter of *ABCD*
    (c) Length of diagonal *BD*

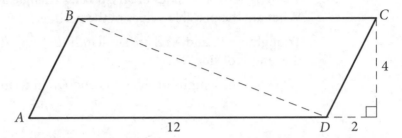

12. The circle with center *O* below has radius 4. Find the following.
    (a) Circumference of the circle
    (b) Length of arc *ABC*
    (c) Area of the shaded region

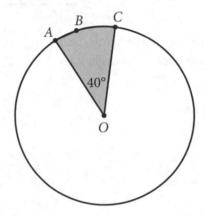

13. The figure below shows two concentric circles, each with center *O*. Given that the larger circle has radius 12 and the smaller circle has radius 7, find the following.
    (a) Circumference of the larger circle
    (b) Area of the smaller circle
    (c) Area of the shaded region

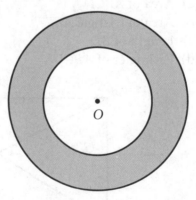

14. For the rectangular solid below, find the following.
    (a) Surface area of the solid
    (b) Length of diagonal *AB*

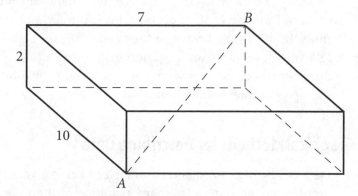

ANSWERS TO GEOMETRY EXERCISES

1. $x = 57$ and $y = 138$

2. $x = 70$ and $y = 125$

3. $z = x + y$

4. $1,440°$

5. $144°$

6. 52 and 59

7. 6

8. $NO = 30$ and $OP = 10\sqrt{34}$

9. 378

10. (a) 50
    (b) 17.5
    (c) $5\sqrt{5}$
    (d) 30

11. (a) 48
    (b) $24 + 4\sqrt{5}$
    (c) $2\sqrt{29}$

12. (a) 8π
    (b) $\dfrac{8\pi}{9}$
    (c) $\dfrac{16\pi}{9}$

13. (a) 24π
    (b) 49π
    (c) 95π

14. (a) 208
    (b) $3\sqrt{17}$

4. DATA ANALYSIS

The goal of data analysis is to understand data well enough to describe past and present trends, predict future events with some certainty, and thereby make better decisions. In this limited review of data analysis, we begin with tools for describing data; follow with tools for understanding counting and probability; review the concepts of distributions of data, random variables, and probability distributions; and end with examples of interpreting data.

4.1   Graphical Methods for Describing Data

Data can be organized and summarized using a variety of methods. Tables are commonly used, and there are many graphical and numerical methods as well. The appropriate type of representation for a collection of data depends in part on the nature of the data, such as whether the data are numerical or nonnumerical. In this section, we review some common graphical methods for describing and summarizing data.

Variables play a major role in algebra because a variable serves as a convenient name for many values at once, and it also can represent a particular value in a given problem to solve. In data analysis, variables also play an important role but with a somewhat different meaning. In data analysis, a **variable** is any characteristic that can vary for the population of individuals or objects being analyzed. For example, both gender and age represent variables among people.

Data are collected from a population after observing either a single variable or observing more than one variable simultaneously. The distribution of a variable, or **distribution of data**, indicates the values of the variable and how frequently the values are observed in the data.

Frequency Distributions

The **frequency**, or **count**, of a particular category or numerical value is the number of times that the category or value appears in the data. A **frequency distribution** is a table or graph that presents the categories or numerical values along with their associated frequencies. The **relative frequency** of a category or a numerical value is the associated frequency divided by the total number of data. Relative frequencies may be expressed in terms of percents, fractions, or decimals. A **relative frequency distribution** is a table or graph that presents the relative frequencies of the categories or numerical values.

Example 4.1.1: A survey was taken to find the number of children in each of 25 families. A list of the values collected in the survey follows.

1 2 0 4 1 3 3 1 2 0 4 5 2 3 2 3 2 4 1 2 3 0 2 3 1

Here are the resulting frequency and relative frequency distributions of the data.

Frequency Distribution

Number of Children	Frequency
0	3
1	5
2	7
3	6
4	3
5	1
Total	25

Relative Frequency Distribution

Number of Children	Relative Frequency
0	12%
1	20%
2	28%
3	24%
4	12%
5	4%
Total	100%

Note that the total for the relative frequencies is 100%. If decimals were used instead of percents, the total would be 1. The sum of the relative frequencies in a relative frequency distribution is always 1.

Bar Graphs

A commonly used graphical display for representing frequencies, or counts, is a **bar graph**, or bar chart. In a bar graph, rectangular bars are used to represent the categories of the data, and the height of each bar is proportional to the corresponding frequency or relative frequency. All of the bars are drawn with the same width, and the bars can be presented either vertically or horizontally. Bar graphs enable comparisons across several categories, making it easy to identify frequently and infrequently occurring categories.

Example 4.1.2:

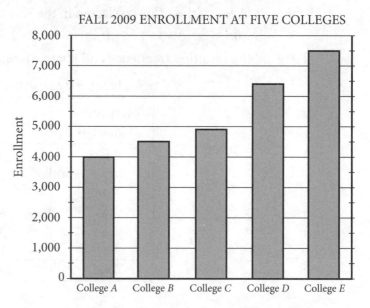

FALL 2009 ENROLLMENT AT FIVE COLLEGES

From the graph, we can conclude that the college with the greatest fall 2009 enrollment was College *E*, and the college with the least enrollment was College *A*. Also, we can estimate that the enrollment for College *D* was about 6,400.

A **segmented bar graph** is used to show how different subgroups or subcategories contribute to an entire group or category. In a segmented bar graph, each bar represents a category that consists of more than one subcategory. Each bar is divided into segments that represent the different subcategories. The height of each segment is proportional to the frequency or relative frequency of the subcategory that the segment represents.

Example 4.1.3:

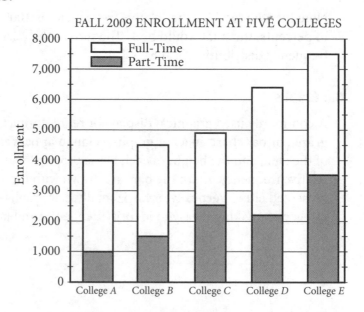

FALL 2009 ENROLLMENT AT FIVE COLLEGES

Different values can be estimated from the segmented bar graph above. For example, for College D, the total enrollment was approximately 6,400 students, the part-time enrollment was approximately 2,200, and the full-time enrollment was approximately 6,400 − 2,200, or 4,200 students.

Bar graphs can also be used to compare different groups using the same categories.

Example 4.1.4:

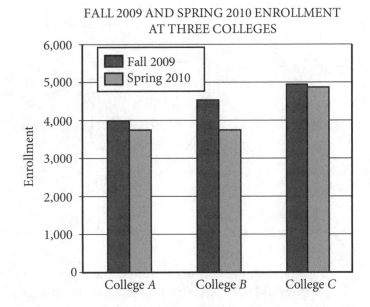

FALL 2009 AND SPRING 2010 ENROLLMENT
AT THREE COLLEGES

Observe that for all three colleges, the fall 2009 enrollment was greater than the spring 2010 enrollment. Also, the greatest decrease in the enrollment from fall 2009 to spring 2010 occurred at College B.

Although bar graphs are commonly used to compare frequencies, as in the examples above, they are sometimes used to compare numerical data that could be displayed in a table, such as temperatures, dollar amounts, percents, heights, and weights. Also, the categories sometimes are numerical in nature, such as years or other time intervals.

Circle Graphs

Circle graphs, often called pie charts, are used to represent data with a relatively small number of categories. They illustrate how a whole is separated into parts. The area of the circle graph representing each category is proportional to the part of the whole that the category represents.

Example 4.1.5:

UNITED STATES PRODUCTION OF PHOTOGRAPHIC EQUIPMENT AND SUPPLIES IN 1971

Total: $3,980 million

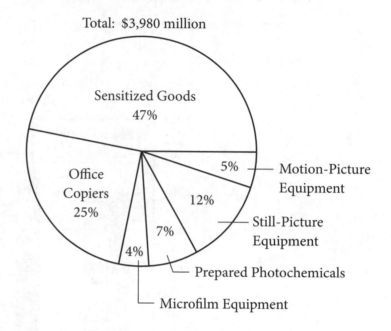

The graph shows that of all United States production of photographic equipment and supplies in 1971, Sensitized Goods was the category with the greatest dollar value.

Each part of a circle graph is called a **sector**. Because the area of each sector is proportional to the percent of the whole that the sector represents, the measure of the central angle of a sector is proportional to the percent of 360 degrees that the sector represents. For example, the measure of the central angle of the sector representing the category Prepared Photochemicals is 7 percent of 360 degrees, or 25.2 degrees.

Histograms

When a list of data is large and contains many different values of a numerical variable, it is useful to organize it by grouping the values into intervals, often called classes. To do this, divide the entire interval of values into smaller intervals of equal length and then count the values that fall into each interval. In this way, each interval has a frequency and a relative frequency. The intervals and their frequencies (or relative frequencies) are often displayed in a **histogram**. Histograms are graphs of frequency distributions that are similar to bar graphs, but they have a number line for the horizontal axis. Also, in a histogram, there are no regular spaces between the bars. Any spaces between bars in a histogram indicate that there are no data in the intervals represented by the spaces.

Example 4.5.1 in section 4.5 illustrates a histogram with 50 bars. Numerical variables with just a few values can also be displayed using histograms, where the frequency or relative frequency of each value is represented by a bar centered over the value, as in the histogram in the following example.

Example 4.1.6: The relative frequency distribution in example 4.1.1 can be displayed as a histogram.

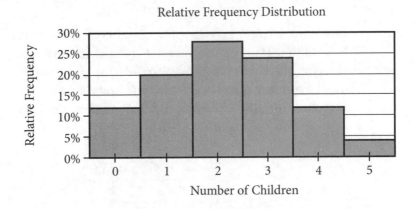

Relative Frequency Distribution

Histograms are useful for identifying the general shape of a distribution of data. Also evident are the "center" and degree of "spread" of the distribution, as well as high-frequency and low-frequency intervals. From the histogram above, you can see that the distribution is shaped like a mound with one peak; that is, the data are frequent in the middle and sparse at both ends. The central values are 2 and 3, and the distribution is close to being symmetric about those values. Because the bars all have the same width, the area of each bar is proportional to the amount of data that the bar represents. Thus, the areas of the bars indicate where the data are concentrated and where they are not.

Finally, note that because each bar has a width of 1, the sum of the areas of the bars equals the sum of the relative frequencies, which is 100% or 1, depending on whether percents or decimals are used. This fact is central to the discussion of probability distributions in section 4.5.

Scatterplots

All examples used thus far have involved data resulting from a single characteristic or variable. These types of data are referred to as **univariate**, that is, data observed for one variable. Sometimes data are collected to study two different variables in the same population of individuals or objects. Such data are called **bivariate** data. We might want to study the variables separately or investigate a relationship between the two variables. If the variables were to be analyzed separately, each of the graphical methods for univariate numerical data presented above could be applied.

To show the relationship between two numerical variables, the most useful type of graph is a **scatterplot**. In a scatterplot, the values of one variable appear on the horizontal axis of a rectangular coordinate system and the values of the other variable appear on the vertical axis. For each individual or object in the data, an ordered pair of numbers is collected, one number for each variable, and the pair is represented by a point in the coordinate system.

A scatterplot makes it possible to observe an overall pattern, or **trend**, in the relationship between the two variables. Also, the strength of the trend as well as striking deviations from the trend are evident. In many cases, a line or a curve that best represents the trend is also displayed in the graph and is used to make predictions about the population.

Example 4.1.7: A bicycle trainer studied 50 bicyclists to examine how the finishing time for a certain bicycle race was related to the amount of physical training in the three months before the race. To measure the amount of training, the trainer developed a training index, measured in "units" and based on the intensity of each bicyclist's training. The data and the trend of the data, represented by a line, are displayed in the scatterplot below.

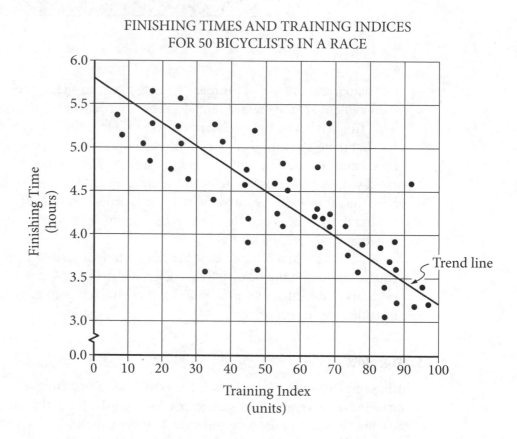

FINISHING TIMES AND TRAINING INDICES
FOR 50 BICYCLISTS IN A RACE

In addition to the given trend line, you can see how scattered or close the data are to the trend line; or to put it another way, you can see how well the trend line fits the data. You can also see that the finishing times generally decrease as the training indices increase and that three or four data are relatively far from the trend.

Several types of predictions can be based on the trend line. For example, it can be predicted, based on the trend line, that a bicyclist with a training index of 70 units would finish the race in approximately 4 hours. This value is obtained by noting that the vertical line at the training index of 70 units intersects the trend line very close to 4 hours.

Another prediction based on the trend line is the number of minutes that a bicyclist can expect to lower his or her finishing time for each increase of 10 training index units. This prediction is basically the ratio of the change in finishing time to the change in training index, or the slope of the trend line. Note that the slope is negative. To estimate the slope, estimate the coordinates of any two points on the line—for instance, the points at the extreme left and right ends of the line: (0, 5.8) and (100, 3.2). The slope is

$$\frac{3.2-5.8}{100-0} = \frac{-2.6}{100} = -0.026$$

which is measured in hours per unit. The slope can be interpreted as follows: the finishing time is predicted to decrease 0.026 hours for every unit by which the training index increases. Since we want to know how much the finishing time decreases for an increase of *10 units*, we multiply the rate by 10 to get 0.26 hour per 10 units. To compute the decrease in *minutes* per 10 units, we multiply 0.26 by 60 to get approximately 16 minutes. Based on the trend line, the bicyclist can expect to decrease the finishing time by 16 minutes for every increase of 10 training index units.

Time Plots

Sometimes data are collected in order to observe changes in a variable over time. For example, sales for a department store may be collected monthly or yearly. A **time plot** (sometimes called a time series) is a graphical display useful for showing changes in data collected at regular intervals of time. A time plot of a variable plots each observation corresponding to the time at which it was measured. A time plot uses a coordinate plane similar to a scatterplot, but the time is always on the horizontal axis, and the variable measured is always on the vertical axis. Additionally, consecutive observations are connected by a line segment to emphasize increases and decreases over time.

Example 4.1.8:

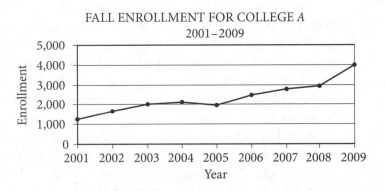

You can observe from the graph that the greatest increase in fall enrollment between consecutive years occurred from 2008 to 2009. One way to determine this is by noting that the slope of the line segment joining the values for 2008 and 2009 is greater than the slopes of the line segments joining all other consecutive years, because the time intervals are regular.

Although time plots are commonly used to compare frequencies, as in the example above, they can be used to compare any numerical data as the data change over time, such as temperatures, dollar amounts, percents, heights, and weights.

4.2 Numerical Methods for Describing Data

Data can be described numerically by various **statistics**, or **statistical measures**. These statistical measures are often grouped in three categories: measures of central tendency, measures of position, and measures of dispersion.

Measures of Central Tendency

Measures of **central tendency** indicate the "center" of the data along the number line and are usually reported as values that represent the data. There are three common measures of central tendency: (i) the **arithmetic mean**—usually called the **average** or simply the **mean**, (ii) the **median**, and (iii) the **mode**.

To calculate the **mean** of n numbers, take the sum of the n numbers and divide it by n.

Example 4.2.1: For the five numbers 6, 4, 7, 10, and 4, the mean is

$$\frac{6+4+7+10+4}{5} = \frac{31}{5} = 6.2$$

When several values are repeated in a list, it is helpful to think of the mean of the numbers as a **weighted mean** of only those values in the list that are *different*.

Example 4.2.2: Consider the following list of 16 numbers.

$$2,\ 4,\ 4,\ 5,\ 7,\ 7,\ 7,\ 7,\ 7,\ 7,\ 8,\ 8,\ 9,\ 9,\ 9,\ 9$$

There are only 6 different values in the list: 2, 4, 5, 7, 8, and 9. The mean of the numbers in the list can be computed as

$$\frac{1(2)+2(4)+1(5)+6(7)+2(8)+4(9)}{1+2+1+6+2+4} = \frac{109}{16} = 6.8125$$

The number of times a value appears in the list, or the frequency, is called the **weight** of that value. So the mean of the 16 numbers is the weighted mean of the values 2, 4, 5, 7, 8, and 9, where the respective weights are 1, 2, 1, 6, 2, and 4. Note that the sum of the weights is the number of numbers in the list, 16.

The mean can be affected by just a few values that lie far above or below the rest of the data, because these values contribute directly to the sum of the data and therefore to the mean. By contrast, the **median** is a measure of central tendency that is fairly unaffected by unusually high or low values relative to the rest of the data.

To calculate the median of n numbers, first order the numbers from least to greatest. If n is odd, then the median is the middle number in the ordered list of numbers. If n is even, then there are *two* middle numbers, and the median is the average of these two numbers.

Example 4.2.3: The five numbers in example 4.2.1 listed in increasing order are 4, 4, 6, 7, 10, so the median is 6, the middle number. Note that if the number 10 in the list is replaced by the number 24, the mean increases from 6.2 to

$$\frac{4+4+6+7+24}{5} = \frac{45}{5} = 9$$

but the median remains equal to 6. This example shows how the median is relatively unaffected by an unusually large value.

The median, as the "middle value" of an ordered list of numbers, divides the list into roughly two equal parts. However, if the median is equal to one of the data values and it is repeated in the list, then the numbers of data above and below the median may be rather different. See example 4.2.2, where the median is 7, but four of the data are less than 7 and six of the data are greater than 7.

The **mode** of a list of numbers is the number that occurs most frequently in the list.

Example 4.2.4: The mode of the numbers in the list 1, 3, 6, 4, 3, 5 is 3. A list of numbers may have more than one mode. For example, the list 1, 2, 3, 3, 3, 5, 7, 10, 10, 10, 20 has two modes, 3 and 10.

Measures of Position

The three most basic **positions**, or locations, in a list of data ordered from least to greatest are the beginning, the end, and the middle. It is useful here to label these as L for the least, G for the greatest, and M for the median. Aside from these, the most common measures of position are **quartiles** and **percentiles**. Like the median M, quartiles and percentiles are numbers that divide the data into roughly equal groups after the data have been ordered from the least value L to the greatest value G. There are three quartile numbers that divide the data into four roughly equal groups, and there are 99 percentile numbers that divide the data into 100 roughly equal groups. As with the mean and median, the quartiles and percentiles may or may not themselves be values in the data.

The **first quartile** Q_1, the **second quartile** Q_2 (which is simply the median M), and the **third quartile** Q_3 divide a group of data into four roughly equal groups as follows. After the data are listed in increasing order, the first group consists of the data from L to Q_1, the second group is from Q_1 to M, the third group is from M to Q_3, and the fourth group is from Q_3 to G. Because the number of data in a list may not be divisible by 4, there are various rules to determine the exact values of Q_1 and Q_3 and some statisticians use different rules, but in all cases $Q_2 = M$. We use perhaps the most common rule, in which $Q_2 = M$ divides the data into two equal parts—the lesser numbers and the greater numbers—and then Q_1 is the median of the lesser numbers and Q_3 is the median of the greater numbers.

Example 4.2.5: To find the quartiles for the list of 16 numbers 2, 4, 4, 5, 7, 7, 7, 7, 7, 7, 8, 8, 9, 9, 9, 9 (already listed in order), first divide the data into two groups of 8 numbers each. The first group is 2, 4, 4, 5, 7, 7, 7, 7 and the second group is 7, 7, 8, 8, 9, 9, 9, 9, so that the second quartile, or median, is $Q_2 = M = 7$. To find the other quartiles, you can take each of the two smaller groups and find *its* median: the first quartile is $Q_1 = 6$ (the average of 5 and 7) and the third quartile is $Q_3 = 8.5$ (the average of 8 and 9).

In example 4.2.5, note that the number 4 is in the lowest 25 percent of the distribution of data. There are different ways to describe this. We can say that 4 is *below* the first quartile, that is, below Q_1; we can also say that 4 is *in* the first quartile. The phrase "*in* a quartile" refers to being *in* one of the four groups determined by Q_1, Q_2, and Q_3.

Percentiles are mostly used for very large lists of numerical data ordered from least to greatest. Instead of dividing the data into four groups, the 99 percentiles $P_1, P_2, P_3, \ldots, P_{99}$ divide the data into 100 groups. Consequently, $Q_1 = P_{25}$, $M = Q_2 = P_{50}$, and $Q_3 = P_{75}$. Because the number of data in a list may not be divisible by 100, statisticians apply various rules to determine values of percentiles.

Measures of Dispersion

Measures of **dispersion** indicate the degree of "spread" of the data. The most common statistics used as measures of dispersion are the range, the interquartile range, and the standard deviation. These statistics measure the spread of the data in different ways.

The **range** of the numbers in a group of data is the difference between the greatest number G in the data and the least number L in the data, that is, $G - L$. For example, given the list 11, 10, 5, 13, 21, the range of the numbers is $21 - 5 = 16$.

The simplicity of the range is useful in that it reflects that maximum spread of the data. However, sometimes a data value is so unusually small or so unusually large in comparison with the rest of the data that it is viewed with suspicion when the data are analyzed—the value could be erroneous or accidental in nature. Such data are called **outliers** because they lie so far out that in most cases, they are ignored when analyzing the data. Unfortunately, the range is directly affected by outliers.

A measure of dispersion that is not affected by outliers is the **interquartile range**. It is defined as the difference between the third quartile and the first quartile, that is, $Q_3 - Q_1$. Thus, the interquartile range measures the spread of the middle half of the data.

Example 4.2.6: In the list of 16 numbers 2, 4, 4, 5, 7, 7, 7, 7, 7, 7, 8, 8, 9, 9, 9, 9, the range is $9 - 2 = 7$, the first quartile is $Q_1 = 6$, and the third quartile is $Q_3 = 8.5$. So the interquartile range for the numbers in this list is $8.5 - 6 = 2.5$.

One way to summarize a group of numerical data and to illustrate its center and spread is to use the five numbers $L, Q_1, Q_2, Q_3,$ and G. These five numbers can be plotted along a number line to show where the four quartile groups lie. Such plots are called **boxplots** or **box-and-whisker plots**, because a box is used to identify each of the two middle quartile groups of data, and "whiskers" extend outward from the boxes to the least and greatest values. The following graph shows the boxplot for the list of 16 numbers in example 4.2.6.

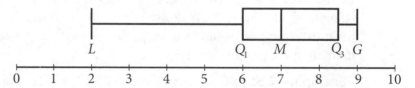

There are a few variations in the way boxplots are drawn—the position of the ends of the boxes can vary slightly, and some boxplots identify outliers with certain symbols—but all boxplots show the center of the data at the median and illustrate the spread of the data in each of the four quartile groups. As such, boxplots are useful for comparing sets of data side by side.

Example 4.2.7: Two large lists of numerical data, list I and list II, are summarized by the following boxplots.

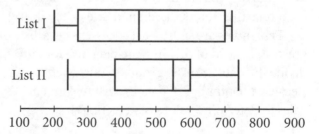

Based on the boxplots, several different comparisons of the two lists can be made. First, the median of list II, which is approximately 550, is greater than the median of list I, which is approximately 450. Second, the two measures of spread, range and interquartile range, are greater for list I than for list II. For list I, these measures are approximately 520 and 430, respectively; and for list II, they are approximately 500 and 220, respectively.

Unlike the range and the interquartile range, the **standard deviation** is a measure of spread that depends on each number in the list. Using the mean as the center of the data, the standard deviation takes into account how much each value differs from the mean and then takes a type of average of these differences. As a result, the more the data are spread away from the mean, the greater the standard deviation; and the more the data are clustered around the mean, the lesser the standard deviation.

The standard deviation of a group of n numerical data is computed by (1) calculating the mean of the n values, (2) finding the difference between the mean and each of the n values, (3) squaring each of the differences, (4) finding the average of the n squared differences, and (5) taking the nonnegative square root of the average squared difference.

Example 4.2.8: For the five data 0, 7, 8, 10, and 10, the standard deviation can be computed as follows. First, the mean of the data is 7, and the squared differences from the mean are

$$(7 - 0)^2, (7 - 7)^2, (7 - 8)^2, (7 - 10)^2, (7 - 10)^2$$

or 49, 0, 1, 9, 9. The average of the five squared differences is $\dfrac{68}{5}$, or 13.6, and the positive square root of 13.6 is approximately 3.7.

Note on terminology: The term "standard deviation" defined above is slightly different from another measure of dispersion, the **sample standard deviation**. The latter term is qualified with the word "sample" and is computed by dividing the sum of the squared differences by $n - 1$ instead of n. The sample standard deviation is only slightly different from the standard deviation but is preferred for technical reasons for a sample of data that is taken from a larger population of data. Sometimes the standard deviation is called the **population standard deviation** to help distinguish it from the sample standard deviation.

Example 4.2.9: Six hundred applicants for several post office jobs were rated on a scale from 1 to 50 points. The ratings had a mean of 32.5 points and a standard deviation of 7.1 points. How many standard deviations above or below the mean is a rating of 48 points? A rating of 30 points? A rating of 20 points?

Solution: Let d be the standard deviation, so $d = 7.1$ points. Note that 1 standard deviation above the mean is

$$32.5 + d = 32.5 + 7.1 = 39.6$$

and 2 standard deviations above the mean is

$$32.5 + 2d = 32.5 + 2(7.1) = 46.7$$

So 48 is a little more than 2 standard deviations above the mean. Since 48 is actually 15.5 points above the mean, the number of standard deviations that 48 is above the mean is $\dfrac{15.5}{7.1} \approx 2.2$. Thus, to answer the question, we first found the difference from the mean and then we divided by the standard deviation. The number of standard deviations that a rating of 30 is away from the mean is

$$\frac{30-32.5}{7.1} = \frac{-2.5}{7.1} \approx -0.4$$

where the negative sign indicates that the rating is 0.4 standard deviation *below* the mean.

The number of standard deviations that a rating of 20 is away from the mean is

$$\frac{20-32.5}{7.1} = \frac{-12.5}{7.1} \approx -1.8$$

where the negative sign indicates that the rating is 1.8 standard deviations *below* the mean.

To summarize:

- 48 points is 15.5 points above the mean, or approximately 2.2 standard deviations above the mean.
- 30 points is 2.5 points below the mean, or approximately 0.4 standard deviation below the mean.
- 20 points is 12.5 points below the mean, or approximately 1.8 standard deviations below the mean.

One more instance, which may seem trivial, is important to note:

- 32.5 points is 0 points from the mean, or 0 standard deviations from the mean.

Example 4.2.9 shows that for a group of data, each value can be located with respect to the mean by using the standard deviation as a ruler. The process of subtracting the mean from each value and then dividing the result by the standard deviation is called **standardization**. Standardization is a useful tool because for each data value, it provides a measure of position relative to the rest of the data independent of the variable for which the data was collected and the units of the variable.

Note that the standardized values 2.2, −0.4, and −1.8 from example 4.2.9 are all between −3 and 3; that is, the corresponding ratings 48, 30, and 20 are all within 3 standard deviations above or below the mean. This is not surprising, based on the following fact about the standard deviation.

In **any group of data**, *most of the data are within about **3** standard deviations above or below the mean.*

Thus, when *any group of data* are standardized, most of the data are transformed to an interval on the number line centered about 0 and extending from about −3 to 3. The mean is always transformed to 0.

4.3 Counting Methods

Uncertainty is part of the process of making decisions and predicting outcomes. Uncertainty is addressed with the ideas and methods of probability theory. Since elementary probability requires an understanding of counting methods, we now turn to a discussion of counting objects in a systematic way before reviewing probability.

When a set of objects is small, it is easy to list the objects and count them one by one. When the set is too large to count that way, and when the objects are related in a patterned or systematic way, there are some useful techniques for counting the objects without actually listing them.

Sets and Lists

The term **set** has been used informally in this review to mean a collection of objects that have some property, whether it is the collection of all positive integers, all points in a circular region, or all students in a school that have studied French. The objects of a set are called **members** or **elements**. Some sets are **finite**, which means that their members can be completely counted. Finite sets can, in principle, have all of their members listed, using curly brackets, such as the set of even digits {0, 2, 4, 6, 8}. Sets that are not finite are called **infinite** sets, such as the set of all integers. A set that has no members is called the **empty set** and is denoted by the symbol $\varnothing$. A set with one or more members is called **nonempty**. If A and B are sets and all of the members of A are also members of B, then A is a **subset** of B. For example, {2, 8} is a subset of {0, 2, 4, 6, 8}. Also, by convention, $\varnothing$ is a subset of every set.

A **list** is like a finite set, having members that can all be listed, but with two differences. In a list, the members are ordered; that is, rearranging the members of a list makes it a different list. Thus, the terms "first element," "second element," etc., make sense in a list. Also, elements can be repeated in a list and the repetitions matter. For example, the lists 1, 2, 3, 2 and 1, 2, 2, 3 are different lists, each with four elements, and they are both different from the list 1, 2, 3, which has three elements.

In contrast to a list, when the elements of a set are given, repetitions are not counted as additional elements and the order of the elements does not matter. For example, the sets {1, 2, 3, 2} and {3, 1, 2} are the same set, which has three elements. For any finite set S, the number of elements of S is denoted by $|S|$. Thus, if $S = \{6.2, -9, \pi, 0.01, 0\}$, then $|S| = 5$. Also, $|\varnothing| = 0$.

Sets can be formed from other sets. If S and T are sets, then the **intersection** of S and T is the set of all elements that are in both S and T and is denoted by $S \cap T$. The **union** of S and T is the set of all elements that are in S or T, or both, and is denoted by $S \cup T$. If sets S and T have no elements in common, they are called **disjoint** or **mutually exclusive**.

A useful way to represent two or three sets and their possible intersections and unions is a **Venn diagram**. In a Venn diagram, sets are represented by circular regions that overlap if they have elements in common but do not overlap if they are disjoint. Sometimes the circular regions are drawn inside a rectangular region, which represents a **universal set**, of which all other sets involved are subsets.

Example 4.3.1: The sets *A*, *B*, and *C* are represented in the Venn diagram below, where *U* represents a universal set.

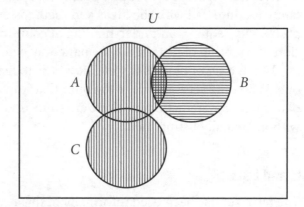

The regions with vertical stripes represent the set $A \cup C$. The regions with horizontal stripes represent the set *B*. The region with both kinds of stripes represents the set $A \cap B$. The sets *B* and *C* are mutually exclusive, often written $B \cap C = \varnothing$.

The example above can be used to illustrate an elementary counting principle involving intersecting sets, called the **inclusion-exclusion principle** for two sets. This principle relates the numbers of elements in the union and intersection of two finite sets: The number of elements in the union of two sets equals the sum of their individual numbers of elements minus the number of elements in their intersection. If the sets in example 4.3.1 are finite, then we have for the union of *A* and *B*,

$$|A \cup B| = |A| + |B| - |A \cap B|$$

Because $A \cap B$ is a subset of both *A* and *B*, the subtraction is necessary to avoid counting the elements in $A \cap B$ twice. For the union of *B* and *C*, we have

$$|B \cup C| = |B| + |C|$$

because $B \cap C = \varnothing$.

Multiplication Principle

Suppose there are two choices to be made sequentially and that the second choice is independent of the first choice. Suppose also that there are *k* different possibilities for the first choice and *m* different possibilities for the second choice. The **multiplication principle** states that under those conditions, there are *km* different possibilities for the pair of choices.

For example, suppose that a meal is to be ordered from a restaurant menu and that the meal consists of one entrée and one dessert. If there are 5 entrées and 3 desserts on the menu, then there are $(5)(3) = 15$ different meals that can be ordered from the menu.

The multiplication principle applies in more complicated situations as well. If there are more than two independent choices to be made, then the number of different possible outcomes of all of the choices is the product of the numbers of possibilities for each choice.

Example 4.3.2: Suppose that a computer password consists of four characters such that the first character is one of the 10 digits from 0 to 9 and each of the next 3 characters is any one of the uppercase letters from the 26 letters of the English alphabet. How many different passwords are possible?

Solution: The description of the password allows repetitions of letters. Thus, there are 10 possible choices for the first character in the password and 26 possible choices for each of the next 3 characters in the password. Therefore, applying the multiplication principle, the number of possible passwords is $(10)(26)(26)(26) = 175{,}760$.

Note that if repetitions of letters are *not* allowed in the password, then the choices are not all independent, but a modification of the multiplication principle can still be applied. There are 10 possible choices for the first character in the password, 26 possible choices for the second character, 25 for the third character because the first letter cannot be repeated, and 24 for the fourth character because the first two letters cannot be repeated. Therefore, the number of possible passwords is $(10)(26)(25)(24) = 156{,}000$.

Example 4.3.3: Each time a coin is tossed, there are 2 possible outcomes—either it lands heads up or it lands tails up. Using this fact and the multiplication principle, you can conclude that if a coin is tossed 8 times, there are $(2)(2)(2)(2)(2)(2)(2)(2) = 2^8 = 256$ possible outcomes.

Permutations and Factorials

Suppose you want to determine the number of different ways the 3 letters A, B, and C can be placed in order from 1st to 3rd. The following is a list of all the possible orders in which the letters can be placed.

ABC   ACB   BAC   BCA   CAB   CBA

There are 6 possible orders for the 3 letters.

Now suppose you want to determine the number of different ways the 4 letters A, B, C, and D can be placed in order from 1st to 4th. Listing all of the orders for 4 letters is time-consuming, so it would be useful to be able to count the possible orders without listing them.

To order the 4 letters, one of the 4 letters must be placed first, one of the remaining 3 letters must be placed second, one of the remaining 2 letters must be placed third, and the last remaining letter must be placed fourth. Therefore, applying the multiplication principle, there are $(4)(3)(2)(1)$, or 24, ways to order the 4 letters.

More generally, suppose n objects are to be ordered from 1st to nth, and we want to count the number of ways the objects can be ordered. There are n choices for the first object, $n - 1$ choices for the second object, $n - 2$ choices for the third object, and so on, until there is only 1 choice for the nth object. Thus, applying the multiplication principle, the number of ways to order the n objects is equal to the product

$$n(n-1)(n-2)\cdots(3)(2)(1)$$

Each order is called a **permutation**, and the product above is called the number of permutations of n objects.

Because products of the form $n(n-1)(n-2)\cdots(3)(2)(1)$ occur frequently when counting objects, a special symbol $n!$, called **n factorial**, is used to denote this product. For example,

$$1! = 1$$
$$2! = (2)(1) = 2$$
$$3! = (3)(2)(1) = 6$$
$$4! = (4)(3)(2)(1) = 24$$

As a special definition, $0! = 1$.

Note that $n! = n(n-1)! = n(n-1)(n-2)! = n(n-1)(n-2)(n-3)!$ and so on.

Example 4.3.4: Suppose that 10 students are going on a bus trip, and each of the students will be assigned to one of the 10 available seats. Then the number of possible different seating arrangements of the students on the bus is

$$10! = (10)(9)(8)(7)(6)(5)(4)(3)(2)(1) = 3,628,800$$

Now suppose you want to determine the number of ways in which you can select 3 of the 5 letters A, B, C, D, and E and place them in order from 1st to 3rd. Reasoning as in the preceding examples, you find that there are $(5)(4)(3)$, or 60, ways to select and order them.

More generally, suppose that k objects will be selected from a set of n objects, where $k \leq n$, and the k objects will be placed in order from 1st to kth. Then there are n choices for the first object, $n - 1$ choices for the second object, $n - 2$ choices for the third object, and so on, until there are $n - k + 1$ choices for the kth object. Thus, applying the multiplication principle, the number of ways to select and order k objects from a set of n objects is $n(n-1)(n-2)\cdots(n-k+1)$. It is useful to note that

$$n(n-1)(n-2)\cdots(n-k+1) = n(n-1)(n-2)\cdots(n-k+1)\frac{(n-k)!}{(n-k)!}$$

$$= \frac{n!}{(n-k)!}$$

This expression represents the number of **permutations of n objects taken k at a time**, that is, the number of ways to select and order k objects out of n objects.

Example 4.3.5: How many different five-digit positive integers can be formed using the digits 1, 2, 3, 4, 5, 6, and 7 if none of the digits can occur more than once in the integer?

Solution: This example asks how many ways there are to order 5 integers chosen from a set of 7 integers. According to the counting principle above, there are $(7)(6)(5)(4)(3) = 2,520$ ways to do this. Note that this is equal to

$$\frac{7!}{(7-5)!} = \frac{(7)(6)(5)(4)(3)(2!)}{2!} = (7)(6)(5)(4)(3).$$

Combinations

Given the five letters A, B, C, D, and E, suppose that you want to determine the number of ways in which you can select 3 of the 5 letters, but unlike before, you do not want to count different orders for the 3 letters. The following is a list of all of the ways in which 3 of the 5 letters can be selected without regard to the order of the letters.

ABC ABD ABE ACD ACE ADE BCD BCE BDE CDE

There are 10 ways of selecting the 3 letters without order. There is a relationship between selecting with order and selecting without order.

The number of ways to select 3 of the 5 letters without order, which is 10, *multiplied by* the number of ways to order the 3 letters, which is 3!, or 6, *is equal to* the number of ways to select 3 of the 5 letters and order them, which is $\dfrac{5!}{2!} = 60$. In short,

$$(\text{number of ways to select without order}) \times (\text{number of ways to order})$$
$$= (\text{number of ways to select with order})$$

This relationship can also be described as follows.

$$(\text{number of ways to select without order}) = \frac{(\text{number of ways to select with order})}{(\text{number of ways to order})}$$

$$= \frac{\dfrac{5!}{2!}}{3!} = \frac{5!}{3!\,2!} = 10$$

More generally, suppose that k objects will be chosen from a set of n objects, where $k \leq n$, but that the k objects will *not* be put in order. The number of ways in which this can be done is called the number of **combinations of n objects taken k at a time** and is given by the formula $\dfrac{n!}{k!(n-k)!}$.

Another way to refer to the number of combinations of n objects taken k at a time is **n choose k**, and two notations commonly used to denote this number are $_nC_k$ and $\dbinom{n}{k}$.

Example 4.3.6: Suppose you want to select a 3-person committee from a group of 9 students. How many ways are there to do this?

Solution: Since the 3 students on the committee are not ordered, you can use the formula for the combination of 9 objects taken 3 at a time, or "9 choose 3":

$$\frac{9!}{3!(9-3)!} = \frac{9!}{3!\,6!} = \frac{(9)(8)(7)}{(3)(2)(1)} = 84$$

Using the terminology of sets, given a set S consisting of n elements, n choose k is simply the number of subsets of S that consist of k elements. The formula $\dfrac{n!}{k!(n-k)!}$ also holds when $k = 0$ and $k = n$.

- n choose 0 is $\dfrac{n!}{0!n!} = 1$, which corresponds to the fact that there is only one subset of S with 0 elements, namely the empty set.

- n choose n is $\dfrac{n!}{n!0!} = 1$, since there is only one subset of S with n elements, namely the set S itself.

Finally, note that n choose k is always equal to n choose $n - k$, because

$$\frac{n!}{(n-k)!(n-(n-k))!} = \frac{n!}{(n-k)!k!} = \frac{n!}{k!(n-k)!}$$

4.4 Probability

Probability is a way of describing uncertainty in numerical terms. In this section we review some of the terminology used in elementary probability theory.

A **probability experiment**, also called a **random experiment**, is an experiment for which the result, or **outcome**, is uncertain. We assume that all of the possible outcomes of an experiment are known before the experiment is performed, but which outcome will actually occur is unknown. The set of all possible outcomes of a random experiment is called the **sample space**, and any particular set of outcomes is called an **event**. For example, consider a cube with faces numbered 1 to 6, called a 6-sided die. Rolling the die once is an experiment in which there are 6 possible outcomes—either 1, 2, 3, 4, 5, or 6 will appear on the top face. The sample space for this experiment is the set of numbers 1, 2, 3, 4, 5, and 6. Two examples of events for this experiment are (i) rolling the number 4, which has only one outcome, and (ii) rolling an odd number, which has three outcomes.

The **probability** of an event is a number from 0 to 1, inclusive, that indicates the likelihood that the event occurs when the experiment is performed. The greater the number, the more likely the event.

Example 4.4.1: Consider the following experiment. A box contains 15 pieces of paper, each of which has the name of one of the 15 students in a class consisting of 7 male and 8 female students, all with different names. The instructor will shake the box for a while and then, without looking, choose a piece of paper at random and read the name. Here the sample space is the set of 15 names. The assumption of **random selection** means that each of the names is **equally likely** to be selected. If this assumption is made, then the probability that any one particular name is selected is equal to $\frac{1}{15}$. For any event E, the probability that E occurs, denoted by $P(E)$, is defined by the ratio

$$P(E) = \frac{\text{the number of names in the event } E}{15}$$

If M is the event that the student selected is male, then $P(M) = \frac{7}{15}$.

In general, for a random experiment with a finite number of possible outcomes, if each outcome is equally likely to occur, then the probability that an event E occurs is defined by the ratio

$$P(E) = \frac{\text{the number of outcomes in the event } E}{\text{the number of possible outcomes in the experiment}}$$

In the case of rolling a 6-sided die, if the die is "fair," then the 6 outcomes are equally likely. So the probability of rolling a 4 is $\frac{1}{6}$, and the probability of rolling an odd number—rolling a 1, 3, or 5—can be calculated as $\frac{3}{6} = \frac{1}{2}$.

The following are general facts about probability.

- If an event E is certain to occur, then $P(E) = 1$.
- If an event E is certain *not* to occur, then $P(E) = 0$.
- If an event E is possible but not certain to occur, then $0 < P(E) < 1$.
- The probability that an event E will not occur is equal to $1 - P(E)$.
- If E is an event, then the probability of E is the sum of the probabilities of the outcomes in E.
- The sum of the probabilities of all possible outcomes of an experiment is 1.

If E and F are two events of an experiment, we consider two other events related to E and F.

- The event that both E and F occur, that is, all outcomes in the set $E \cap F$.
- The event that E or F, or both, occur, that is, all outcomes in the set $E \cup F$.

Events that cannot occur at the same time are said to be **mutually exclusive**. For example, if a 6-sided die is rolled once, the event of rolling an odd number and the event of rolling an even number are mutually exclusive. But rolling a 4 and rolling an even number are not mutually exclusive, since 4 is an outcome that is common to both events.

For events E and F, we have the following rules.

- $P(E \text{ or } F, \text{ or both, occur}) = P(E) + P(F) - P(\text{both } E \text{ and } F \text{ occur})$, which is the inclusion-exclusion principle applied to probability.
- If E and F are mutually exclusive, then $P(\text{both } E \text{ and } F \text{ occur}) = 0$, and therefore, $P(E \text{ or } F, \text{ or both, occur}) = P(E) + P(F)$.

- E and F are said to be **independent** if the occurrence of either event does not affect the occurrence of the other. If two events E and F are independent, then $P(\text{both } E \text{ and } F \text{ occur}) = P(E)P(F)$. For example, if a fair 6-sided die is rolled twice, the event E of rolling a 3 on the first roll and the event F of rolling a 3 on the second roll are independent, and the probability of rolling a 3 on both rolls is $P(E)P(F) = \left(\dfrac{1}{6}\right)\left(\dfrac{1}{6}\right) = \dfrac{1}{36}$. In this example, the experiment is actually "rolling the die twice," and each outcome is an ordered pair of results like "4 on the first roll and 1 on the second roll." But event E restricts only the first roll—to a 3—having no effect on the second roll; similarly, event F restricts only the second roll—to a 3—having no effect on the first roll.

Note that if $P(E) \neq 0$ and $P(F) \neq 0$, then events E and F cannot be both mutually exclusive and independent. For if E and F are independent, then $P(\text{both } E \text{ and } F \text{ occur}) = P(E)P(F) \neq 0$; but if E and F are mutually exclusive, then $P(\text{both } E \text{ and } F \text{ occur}) = 0$.

It is common to use the shorter notation "E and F" instead of "both E and F occur" and use "E or F" instead of "E or F, or both, occur." With this notation, we have the following rules.

- $P(E \text{ or } F) = P(E) + P(F) - P(E \text{ and } F)$
- $P(E \text{ or } F) = P(E) + P(F)$ if E and F are mutually exclusive.
- $P(E \text{ and } F) = P(E)P(F)$ if E and F are independent.

Example 4.4.2: If a fair 6-sided die is rolled once, let E be the event of rolling a 3 and let F be the event of rolling an odd number. These events are *not* independent. This is because rolling a 3 makes certain that the event of rolling an odd number occurs. Note that $P(E \text{ and } F) \neq P(E)P(F)$, since

$$P(E \text{ and } F) = P(E) = \frac{1}{6} \text{ and } P(E)P(F) = \left(\frac{1}{6}\right)\left(\frac{1}{2}\right) = \frac{1}{12}$$

Example 4.4.3: A 12-sided die, with faces numbered 1 to 12, is to be rolled once, and each of the 12 possible outcomes is equally likely to occur. The probability of rolling a 4 is $\dfrac{1}{12}$, so the probability of rolling a number that is *not* a 4 is $1 - \dfrac{1}{12} = \dfrac{11}{12}$. The probability of rolling a number that is either a multiple of 5—a 5 or a 10—or an odd number—a 1, 3, 5, 7, 9, or 11—is equal to

$$P(\text{multiple of 5}) + P(\text{odd}) - P(\text{multiple of 5 and odd}) = \frac{2}{12} + \frac{6}{12} - \frac{1}{12}$$

$$= \frac{7}{12}$$

Another way to calculate this probability is to notice that rolling a number that is either a multiple of 5 (5 or 10) or an odd number (1, 3, 5, 7, 9, or 11) is the same as rolling one of 1, 3, 5, 7, 9, 10, and 11, which are 7 equally likely outcomes. So by using the ratio formula to calculate the probability, the required probability is $\dfrac{7}{12}$.

Example 4.4.4: Consider an experiment with events A, B, and C for which $P(A) = 0.23$, $P(B) = 0.40$, and $P(C) = 0.85$. Suppose that events A and B are mutually exclusive and events B and C are independent. What are the probabilities $P(A \text{ or } B)$ and $P(B \text{ or } C)$?

Solution: Since A and B are mutually exclusive,

$$P(A \text{ or } B) = P(A) + P(B) = 0.23 + 0.40 = 0.63$$

Since B and C are independent, $P(B \text{ and } C) = P(B)P(C)$. So,

$$P(B \text{ or } C) = P(B) + P(C) - P(B \text{ and } C) = P(B) + P(C) - P(B)P(C)$$

Therefore,

$$P(B \text{ or } C) = 0.40 + 0.85 - (0.40)(0.85) = 1.25 - 0.34$$
$$= 0.91$$

Example 4.4.5: Suppose that there is a 6-sided die that is weighted in such a way that each time the die is rolled, the probabilities of rolling any of the numbers from 1 to 5 are all equal, but the probability of rolling a 6 is twice the probability of rolling a 1. When you roll the die once, the 6 outcomes are *not equally likely*. What are the probabilities of the 6 outcomes?

Solution: Using the notation $P(1)$ for the probability of rolling a 1, let $p = P(1)$. Then each of the probabilities of rolling a 2, 3, 4, or 5 is equal to p, and the probability of rolling a 6 is $2p$. Therefore, since the sum of the probabilities of all possible outcomes is 1, it follows that

$$1 = P(1) + P(2) + P(3) + P(4) + P(5) + P(6) = p + p + p + p + p + 2p$$
$$= 7p$$

So the probability of rolling each of the numbers from 1 to 5 is $p = \dfrac{1}{7}$, and the probability of rolling a 6 is $\dfrac{2}{7}$.

Example 4.4.6: Suppose that you roll the weighted 6-sided die from example 4.4.5 twice. What is the probability that the first roll will be an odd number and the second roll will be an even number?

Solution: To calculate the probability that the first roll will be odd and the second roll will be even, note that these two events are independent. To calculate the probability that both occur, you must multiply the probabilities of the two independent events. First compute the individual probabilities.

$$P(\text{odd}) = P(1) + P(3) + P(5) = \frac{3}{7}$$

$$P(\text{even}) = P(2) + P(4) + P(6) = \frac{4}{7}$$

Then, $P(\text{first roll is odd and second roll is even}) = P(\text{odd})P(\text{even}) = \left(\dfrac{3}{7}\right)\left(\dfrac{4}{7}\right) = \dfrac{12}{49}$.

Two events that happen sequentially are not always independent. The occurrence of one event may affect the occurrence of a following event. In that case, the probability that *both* events happen is equal to the probability that the first event happens multiplied by the probability that *given that the first event has already happened*, the second event happens as well.

Example 4.4.7: A box contains 5 orange disks, 4 red disks, and 1 blue disk. You are to select two disks at random and without replacement from the box. What is the probability that the first disk you select will be red and the second disk you select will be orange?

Solution: To solve, you need to calculate the following two probabilities and then multiply them.

- The probability that the first disk selected from the box will be red
- The probability that the second disk selected from the box will be orange, given that the first disk selected from the box is red

The probability that the first disk you select will be red is $\frac{4}{10} = \frac{2}{5}$. If the first disk you select is red, there will be 5 orange disks, 3 red disks, and 1 blue disk left in the box, for a total of 9 disks. Therefore, the probability that the second disk you select will be orange, given that the first disk you selected is red, is $\frac{5}{9}$. Multiply the two probabilities to get $\left(\frac{2}{5}\right)\left(\frac{5}{9}\right) = \frac{2}{9}$.

4.5 Distributions of Data, Random Variables, and Probability Distributions

In data analysis, variables whose values depend on chance play an important role in linking distributions of data to probability distributions. Such variables are called random variables. We begin with a review of distributions of data.

Distributions of Data

Recall that relative frequency distributions given in a table or histogram are a common way to show how numerical data are distributed. In a histogram, the areas of the bars indicate where the data are concentrated. The histogram in example 4.1.6 illustrates a small group of data, with only 6 possible values and only 25 data altogether. Many groups of data are much larger than 25 and have many more than 6 possible values, which are often measurements of quantities like length, money, and time.

Example 4.5.1: The lifetimes of 800 electric devices were measured. Because the lifetimes had many different values, the measurements were grouped into 50 intervals, or **classes**, of 10 hours each: 601–610 hours, 611–620 hours, . . . , 1,091–1,100 hours. The resulting relative frequency distribution, as a histogram, has 50 thin bars and many different bar heights, as shown below

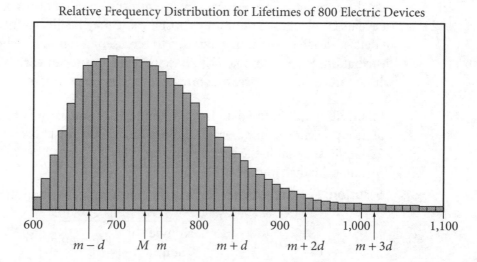

Relative Frequency Distribution for Lifetimes of 800 Electric Devices

Note that the tops of the bars of the histogram have a relatively smooth appearance and begin to look like a curve. In general, histograms that represent very large data sets with many classes appear to have smooth shapes. Consequently, the distribution can be modeled by a smooth curve that is close to the tops of the bars. Such a model retains the shape of the distribution but is independent of classes.

Recall from example 4.1.6 that the sum of the areas of the bars of a relative frequency histogram is 1. Although the units on the horizontal axis of a histogram vary from one data set to another, the vertical scale can be adjusted (stretched or shrunk) so that the sum of the areas of the bars is 1. With this vertical scale adjustment, the area under the curve that models the distribution is also 1. This model curve is called a **distribution curve**, but it has other names as well, including **density curve** and **frequency curve**.

The purpose of the distribution curve is to give a good illustration of a large distribution of numerical data that doesn't depend on specific classes. To achieve this, the main property of a distribution curve is that the area under the curve in any vertical slice, just like a histogram bar, represents the proportion of the data that lies in the corresponding interval on the horizontal axis, which is at the base of the slice.

Before leaving this histogram, note that the mean m and the median M of the data are marked on the horizontal axis. Also, several standard deviations above and below the mean are marked, where d is the standard deviation of the data. The standard deviation marks show how most of the data are within about 3 standard deviations above or below the mean [that is, between the numbers $m - 3d$ (not shown) and $m + 3d$].

Finally, regarding the mean and the median, recall that the median splits the data into a lower half and an upper half, so that the sum of the areas of the bars to the left of M is the same as the sum of the areas to the right. On the other hand, m takes into account the exact value of each of the data, not just whether a value is high or low. The nature of the mean is such that if an imaginary fulcrum were placed somewhere under the horizontal axis in order to balance the distribution perfectly, the balancing position would be exactly at m. That is why m is somewhat to the right of M. The balance point at m takes into account *how high* the few very high values are (to the far right), while M just counts them as "high." To summarize, the median is the "halving point" and the mean is the "balance point."

Random Variables

When analyzing data, it is common to choose a value of the data at random and consider that choice as a random experiment, as introduced in section 4.4. Then, the probabilities of events involving the randomly chosen value may be determined. Given a distribution of data, a variable, say X, may be used to represent a randomly chosen value from the distribution. Such a variable X is an example of a **random variable**, which is a variable whose value is a numerical outcome of a random experiment.

Example 4.5.2: In the data from example 4.1.1 consisting of numbers of children, let X represent the number of children in a randomly chosen family among the 25 families. What is the probability that $X = 3$? That $X > 3$? That X is less than the mean of the distribution?

Solution: For convenience, here is the frequency distribution of the data.

Number of Children	Frequency
0	3
1	5
2	7
3	6
4	3
5	1
Total	25

Since there are 6 families with 3 children and each of the 25 families is equally likely to be chosen, the probability that a family with 3 children will be chosen is $\dfrac{6}{25}$. That is, $X = 3$ is an event, and its probability is $P(X = 3) = \dfrac{6}{25}$, or 0.24. It is common to use the shorter notation $P(3)$ instead of $P(X = 3)$, so you could write $P(3) = 0.24$. Note that in the histogram shown below, the area of the bar corresponding to $X = 3$ as a proportion of the combined areas of all of the bars is equal to this probability. This indicates how probability is related to area in a histogram for a relative frequency distribution.

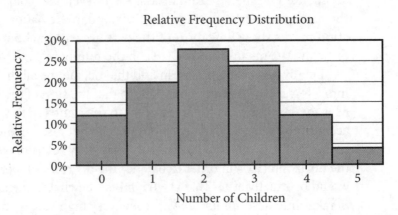

Relative Frequency Distribution

As for the event $X > 3$, it is the same as the event "$X = 4$ or $X = 5$". Because $X = 4$ and $X = 5$ are mutually exclusive events, we can use the rules of probability from section 4.4.

$$P(X > 3) = P(4) + P(5) = \frac{3}{25} + \frac{1}{25} = 0.12 + 0.04 = 0.16$$

For the last question, first compute the mean of the distribution.

$$\frac{0(3) + 1(5) + 2(7) + 3(6) + 4(3) + 5(1)}{25} = \frac{54}{25} = 2.16$$

Then,

$$P(X < 2.16) = P(0) + P(1) + P(2) = \frac{3}{25} + \frac{5}{25} + \frac{7}{25} = \frac{15}{25} = 0.6$$

A table showing all 6 possible values of X and their probabilities is called the **probability distribution** of the random variable X.

Probability Distribution of the Random Variable X

X	$P(X)$
0	0.12
1	0.20
2	0.28
3	0.24
4	0.12
5	0.04

Note that the probabilities are simply the relative frequencies of the 6 possible values expressed as decimals instead of percents. The following statement indicates a fundamental link between data distributions and probability distributions.

For a random variable that represents a randomly chosen value from a distribution of data, the probability distribution of the random variable is the same as the relative frequency distribution of the data.

Because the probability distribution and the relative frequency distribution are essentially the same, the probability distribution can be represented by a histogram. Also, all of the descriptive statistics—such as mean, median, and standard deviation—that apply to the distribution of data also apply to the probability distribution. For example, we say that the probability distribution above has a mean of 2.16, a median of 2, and a standard deviation of about 1.3, since the 25 data values have these statistics, as you can check.

These statistics are similarly defined for the random variable X above. Thus, we would say that the **mean of the random variable X** is 2.16. Another name for the mean of a random variable is **expected value**. So we would also say that the expected value of X is 2.16. Note that the mean of X can be expressed in terms of probabilities as follows.

$$\frac{0(3) + 1(5) + 2(7) + 3(6) + 4(3) + 5(1)}{25} = 0\left(\frac{3}{25}\right) + 1\left(\frac{5}{25}\right) + 2\left(\frac{7}{25}\right) + 3\left(\frac{6}{25}\right) + 4\left(\frac{3}{25}\right) + 5\left(\frac{1}{25}\right)$$

$$= 0P(0) + 1P(1) + 2P(2) + 3P(3) + 4P(4) + 5P(5)$$

which is the sum of the products $XP(X)$, that is, the sum of each value of X multiplied by its corresponding probability $P(X)$.

The preceding example involves a common type of random variable—one that represents a randomly chosen value from a distribution of data. However, the concept of a random variable is more general. A random variable can be any quantity whose value is the result of a random experiment. The possible values of the random variable are the same as the outcomes of the experiment. So any random experiment with numerical outcomes naturally has a random variable associated with it, as in the following example.

Example 4.5.3: Let Y represent the outcome of the experiment in example 4.4.5 of rolling a weighted 6-sided die. Then Y is a random variable with 6 possible values, the numbers 1 through 6. Each value of Y has a probability, which is listed in the probability distribution of the random variable Y and is shown in a histogram for Y.

Probability Distribution of the Random Variable Y

X	1	2	3	4	5	6
$P(Y)$	$\dfrac{1}{7}$	$\dfrac{1}{7}$	$\dfrac{1}{7}$	$\dfrac{1}{7}$	$\dfrac{1}{7}$	$\dfrac{2}{7}$

Histogram for the Random Variable Y

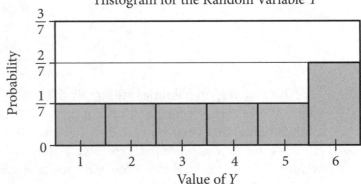

The mean, or expected value, of Y can be computed as

$$P(1) + 2P(2) + 3P(3) + 4P(4) + 5P(5) + 6P(6) = \left(\frac{1}{7}\right) + 2\left(\frac{1}{7}\right) + 3\left(\frac{1}{7}\right) + 4\left(\frac{1}{7}\right) + 5\left(\frac{1}{7}\right) + 6\left(\frac{2}{7}\right)$$

$$= \frac{1}{7} + \frac{2}{7} + \frac{3}{7} + \frac{4}{7} + \frac{5}{7} + \frac{12}{7}$$

$$= \frac{27}{7} \approx 3.86$$

Both of the random variables X and Y above are examples of **discrete random variables** because their values consist of discrete points on a number line.

A basic fact about probability from section 4.4 is that the sum of the probabilities of all possible outcomes of an experiment is 1, which can be confirmed by adding all of the probabilities in each of the probability distributions for the random variables X and Y above. Also, the sum of the areas of the bars in a histogram for the probability distribution of a random variable is 1. This fact is related to a fundamental link between the areas of the bars of a histogram and the probabilities of a discrete random variable.

In the histogram for a random variable, the area of each bar is proportional to the probability represented by the bar.

If the die in example 4.4.5 were a fair die instead of weighted, then the probability of each of the outcomes would be $\frac{1}{6}$, and consequently, each of the bars in the histogram would have the same height. Such a flat histogram indicates a **uniform distribution**, since the probability is distributed uniformly over all possible outcomes.

The Normal Distribution

Many natural processes yield data that have a relative frequency distribution shaped somewhat like a bell, as in the distribution below with mean m and standard deviation d.

Approximately Normal Relative Frequency Distribution

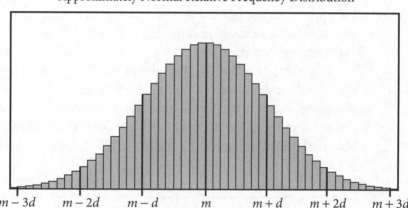

Such data are said to be **approximately normally distributed** and have the following properties.

- The mean, median, and mode are all nearly equal.
- The data are grouped fairly symmetrically about the mean.
- About two-thirds of the data are within 1 standard deviation of the mean.
- Almost all of the data are within 2 standard deviations of the mean.

As stated above, you can always associate a random variable X with a distribution of data by letting X be a randomly chosen value from the distribution. If X is such a random variable for the distribution above, we say that X is approximately normally distributed.

As described in example 4.5.1, relative frequency distributions are often approximated using a smooth curve—a distribution curve or density curve—for the tops of the bars in the histogram. The region below such a curve represents a distribution, called a **continuous probability distribution**. There are many different continuous probability distributions, but the most important one is the **normal distribution**, which has a bell-shaped curve like the one shown in the figure below.

Normal Distribution

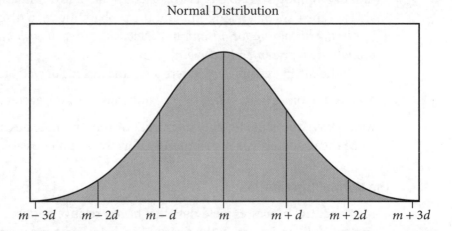

$$m-3d \qquad m-2d \qquad m-d \qquad m \qquad m+d \qquad m+2d \qquad m+3d$$

Just as a data distribution has a mean and standard deviation, the normal probability distribution has a mean and standard deviation. Also, the properties listed above for the approximately normal distribution of data hold for the normal distribution, except that the mean, median, and mode are exactly the same and the distribution is perfectly symmetric about the mean.

A normal distribution, though always shaped like a bell, can be centered around any mean and can be spread out to a greater or lesser degree, depending on the standard deviation. Below are three normal distributions that have different centers and spreads. From left to right, the means of the three distributions are −10, 1, and 20; and the standard deviations are 5, 10, and 2.

Three Normal Distributions

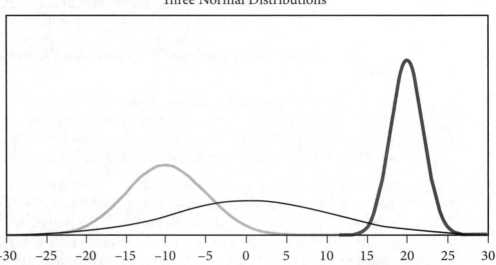

$$-30 \quad -25 \quad -20 \quad -15 \quad -10 \quad -5 \quad 0 \quad 5 \quad 10 \quad 15 \quad 20 \quad 25 \quad 30$$

As mentioned earlier, areas of the bars in a histogram for a discrete random variable correspond to probabilities for the values of the random variable; the sum of the areas is 1 and the sum of the probabilities is 1. This is also true for a continuous probability distribution: the area of the region under the curve is 1, and the areas of vertical slices of the region—similar to the bars of a histogram—are equal to probabilities of a random variable associated with the distribution. Such a random variable is called a **continuous random variable**, and it plays the same role as a random variable that represents a randomly chosen value from a distribution of data. The main difference is that we seldom consider the event in which a continuous random variable is equal to a single value like $X = 3$; rather, we consider events that are described by intervals of values such as $1 < X < 3$ and $X > 10$. Such events correspond to vertical slices under a continuous probability distribution, and the areas of the vertical slices are the probabilities of the corresponding events. (Consequently, the probability of an event such as $X = 3$ would correspond to the area of a line segment, which is 0.)

Example 4.5.4: If W is a random variable that is normally distributed with a mean of 5 and a standard deviation of 2, what is $P(W > 5)$? Approximately what is $P(3 < W < 7)$? Which of the four numbers 0.5, 0.1, 0.05, or 0.01 is the best estimate of $P(W < -1)$?

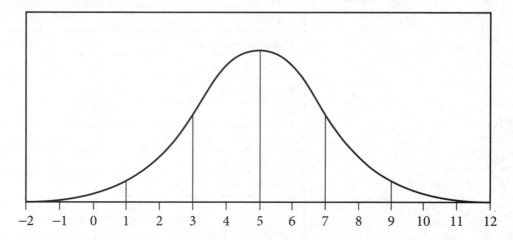

Solution: Since the mean of the distribution is 5, and the distribution is symmetric about the mean, the event $W > 5$ corresponds to exactly half of the area under the normal distribution. So $P(W > 5) = \dfrac{1}{2}$.

For the event $3 < W < 7$, note that since the standard deviation of the distribution is 2, the values 3 and 7 are one standard deviation below and above the mean, respectively. Since about two-thirds of the area is within one standard deviation of the mean, $P(3 < W < 7)$ is approximately $\dfrac{2}{3}$.

For the event $W < -1$, note that -1 is 3 standard deviations below the mean. Since the graph makes it fairly clear that the area of the region under the normal curve to the left of -1 is much less than 5 percent of all of the area, the best of the four estimates given for $P(W < -1)$ is 0.01.

The **standard normal distribution** is a normal distribution with a mean of 0 and standard deviation equal to 1. To transform a normal distribution with a mean of m and a standard deviation of d to a standard normal distribution, you standardize the values (as explained below example 4.2.9); that is, you subtract m from any observed value of the normal distribution and then divide the result by d.

Very precise values for probabilities associated with normal distributions can be computed using calculators, computers, or statistical tables for the standard normal distribution. For example, more precise values for $P(3 < W < 7)$ and $P(W < -1)$ are 0.683 and 0.0013. Such calculations are beyond the scope of this review.

4.6 Data Interpretation Examples

Example 4.6.1:

DISTRIBUTION OF CUSTOMER COMPLAINTS
RECEIVED BY AIRLINE P, 2003 AND 2004

Category	2003	2004
Flight problem	20.0%	22.1%
Baggage	18.3	21.8
Customer service	13.1	11.3
Oversales of seats	10.5	11.8
Refund problem	10.1	8.1
Fare	6.4	6.0
Reservation and ticketing	5.8	5.6
Tours	3.3	2.3
Smoking	3.2	2.9
Advertising	1.2	1.1
Credit	1.0	0.8
Special passenger accommodation	0.9	0.9
Other	6.2	5.3
Total	100.0%	100.0%
Total number of complaints	22,998	13,278

(a) Approximately how many complaints concerning credit were received by Airline P in 2003?
(b) By approximately what percent did the total number of complaints decrease from 2003 to 2004?
(c) Based on the information in the table, which of the following statements are true?
    I. In each of the years 2003 and 2004, complaints about flight problems, baggage, and customer service together accounted for more than 50 percent of all customer complaints received by Airline P.
    II. The number of special passenger accommodation complaints was unchanged from 2003 to 2004.
    III. From 2003 to 2004, the number of flight problem complaints increased by more than 2 percent.

Solutions:

(a) According to the table, in 2003, 1 percent of the total number of complaints concerned credit. Therefore, the number of complaints concerning credit is equal to 1 percent of 22,998. By converting 1 percent to its decimal equivalent, you obtain that the number of complaints in 2003 is equal to (0.01)(22,998), or about 230.

(b) The decrease in the total number of complaints from 2003 to 2004 was

22,998 – 13,278, or 9,720. Therefore, the percent decrease was $\left(\dfrac{9,720}{22,998}\right)(100\%)$, or approximately 42 percent.

(c) Since $20.0 + 18.3 + 13.1$ and $22.1 + 21.8 + 11.3$ are both greater than 50, statement I is true. For statement II, the *percent* of special passenger accommodation complaints *did* remain the same from 2003 to 2004, but the *number* of such complaints decreased because the total number of complaints decreased. Thus, statement II is false. For statement III, the *percents* shown in the table for flight problems do in fact increase by more than 2 percentage points, but the bases of the percents are different. The total number of complaints in 2004 was much lower than the total number of complaints in 2003, and clearly 20 percent of 22,998 is greater than 22.1 percent of 13,278. So, the number of flight problem complaints actually decreased from 2003 to 2004, and statement III is false.

Example 4.6.2:

UNITED STATES PRODUCTION OF PHOTOGRAPHIC
EQUIPMENT AND SUPPLIES IN 1971

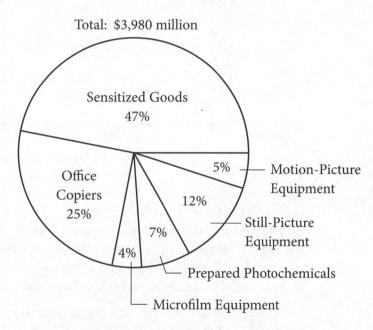

Total: $3,980 million

(a) Approximately what was the ratio of the value of sensitized goods to the value of still-picture equipment produced in 1971 in the United States?

(b) If the value of office copiers produced in 1971 was 30 percent greater than the corresponding value in 1970, what was the value of office copiers produced in 1970?

Solutions:

(a) The ratio of the value of sensitized goods to the value of still-picture equipment is equal to the ratio of the corresponding percents shown because the percents have the same base, which is the total value. Therefore, the ratio is 47 to 12, or approximately 4 to 1.

(b) The value of office copiers produced in 1971 was 0.25 times $3,980 million, or $995 million. Therefore, if the corresponding value in 1970 was x million dollars, then $1.3x = 995$ million. Solving for x yields $x = \dfrac{995}{1.3} \approx 765$, so the value of office copiers produced in 1970 was approximately $765 million.

Example 4.6.3:

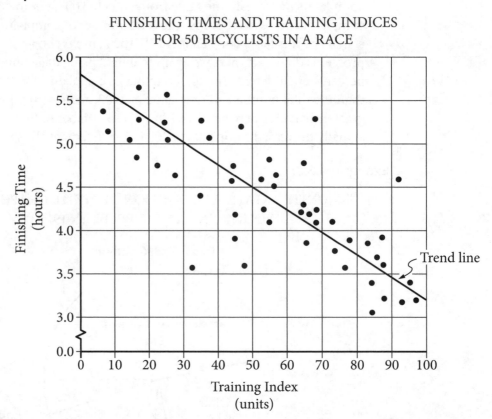

FINISHING TIMES AND TRAINING INDICES FOR 50 BICYCLISTS IN A RACE

A bicycle trainer studied 50 bicyclists to examine how the finishing time for a certain bicycle race was related to the amount of physical training in the three months before the race. To measure the amount of training, the trainer developed a training index, measured in "units" and based on the intensity of each bicyclist's training. The data and the trend of the data, represented by a line, are displayed in the scatterplot above.

(a) How many of the 50 bicyclists had both a training index less than 50 units and a finishing time less than 4.5 hours?

(b) What percent of the 10 fastest bicyclists in the race had a training index less than 90 units?

Solutions:

(a) The number of bicyclists who had both a training index less than 50 units and a finishing time less than 4.5 hours is equal to the number of points on the graph to the left of 50 and below 4.5. Since there are five data points that are both to the left of 50 units and below 4.5 hours, the correct answer is five.

(b) The 10 lowest data points represent the 10 fastest bicyclists. Of these 10 data points, 3 points are to the right of 90 units, so the number of points to the left of 90 units is 7, which represents 70 percent of the 10 fastest bicyclists.

Example 4.6.4:

TRAVELERS SURVEYED: 250

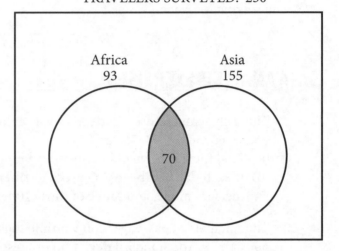

In a survey of 250 European travelers, 93 have traveled to Africa, 155 have traveled to Asia, and of these two groups, 70 have traveled to both continents, as illustrated in the Venn diagram above.

(a) How many of the travelers surveyed have traveled to Africa but <u>not</u> to Asia?

(b) How many of the travelers surveyed have traveled to <u>at least one</u> of the two continents of Africa and Asia?

(c) How many of the travelers surveyed have traveled <u>neither</u> to Africa <u>nor</u> to Asia?

Solutions: In the Venn diagram, the rectangular region represents the set of all travelers surveyed; the two circular regions represent the two sets of travelers to Africa and Asia, respectively; and the shaded region represents the subset of those who have traveled to both continents.

(a) The set described here is represented by *the part of the left circle that is not shaded*. This description suggests that the answer can be found by taking the shaded part away from the first circle—in effect, subtracting the 70 from the 93, to get 23 travelers who have traveled to Africa but not to Asia.

(b) The set described here is represented by that part of the rectangle that is *in at least one of the two circles*. This description suggests adding the two numbers 93 and 155. But the 70 travelers who have traveled to both continents would be counted twice in the sum $93 + 155$. To correct the double counting, subtract 70 from the sum so that these 70 travelers are counted only once:

$$93 + 155 - 70 = 178$$

(c) The set described here is represented by the part of the rectangle that is *not in either circle*. Let N be the number of these travelers. Note that the entire rectangular region has two main nonoverlapping parts: the part *outside* the circles and the part *inside* the circles. The first part represents N travelers and the second part represents $93 + 155 - 70 = 178$ travelers (from question (b)). Therefore,

$$250 = N + 178$$

and solving for N yields

$$N = 250 - 178 = 72$$

DATA ANALYSIS EXERCISES

1. The daily temperatures, in degrees Fahrenheit, for 10 days in May were 61, 62, 65, 65, 65, 68, 74, 74, 75, and 77.
   (a) Find the mean, median, mode, and range of the temperatures.
   (b) If each day had been 7 degrees warmer, what would have been the mean, median, mode, and range of those 10 temperatures?

2. The numbers of passengers on 9 airline flights were 22, 33, 21, 28, 22, 31, 44, 50, and 19. The standard deviation of these 9 numbers is approximately equal to 10.2.
   (a) Find the mean, median, mode, range, and interquartile range of the 9 numbers.
   (b) If each flight had had 3 times as many passengers, what would have been the mean, median, mode, range, interquartile range, and standard deviation of the 9 numbers?
   (c) If each flight had had 2 fewer passengers, what would have been the interquartile range and standard deviation of the 9 numbers?

3. A group of 20 values has a mean of 85 and a median of 80. A different group of 30 values has a mean of 75 and a median of 72.
   (a) What is the mean of the 50 values?
   (b) What is the median of the 50 values?

4. Find the mean and median of the values of the random variable X, whose relative frequency distribution is given in the table below.

X	Relative Frequency
0	0.18
1	0.33
2	0.10
3	0.06
4	0.33

5. Eight hundred insects were weighed, and the resulting measurements, in milligrams, are summarized in the boxplot below.

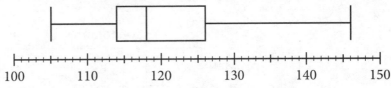

(a) What are the range, the three quartiles, and the interquartile range of the measurements?

(b) If the 80th percentile of the measurements is 130 milligrams, about how many measurements are between 126 milligrams and 130 milligrams?

6. In how many different ways can the letters in the word STUDY be ordered?

7. Martha invited 4 friends to go with her to the movies. There are 120 different ways in which they can sit together in a row of 5 seats, one person per seat. In how many of those ways is Martha sitting in the middle seat?

8. How many 3-digit positive integers are odd and do not contain the digit 5?

9. From a box of 10 lightbulbs, you are to remove 4. How many different sets of 4 lightbulbs could you remove?

10. A talent contest has 8 contestants. Judges must award prizes for first, second, and third places, with no ties.

(a) In how many different ways can the judges award the 3 prizes?

(b) How many different groups of 3 people can get prizes?

11. If an integer is randomly selected from all positive 2-digit integers, what is the probability that the integer chosen has

(a) a 4 in the tens place?

(b) at least one 4 in the tens place or the units place?

(c) no 4 in either place?

12. In a box of 10 electrical parts, 2 are defective.

(a) If you choose one part at random from the box, what is the probability that it is not defective?

(b) If you choose two parts at random from the box, without replacement, what is the probability that both are defective?

13. The table below shows the distribution of a group of 40 college students by gender and class.

	Sophomores	Juniors	Seniors
Males	6	10	2
Females	10	9	3

If one student is randomly selected from this group, find the probability that the student chosen is
(a) not a junior
(b) a female or a sophomore
(c) a male sophomore or a female senior

14. Let A, B, C, and D be events for which $P(A \text{ or } B) = 0.6$, $P(A) = 0.2$, $P(C \text{ or } D) = 0.6$, and $P(C) = 0.5$. The events A and B are mutually exclusive, and the events C and D are independent.
(a) Find $P(B)$
(b) Find $P(D)$

15. Lin and Mark each attempt independently to decode a message. If the probability that Lin will decode the message is 0.80 and the probability that Mark will decode the message is 0.70, find the probability that
(a) both will decode the message
(b) at least one of them will decode the message
(c) neither of them will decode the message

16.

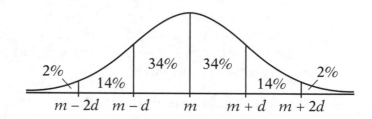

The figure above shows a normal distribution with mean m and standard deviation d, including approximate percents of the distribution corresponding to the six regions shown.

Suppose the heights of a population of 3,000 adult penguins are approximately normally distributed with a mean of 65 centimeters and a standard deviation of 5 centimeters.
(a) Approximately how many of the adult penguins are between 65 centimeters and 75 centimeters tall?
(b) If an adult penguin is chosen at random from the population, approximately what is the probability that the penguin's height will be less than 60 centimeters? Give your answer to the nearest 0.05.

17.

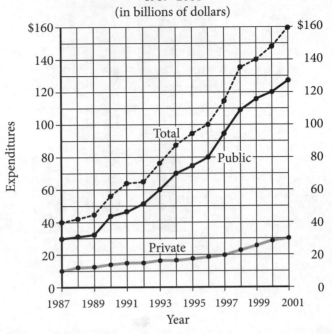

PUBLIC AND PRIVATE SCHOOL EXPENDITURES
1987–2001
(in billions of dollars)

(a) For which year did total expenditures increase the most from the year before?

(b) For 2001, private school expenditures were approximately what percent of total expenditures?

18.

DISTRIBUTION OF WORKFORCE BY OCCUPATIONAL CATEGORY
FOR REGION *Y* IN 2011 AND PROJECTED FOR 2025

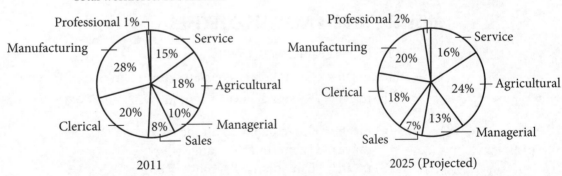

(a) In 2011, how many categories each comprised more than 25 million workers?

(b) What is the ratio of the number of workers in the Agricultural category in 2011 to the projected number of such workers in 2025 ?

(c) From 2011 to 2025, there is a projected increase in the number of workers in which of the following categories?

I. Sales   II. Service   III. Clerical

19.

A FAMILY'S EXPENDITURES AND SAVINGS
AS A PERCENT OF ITS GROSS ANNUAL INCOME*

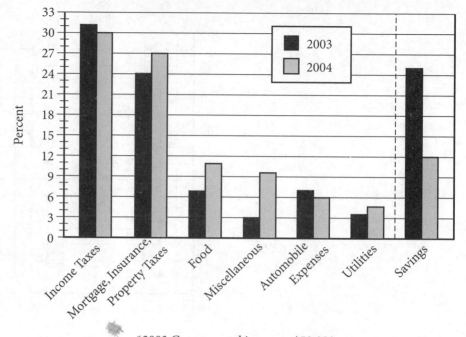

*2003 Gross annual income: $50,000
2004 Gross annual income: $45,000

(a) In 2003 the family used a total of 49 percent of its gross annual income for two of the categories listed. What was the total amount of the family's income used for those same categories in 2004?

(b) Of the seven categories listed, which category of expenditure had the greatest percent increase from 2003 to 2004 ?

ANSWERS TO DATA ANALYSIS EXERCISES

1. In degrees Fahrenheit, the statistics are
   (a) mean = 68.6, median = 66.5, mode = 65, range = 16
   (b) mean = 75.6, median = 73.5, mode = 72, range = 16

2. (a) mean = 30, median = 28, mode = 22,
      range = 31, interquartile range = 17
   (b) mean = 90, median = 84, mode = 66,
      range = 93, interquartile range = 51,

   $$\text{standard deviation} = 3\sqrt{\frac{940}{9}} \approx 30.7$$

   (c) interquartile range = 17, standard deviation ≈ 10.2

3. (a) mean = 79
   (b) The median cannot be determined from the information given.

4. mean = 2.03, median = 1

5. (a) range = 41, Q_1 = 114, Q_2 = 118, Q_3 = 126, interquartile range = 12
    (b) 40 measurements

6. 5! = 120

7. 24

8. 288

9. 210

10. (a) 336   (b) 56

11. (a) $\dfrac{1}{9}$ (b) $\dfrac{1}{5}$ (c) $\dfrac{4}{5}$

12. (a) $\dfrac{4}{5}$ (b) $\dfrac{1}{45}$

13. (a) $\dfrac{21}{40}$ (b) $\dfrac{7}{10}$ (c) $\dfrac{9}{40}$

14. (a) 0.4   (b) 0.2

15. (a) 0.56   (b) 0.94   (c) 0.06

16. (a) 1,440   (b) 0.15

17. (a) 1998   (b) 19%

18. (a) Three   (b) 9 to 14, or $\dfrac{9}{14}$ (c) I, II, and III

19. (a) $17,550   (b) Miscellaneous

Mathematical Conventions for the Quantitative Reasoning Measure of the *GRE®* revised General Test

Your goals for this material	⇒ Check your understanding of common mathematical conventions, notation, and terminology ⇒ Learn the conventions that are particular to the *GRE®* Quantitative Reasoning measure

The mathematical symbols and terminology used in the Quantitative Reasoning measure of the test are conventional at the high school level, and most of these appear in the Math Review (Appendix A). Whenever nonstandard or special notation or terminology is used in a test question, it is explicitly introduced in the question. However, there are some particular assumptions about numbers and geometric figures that are made throughout the test. These assumptions appear in the test at the beginning of the Quantitative Reasoning sections, and they are elaborated below.

Also, some notation and terminology, while standard at the high school level in many countries, may be different from those used in other countries or from those used at higher or lower levels of mathematics. Such notation and terminology are clarified below. Because it is impossible to ascertain which notation and terminology should be clarified for an individual test taker, more material than necessary may be included.

Finally, there are some guidelines for how certain information given in test questions should be interpreted and used in the context of answering the questions—information such as certain words, phrases, quantities, mathematical expressions, and displays of data. These guidelines appear at the end.

Numbers and Quantities

- All numbers used in the test questions are real numbers. In particular, integers and both rational and irrational numbers are to be considered, but imaginary numbers are not. This is the main assumption regarding numbers. Also, all quantities are real numbers, although quantities may involve units of measurement.

- Numbers are expressed in base 10 unless otherwise noted, using the 10 digits 0 through 9 and a period to the right of the ones digit, or units digit, for the decimal point. Also, in numbers that are 1,000 or greater, commas are used to separate groups of three digits to the left of the decimal point.

- When a positive integer is described by the number of its digits, e.g., a two-digit integer, the digits that are counted include the ones digit and all the digits further to the left, where the left-most digit is not 0. For example, 5,000 is a four-digit integer, whereas 031 is not considered to be a three-digit integer.

- Some other conventions involving numbers: *one billion* means 1,000,000,000, or 10^9 (not 10^{12}, as in some countries); *one dozen* means 12; the Greek letter π represents the ratio of the circumference of a circle to its diameter and is approximately 3.14.

- When a positive number is to be rounded to a certain decimal place and the number is halfway between the two nearest possibilities, the number should be rounded to the greater possibility. For example, 23.5 rounded to the nearest integer is 24, and 123.985 rounded to the nearest 0.01 is 123.99. When the number to be rounded is negative, the number should be rounded to the lesser possibility. For example, −36.5 rounded to the nearest integer is −37.

- Repeating decimals are sometimes written with a bar over the digits that repeat, as in $\dfrac{25}{12} = 2.08\overline{3}$ and $\dfrac{1}{7} = 0.\overline{142857}$.

- If r, s, and t are integers and $rs = t$, then r and s are *factors*, or *divisors*, of t; also, t is a *multiple* of r (and of s) and t is *divisible* by r (and by s). The factors of an integer include positive and negative integers. For example, −7 is a factor of 35, 8 is a factor of −40, and the integer 4 has six factors: −4, −2, −1, 1, 2, and 4. The terms *factor*, *divisor*, and *divisible* are used only when r, s, and t are integers. However, the term *multiple* can be used with any real numbers s and t provided r is an integer. For example, 1.2 is a multiple of 0.4, and -2π is a multiple of π.

- The *least common multiple* of two nonzero integers a and b is the least positive integer that is a multiple of both a and b. The *greatest common divisor* (or *greatest common factor*) of a and b is the greatest positive integer that is a divisor of both a and b.

- If an integer n is divided by a nonzero integer d resulting in a quotient q with remainder r, then $n = qd + r$, where $0 \le r < |d|$. Furthermore, $r = 0$ if and only if n is a multiple of d. For example, when 20 is divided by 7, the quotient is 2 and the remainder is 6; when 21 is divided by 7, the quotient is 3 and the remainder is 0; and when −17 is divided by 7, the quotient is −3 and the remainder is 4.

- A *prime number* is an integer greater than 1 that has only two positive divisors: 1 and itself. The first five prime numbers are 2, 3, 5, 7, and 11. A *composite number* is an integer greater than 1 that is not a prime number. The first five composite numbers are 4, 6, 8, 9, and 10.

- Odd and even integers are not necessarily positive; for example, −7 is odd, and −18 and 0 are even.

- The integer 0 is neither positive nor negative.

Mathematical Expressions, Symbols, and Variables

- As is common in algebra, italic letters like x are used to denote numbers, constants, and variables. Letters are also used to label various objects, such as line ℓ, point P, function f, set S, list T, event E, random variable X, Brand X, City Y, and Company Z. The meaning of a letter is determined by the context.

- When numbers, constants, or variables are given, their possible values are all real numbers unless otherwise restricted. It is common to restrict the possible values in various ways. Here are some examples: n is a nonzero integer; $1 \le x < \pi$; and T is the tens digits of a two-digit positive integer, so T is an integer from 1 to 9.

- Standard mathematical symbols at the high school level are used. These include the arithmetic operations $+, -, \times$, and $\div$, though multiplication is usually denoted by juxtaposition, often with parentheses, e.g., $2y$ and $(3)(4.5)$; and division is usually denoted with a horizontal fraction bar, e.g., $\dfrac{w}{3}$. Sometimes mixed numbers, or mixed fractions, are used, like $4\dfrac{3}{8}$ and $-10\dfrac{1}{2}$. These two numbers are equal to $\dfrac{35}{8}$ and $-\dfrac{21}{2}$, respectively. Exponents are also used, e.g., $2^{10} = 1{,}024$, $10^{-2} = \dfrac{1}{100}$, and $x^0 = 1$ for all nonzero numbers x.

- Mathematical expressions are to be interpreted with respect to *order of operations*, which establishes which operations are performed before others in an expression. The order is as follows: parentheses; exponentiation; negation; multiplication and division (from left to right); addition and subtraction (from left to right). For example, the value of the expression $1 + 2 \times 4$ is 9, because the expression is evaluated by first multiplying 2 and 4 and then adding 1 to the result. Also, -3^2 means "the negative of '3 squared'" because exponentiation takes precedence over negation. Therefore, $-3^2 = -9$, but $(-3)^2 = 9$ because parentheses take precedence over exponentiation.

- Here are examples of other standard symbols with their meanings:

    $x \le y$ x is less than or equal to y
    $x \ne y$ x and y are not equal
    $x \approx y$ x and y are approximately equal
    $|x|$ the absolute value of x
    $\sqrt{x}$ the nonnegative square root of x, where $x \ge 0$
    $-\sqrt{x}$ the nonpositive square root of x, where $x \ge 0$
    $n!$ the product of all positive integers less than or equal to n, where n is any positive integer and, as a special definition, $0! = 1$.
    $\ell \,\|\, m$ lines ℓ and m are parallel
    $\ell \perp m$ lines ℓ and m are perpendicular

- Because all numbers are assumed to be real, some expressions are not defined. For example, for every number x, the expression $\dfrac{x}{0}$ is not defined; if $x < 0$, then $\sqrt{x}$ is not defined; and 0^0 is not defined.

- Sometimes special symbols or notation are introduced in a question. Here are two examples:

  The operation $\lozenge$ is defined for all integers r and s by $r \lozenge s = \dfrac{rs}{1+r^2}$.

  The operation $\sim$ is defined for all nonzero numbers x by $\sim x = -\dfrac{1}{x}$.

- Sometimes juxtaposition of letters does *not* denote multiplication, as in "consider a three-digit integer denoted by XYZ, where X, Y, and Z are digits." The meaning is taken from the context.

- Standard function notation is used in the test. For example, "the function g is defined for all $x \geq 0$ by $g(x) = 2x + \sqrt{x}$." If the domain of a function f is not given explicitly, it is assumed to be the set of all real numbers x for which $f(x)$ is a real number. If f and g are two functions, then the *composition* of g with f is denoted by $g(f(x))$.

Geometry

- In questions involving geometry, the conventions of plane (or Euclidean) geometry are followed, including the assumption that the sum of the measures of the interior angles of a triangle is 180 degrees.

- Lines are assumed to be "straight" lines that extend in both directions without end.

- Angle measures are in degrees and are assumed to be positive and less than or equal to 360 degrees.

- When a square, circle, polygon, or other closed geometric figure is described in words but not shown, the figure is assumed to enclose a convex region. It is also assumed that such a closed geometric figure is not just a single point or a line segment. For example, a quadrilateral **cannot** be any of the following:

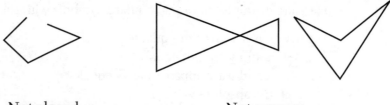

Not closed   Not convex

- The phrase *area of a rectangle* means the area of the region enclosed by the rectangle. The same terminology applies to circles, triangles, and other closed figures.

- The *distance between a point and a line* is the length of the perpendicular line segment from the point to the line, which is the shortest distance between the point and the line. Similarly, the *distance between two parallel lines* is the distance between a point on one line and the other line.

- In a geometric context, the phrase *similar triangles* (or other figures) means that the figures have the same shape. See the Geometry section of the Math Review for further explanation of the terms *similar* and *congruent*.

Geometric Figures

- Geometric figures consist of points, lines, line segments, curves (such as circles), angles, and regions; also included are labels, and markings or shadings that identify these objects or their sizes. A point is indicated by a dot, a label, or the intersection of two or more lines or curves. Points, lines, angles, etc., that are shown as distinct are indeed distinct. All figures are assumed to lie in a plane unless otherwise indicated.

- If points A, B, and C do not lie on the same line, then line segments AB and BC form two angles with vertex B—one angle with measure less than 180° and the other with measure greater than 180°, as shown below. Unless otherwise indicated, angle ABC, also denoted by $\angle ABC$ or $\angle B$, refers to the *smaller* of the two angles.

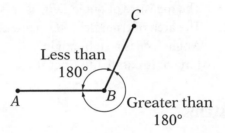

- The notation AB may mean the line segment with endpoints A and B, or it may mean the length of the line segment. The meaning can be determined from the context.

- Geometric figures **are not necessarily** drawn to scale. That is, you should **not** assume that quantities such as lengths and angle measures are as they appear in a figure. However, you should assume that lines shown as straight are actually straight, and when curves are shown, you should assume they are not straight. Also, assume that points on a line or a curve are in the order shown, points shown to be on opposite sides of a line or curve are so oriented, and more generally, assume all geometric objects are in the relative positions shown. For questions with geometric figures, you should base your answers on geometric reasoning, not on estimating or comparing quantities by sight or by measurement.

- To illustrate some of these conventions, consider the geometric figure below.

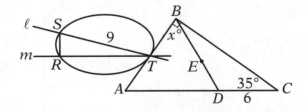

The following can be determined from the figure.
- ABD and DBC are triangles, and points R, S, and T lie on the closed curve.
- Points A, D, and C lie on a straight line, so ABC is a triangle with sides AB, BC, and AC.
- Point D is a distinct point between points A and C.
- Points A and S are on opposite sides of line m.

- Point E is on BD.
- $AD < AC$
- $ST = 9$, $DC = 6$, and the measure of angle C is 35 degrees.
- Angle ABC is a right angle, as indicated by the small square symbol at point B.
- The measure of angle ABD is x degrees, and $x < 90$.
- Line ℓ intersects the closed curve at points S and T, and the curve is tangent to AB at T.
- The area of the region enclosed by the curve is greater than the area of triangle RST.

The following **cannot** be determined from the figure.

- $AD > DC$
- The measures of angles BAD and BDA are equal.
- The measure of angle DBC is less than x degrees.
- The area of triangle ABD is greater than the area of triangle DBC.
- Angle SRT is a right angle.
- Line m is parallel to line AC.

Coordinate Systems

- Coordinate systems, such as xy-planes and number lines, **are** drawn to scale. Therefore, you can read, estimate, or compare quantities in such figures by sight or by measurement, including geometric figures that appear in coordinate systems.
- The positive direction of a number line is to the right.
- As in geometry, distances in a coordinate system are nonnegative.
- The rectangular coordinate plane, or rectangular coordinate system, commonly known as the xy-plane, is shown below. The x-axis and y-axis intersect at the origin O, and they partition the plane into four quadrants. Each point in the xy-plane has coordinates (x, y) that give its location with respect to the axes; for example, the point $P(2, -8)$ is located 2 units to the right of the y-axis and 8 units below the x-axis. The units on the x-axis have the same length as the units on the y-axis, unless otherwise noted.

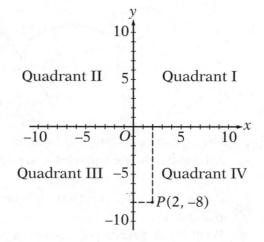

- Intermediate grid lines or tick marks in a coordinate system are evenly spaced unless otherwise noted.
- The term *x-intercept* refers to the *x*-coordinate of the point at which a graph in the *xy*-plane intersects the *x*-axis. The term *y-intercept* is used analogously. Sometimes the terms *x-intercept* and *y-intercept* refer to the actual intersection points.

Sets, Lists, and Sequences

- Sets of numbers or other elements appear in some questions. Some sets are infinite, such as the set of integers; other sets are finite and may have all of their elements listed within curly brackets, such as the set $\{2, 4, 6, 8\}$. When the elements of a set are given, repetitions are *not* counted as additional elements and the order of the elements is *not* relevant. Elements are also called *members*. A set with one or more members is called *nonempty*; there is a set with no members, called the *empty set* and denoted by $\varnothing$. If A and B are sets, then the *intersection* of A and B, denoted by $A \cap B$, is the set of elements that are in both A and B, and the *union* of A and B, denoted by $A \cup B$, is the set of elements that are in A or B, or both. If all of the elements in A are also in B, then A is a *subset* of B. By convention, the empty set is a subset of every set. If A and B have no elements in common, they are called *disjoint* sets or *mutually exclusive* sets.
- Lists of numbers or other elements are also used in the test. When the elements of a list are given, repetitions *are* counted as additional elements and the order of the elements *is* relevant. For example, the list $3, 1, 2, 3, 3$ contains five numbers, and the first, fourth, and last numbers in the list are each 3.
- The terms *data set* and *set of data* are not sets in the mathematical sense given above. Rather they refer to a list of data because there may be repetitions in the data, and if there are repetitions, they would be relevant.
- Sequences are lists that often have an infinite number of elements, or terms. The terms of a sequence are often represented by a fixed letter along with a subscript that indicates the order of a term in the sequence. For example, $a_1, a_2, a_3, \ldots$, $a_n, \ldots$ represents an infinite sequence in which the first term is a_1, the second term is a_2, and more generally, the *n*th term is a_n for every positive integer n. Sometimes the *n*th term of a sequence is given by a formula, such as $b_n = 2^n + 1$. Sometimes the first few terms of a sequence are given explicitly, as in the following sequence of consecutive even negative integers: $-2, -4, -6, -8, -10, \ldots$.
- Sets of consecutive integers are sometimes described by indicating the first and last integer, as in "the integers from 0 to 9, inclusive." This phrase refers to 10 integers, with or without "inclusive" at the end. Thus, the phrase "during the years from 1985 to 2005" refers to 21 years.

Data and Statistics

- Numerical data are sometimes given in lists and sometimes displayed in other ways, such as in tables, bar graphs, or circle graphs. Various statistics, or measures of data, appear in questions: measures of central tendency—mean, median, and mode; measures of position—quartiles and percentiles; and measures of dispersion—standard deviation, range, and interquartile range.

- The term *average* is used in two ways, with and without the qualification "(arithmetic mean)." For a list of data, the *average* (*arithmetic mean*) of the data is the sum of the data divided by the number of data. The term *average* does not refer to either *median* or *mode* in the test. Without the qualification of "arithmetic mean," *average* can refer to a rate or the ratio of one quantity to another, as in "average number of miles per hour" or "average weight per truckload."

- When *mean* is used in the context of data, it means *arithmetic mean*.

- The *median* of an odd number of data is the middle number when the data are listed in increasing order; the *median* of an even number of data is the arithmetic mean of the two middle numbers when the data are listed in increasing order.

- For a list of data, the *mode* of the data is the most frequently occurring number in the list. Thus, there may be more than one mode for a list of data.

- For data listed in increasing order, the *first quartile*, *second quartile*, and *third quartile* of the data are three numbers that divide the data into four groups that are roughly equal in size. The first group of numbers is from the least number up to the first quartile. The second group is from the first quartile up to the second quartile, which is also the median of the data. The third group is from the second quartile up to the third quartile, and the fourth group is from the third quartile up to the greatest number. Note that the four groups themselves are sometimes referred to as quartiles—*first quartile*, *second quartile*, *third quartile*, and *fourth quartile*. The latter usage is clarified by the word "in" as in the phrase "the cow's weight is *in* the third quartile of the weights of the herd."

- For data listed in increasing order, the *percentiles* of the data are 99 numbers that divide the data into 100 groups that are roughly equal in size. The 25th percentile equals the first quartile; the 50th percentile equals the second quartile, or median; and the 75th percentile equals the third quartile.

- For a list of data, where the arithmetic mean is denoted by m, the *standard deviation* of the data refers to the nonnegative square root of the mean of the squared differences between m and each of the data. This statistic is also known as the *population standard deviation* and is not to be confused with the *sample standard deviation*.

- For a list of data, the *range* of the data is the greatest number in the list minus the least number. The *interquartile range* of the data is the third quartile minus the first quartile.

Data Distributions and Probability Distributions

- Some questions display data in *frequency distributions*, where discrete data values are repeated with various frequencies, or where preestablished intervals of possible values are assigned frequencies corresponding to the numbers of data in the intervals. For example, the lifetimes, rounded to the nearest hour, of 300 lightbulbs could be in the following 10 intervals: 501–550 hours, 551–600 hours, 601–650 hours, . . . , 951–1,000 hours; consequently, each of the intervals would have a number, or frequency, of lifetimes, and the sum of the 10 frequencies is 300.

- Questions may involve *relative frequency distributions*, where each frequency of a frequency distribution is divided by the total number of data in the distribution, resulting in a relative frequency. In the example above, the 10 frequencies of the 10 intervals would each be divided by 300, yielding 10 relative frequencies.
- When a question refers to a random selection or a random sample, all possible samples of equal size have the same probability of being selected unless there is information to the contrary.
- Some questions describe *probability experiments*, or *random experiments*, that have a finite number of possible *outcomes*. In a random experiment, any particular set of outcomes is called an *event*, and every event E has a *probability*, denoted by $P(E)$, where $0 \leq P(E) \leq 1$. If each outcome of an experiment is equally likely, then the probability of an event E is defined as the following ratio:

$$P(E) = \frac{\text{the number of outcomes in the event } E}{\text{the number of possible outcomes in the experiment}}$$

- If E and F are two events in an experiment, then "E and F" is an event, which is the set of outcomes that are in the intersection of events E and F. Another event is "E or F," which is the set of outcomes that are in the union of events E and F.
- If E and F are two events and E and F are mutually exclusive, then $P(E \text{ and } F) = 0$.
- If E and F are two events such that the occurrence of either event does not affect the occurrence of the other, then E and F are said to be *independent* events. Events E and F are independent if and only if $P(E \text{ and } F) = P(E)P(F)$.
- A *random variable* is a variable that represents values resulting from a random experiment. The values of the random variable may be the actual outcomes of the experiment if the outcomes are numerical, or the random variable may be related to the outcomes more indirectly. In either case, random variables can be used to describe events in terms of numbers.
- A random variable from an experiment with only a finite number of possible outcomes also has only a finite number of values and is called a *discrete random variable*. When the values of a random variable form a continuous interval of real numbers, such as all of the numbers between 0 and 2, the random variable is called a *continuous random variable*.
- Every value of a discrete random variable X, say $X = a$, has a probability denoted by $P(a)$. A histogram (or a table) showing all of the values of X and their probabilities $P(X)$ is called the *probability distribution* of X. The *mean of the random variable X* is the sum of the products $XP(X)$ for all values of X.
- The mean of a random variable X is also called the *expected value* of X or the *mean of the probability distribution* of X.
- For a continuous random variable X, every interval of values, say $a \leq X \leq b$, has a probability, which is denoted by $P(a \leq X \leq b)$. The *probability distribution* of X can be described by a curve in the xy–plane that mimics the tops of the bars of a histogram, only smoother. The curve is the graph of a function f whose values are nonnegative and whose graph is therefore above the x-axis. The curve $y = f(x)$ is related to the probability of each interval $a \leq X \leq b$ in the following way: $P(a \leq X \leq b)$ is equal to the area of the region that is below the curve, above the x-axis, and between the vertical lines $x = a$ and $x = b$. The area of the entire region under the curve is 1.

- The *mean of a continuous random variable X* is the point *m* on the *x*-axis at which region under the distribution curve would perfectly balance if a fulcrum were placed at $x = m$. The *median of X* is the point *M* on the *x*-axis at which the line $x = M$ divides the region under the distribution curve into two regions of equal area.
- The *standard deviation of a random variable X* is a measure of dispersion, which indicates how spread out the probability distribution of *X* is from its mean. It is also called the *standard deviation of the probability distribution* of *X*.
- The most important probability distribution is the *normal distribution*, whose distribution curve is shaped like a bell. A random variable *X* with this distribution is called *normally distributed*. The curve is symmetric about the line $x = m$, where *m* is the mean as well as the median. The right and left tails of the distribution become ever closer to the *x*-axis but never touch it.
- The *standard normal distribution* has mean 0 and standard deviation 1. The following figure shows the distribution, including approximate probabilities corresponding to the six intervals shown.

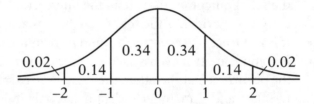

Graphical Representations of Data

- Graphical data presentations, such as bar graphs, circle graphs, and line graphs, **are** drawn to scale; therefore, you can read, estimate, or compare data values by sight or by measurement.
- Standard conventions apply to graphs of data unless otherwise indicated. For example, a circle graph represents 100 percent of the data indicated in the graph's title, and the areas of the individual sectors are proportional to the percents they represent. Scales, grid lines, dots, bars, shadings, solid and dashed lines, legends, etc., are used on graphs to indicate the data. Sometimes, scales that do not begin at 0 are used, and sometimes broken scales are used.
- In Venn diagrams, various sets of objects are represented by circular regions and by regions formed by intersections of the circles. In some Venn diagrams, all of the circles are inside a rectangular region that represents a universal set. A number placed in a region is the number of elements in the subset represented by the smallest region containing the number, unless otherwise noted. Sometimes a number is placed above a circle to indicate the number of elements in the entire circle.

Miscellaneous Guidelines for Interpreting and Using Information in Test Questions

- Numbers given in a question are to be used as exact numbers, even though in some real-life settings they are likely to have been rounded. For example, if a question states that "30 percent of the company's profit was from health products," then 30 is to be used as an exact number; it is not to be treated as though it were a nearby number, say 29 or 30.1, that has been rounded up or down.

- An integer that is given as the number of certain objects, whether in a real-life or pure-math setting, is to be taken as the total number of such objects. For example, if a question states that "a bag contains 50 marbles, and 23 of the marbles are red," then 50 is to be taken as the total number of marbles in the bag and 23 is to be taken as the total number of red marbles in the bag, so that the other 27 marbles are not red. Fractions and percents are understood in a similar way, so "one-fifth, or 20 percent, of the 50 marbles in the bag are green" means 10 marbles in the bag are green and 40 marbles are not green.

- When a multiple-choice question asks for an approximate quantity without stipulating a degree of approximation, the correct answer is the choice that is closest in value to the quantity that can be computed from the information given.

- Unless otherwise indicated, the phrase "difference between two quantities" is assumed to mean "positive difference," that is, the greater quantity minus the lesser quantity. For example, "for which two consecutive years was the difference in annual rainfall least?" means "for which two consecutive years was the *absolute value of the difference* in annual rainfall least?"

- When the term *profit* is used in a question, it refers to *gross profit*, which is the sales revenue minus the cost of production. The profit does not involve any other amounts unless they are explicitly given.

- The common meaning of terms such as *months* and *years* and other everyday terms are assumed in questions where the terms appear.

- In questions involving real-life scenarios in which a variable is given to represent a number of existing objects or another nonnegative amount, the context implies that the variable is greater than 0. For example, "Jane sold x rugs and deposited her profit of y dollars into her savings account" implies that x and y are greater than 0.

- Some quantities may involve units, such as inches, pounds, and Celsius degrees, while other quantities are pure numbers. Any units of measurement, such as English units or metric units, may be used. However, if an answer to a question requires converting one unit of measurement to another, then the relationship between the units is given in the question, unless the relationship is a common one, such as the relationships between minutes and hours, dollars and cents, and metric units like centimeters and meters.

- In any question, there may be some information that is not needed for obtaining the correct answer.

- When reading questions, do not introduce unwarranted assumptions. For example, if a question describes a trip that begins and ends at certain times, the intended answer will assume that the times are unaffected by crossing time zones or by changes to the local time for daylight savings, unless those matters are explicitly mentioned. As another example, do not consider sales taxes on purchases unless explicitly mentioned.

- The display of data in a Data Interpretation set of questions is the same for each question in the set. Also, the display may contain more than one graph or table. Each question will refer to some of the data, but it may happen that some part of the data will have no question that refers to it.

- In a Data Interpretation set of questions, each question should be considered separately from the others. No information except what is given in the display of data should be carried over from one question to another.

- In many questions, mathematical expressions and words appear together in a phrase. In such a phrase, each mathematical expression should be interpreted *separately* from the words before it is interpreted *along with* the words. For example, if n is an integer, then the phrase "the sum of the first two consecutive integers greater than $n+6$" means $(n+7)+(n+8)$; it does not mean "the sum of the first two consecutive integers greater than n" plus 6, or $(n+1)+(n+2)+6$. That is, the expression $n+6$ should be interpreted first, separately from the words. However, in a phrase like "the function g is defined for all $x \geq 0$," the phrase "for all $x \geq 0$" is a mathematical shorthand for "for all numbers x such that $x \geq 0$."